Best Wi.

The Chirp Club

HAIL TO
THE CHIEFS

BOB GRETZ

SAGAMORE PUBLISHING
Champaign, IL

Production Manager: Susan M. McKinney
Dustjacket and
  photo insert design: Michelle R. Dressen and Amy Todd
Editor: Susan M. McKinney
Proofreader: Phyllis L. Bannon

Library of Congress Catalog Number: 94-67274
ISBN: 1-57167-002-5

Printed in the United States

To Robin, Lauren and Elizabeth for putting up with so much.
And to Al, Phyllis, Sharon and Brian for giving so much.

ᢞ

In memory of

Albert R. Gretz, Sr.

1905-1994

CONTENTS

ACKNOWLEDGMENTS

As with any creative work, there are many people to thank in the process of taking an idea and turning it into the book you now hold in your hands.

And it must start with the folks at Sagamore Publishing, especially Joe Bannon, Sr. and Joe Bannon, Jr., for their help and willingness to go forward on this project before the Chiefs won a single football game in 1993. Thanks to Susan McKinney for shepherding the book through the publication process. And thanks to Hank Young and Young Company for the great photos.

Over 13 years of hanging around the Chiefs franchise, many people have been especially helpful and a joy to work with, folks like Marv Levy, Dorothy Levy, Walt and Jane Corey, John and Arlene Mackovic, Les and Joyce Miller, and Kansas City true sporting superstars, George and Chip Toma. They deserve a share of the good stuff that seldom came their way with the Chiefs.

This book would not have been possible without the candor and cooperation of Carl Peterson, Marty Schottenheimer, Tim Connolly, Denny Thum, Lynn Stiles, Terry Bradway, the coaching staff, Mike Davidson, and so many others at Arrowhead Stadium.

As a member of the media, I spend most of my time bothering the folks in the Chiefs public relations department, and a finer group cannot be found in the National Football League. Special thanks to Bob Moore, Jim Carr, Brenda Sniezek, Eileen Normile, Julie Garney, Candy Knabe, and Joel Badzinski. And gratitude towards a host of public relations folks of seasons past whose help is remembered: Bob Sprenger, Doug Kelly, Gary

Heise, Phyllis Bixler, Cheryl Forbis, Anita McDonald, Efie Protopappas, Laura Milborn, Susan Kapsch-Frerking, Theotis Brown, Cedric Fullard, Ronald Mott, Shawn Barnes, Scott Smith, Joe Horak, Kim Huthoefer, Becky Edwards, and Kem Hammeren.

"Thank you" to all the folks at KCFX-FM and the Chiefs Radio Network, especially the boys in the booth — Kevin Harlan, Len Dawson, Bill Grigsby, Jay Copeland, and Dan Israel — who make game day so much fun each week. Special thanks to Dan Israel for helping me find the entrance ramp on the "Information Highway."

And there are a host of friends who have helped in so many ways, not only with this book, but with life. THANK YOU:

Hank Young, Kelly Fray, David Naster, Chuck Rubin, Joe MacCabe, Ron and Lee Labinski, Will Rudd, Mark and Donna Anderson, Jeff Anderson, Michael Anderson, Bill Anderson, the Augustines of Downingtown, the Strachans of Johnstown, the Gretzs of Grand Rapids, the Laskys of Cheswick, Kent and Gina Pulliam, Wick and Bev Divelbiss, Mickey Curtis, Nan Dinsmore-Ellis, Jessica Rogers, Jo-Ann Barnas, Ed Bouchette, Ron Cook, and Joe Gordon.

And thanks to you for reading this book.

INTRODUCTION

George Santayana never played a down for the Kansas City Chiefs. He never played for any National Football League team. If Santayana knew anything about football, it was only the soccer played in his native Spain.

However, Santayana is an important figure in understanding what has happened to the Chiefs franchise over the last 25 years, especially the success experienced in 1993. A philosopher and poet who immigrated to the United States in the late 1880s, Santayana spent more than 20 years teaching philosophy at Harvard University. The most popular of his thoughts came from his book *The Life of Reason.*

Published in 1905, Santayana wrote: *"Those who cannot remember the past are condemned to repeat it."*

It is simply impossible to comprehend what the Chiefs have become in the 1990s — one of pro football's best franchises on and off the field — without understanding that in the 1970s and 1980s, they were one of the laughingstock teams of the National Football League. Or, that in the 1960s, they were the flagship franchise of the most successful alternative sports league of the last 90 years, the American Football League.

Chiefs owner Lamar Hunt created the AFL in 1960 and saw it through to a complete merger with the NFL in 1970. In 10 years of league play, the Chiefs won more games (87) and championships (3) than any of the eight original franchises. The Chiefs were in the first AFL-NFL Championship Game, losing to the Green Bay Packers at the Los Angeles Coliseum in a game that would become known as Super Bowl 1. Three years later, the Chiefs won Super Bowl 4, beating the Minnesota Vikings in what was the final game involving an AFL team.

Beginning in 1972 and over the next 16 years, Hunt's team became inept on the field of play and fans avoided Arrowhead Stadium in droves. History repeated itself again and again, as five head coaching changes brought increasing disappointment and frustration. From 1972 through 1988, the Chiefs lost nearly three of every five games they played (101-148-3) and made the playoffs one time (1986). The number of seats held by season ticket holders fell by more than 46,000 and actual attendance was off nearly 22,000 per game. Through all this misery, the same front-office executives ran the team: president Jack Steadman and general manager Jim Schaaf.

On December 19, 1988, Hunt finally heeded the words of Santayana. This time there would be no repeating; this time he did not fire his head coach. Hunt removed Steadman and Schaaf, replacing them with one man: Carl Peterson. A month later, Peterson named Marty Schottenheimer as the Chiefs' newest head coach.

Since then, the Kansas City Chiefs have not repeated the mistakes of the past. Rather, they are duplicating the success of the 1960s and again have become one of the league's most popular and successful franchises. The Chiefs are one of three NFL teams to make the playoffs in all four seasons of the 1990s, and one of three teams to win 10 or more games in each season of this decade.

The success of the 1990s has created two very different types of Chiefs fans. There are those who survived the dark years, where frustration waited on every kickoff. And there are those who have signed on with the arrival of Peterson and Schottenheimer, who know nothing of the ineptitude that was once so much a part of Chiefs football.

Both groups rejoiced in 1993 when, for the first time in 22 years, the Chiefs won the American Football Conference Western Division championship and, for the first time in 24 years, played in the AFC Championship Game.

They became America's darlings in the chase to Super Bowl 28 in Atlanta's Georgia Dome. With a 37-year-old Joe Montana, rescued from the sidelines of the San Francisco 49ers and a 33-year-old Marcus Allen, saved from the doghouse of the Los Angeles Raiders, the Chiefs return to excellence excited the league, networks, national media and fans.

"For a few weeks there was a real question about just who was America's Team," said Peterson, referring to the nickname the Dallas Cowboys have carried for the last 15 years. "There were a lot of people around the country rooting for the Kansas City Chiefs."

The glory days are no longer dust-covered and tarnished after seasons of misfortune. There are now tangible successes that can be celebrated and discussed at length over the office coffee pot or in sports bars over the weekend. The key events on Kansas City's fall social calendar have become pre-game tailgate parties in the parking lots at Arrowhead Stadium. Identifying oneself as a Chiefs fan is no longer an invitation for derision; bumper stickers sent each year to season ticket holders now are displayed proudly on vehicles all over the metropolitan area.

A visit to any Kansas City area shopping mall reveals hundreds of jackets, caps, T-shirts and the like, and they are not just being worn by children, but also by adults. Each year NFL Properties, Inc., the league's marketing and licensing arm, keeps track of the merchandise sold around the world and ranks the 28 teams by the dollar amounts sold in their colors and with their logo. In 1988, the Chiefs were dead last, No. 28. Even fans of perpetually hapless franchises like Tampa Bay, Indianapolis and Phoenix bought more merchandise that year than the lowly Chiefs. In 1993, the Chiefs ranked ninth in sales volume, the highest position in franchise history.

A ticket to a Chiefs game at Arrowhead Stadium has become a valuable commodity. Season ticket sales were stopped at 69,219 for 1993, compared to the 26,594 sold in 1988. All 11 Chiefs home games — two preseason, eight regular season, one postseason — were sellouts. In-house attendance during the regular season totaled 606,222, the first time the team went over the 600,000 mark and average attendance was 75,777, the highest in team's history. The Chiefs open the 1994 season with a streak of 25 consecutive sellouts for regular season and postseason games. An unbelievable *99 percent* of Chiefs season ticket holders renewed their seats for 1994.

The scarcity of available seats has created a bigger fan base for the Chiefs, because with the sold-out games comes a lifting of the NFL's television blackout rule (a game must be sold-out 72 hours before kickoff or it cannot be shown on live television in

xi

that community.) All 16 of the Chiefs regular season games now can be viewed from the comfort of the living room, and they have become a prime-time team, playing four games under the lights for national TV in 1993 and a host of Sunday games that have been national broadcasts on NBC.

Kansas City television station WDAF (Channel 4) carried the bulk of the team's games because of its affiliation with NBC, and the Chiefs brought huge ratings throughout the season. According to the Arbitron ratings service, among those households watching television on Sunday afternoons, 72 percent were tuned to Chiefs games on WDAF. Among adults (25-54 years), the rating increased to 77 percent of the TVs in use.

Radio station KCFX-FM (101), the flagship station of the Chiefs Radio Network, experienced ratings success that it never could have achieved with its music format. During the Fall 1993 Arbitron ratings period, 29 percent of those listening to the radio on Sunday afternoons were tuned into the Chiefs game. Among adults, the rating increased to 38 percent of the radios in use.

On most Sundays then, nearly eight out of every 10 adults watching television and nearly four out of every 10 adults listening to the radio had the Chiefs game on.

If a fan of the Chiefs wanted to do more than watch or listen, he can now read about the team in the weekly newspaper *Chiefs Report*. After selling 1,700 copies a week during its first year of operation in 1992, *Chiefs Report* sold 8,000 copies a week during the 1993 season, and had subscribers in Australia, Japan, England, Panama, Mexico, Canada, Sweden and Spain.

Chiefs fans are popping up throughout the United States. One of the largest contingents (120 fans) meets each week in Atlanta, Georgia to watch the games on television. There is another fan club in Washington D.C. that includes U.S. Senator Christopher "Kit" Bond of Missouri. There are more than 50 fan clubs in 26 states and one in Germany

On the field of play, the Chiefs do not win every game; they even lose some they are expected to win. There are times when the bodies are there but the minds are elsewhere. But there are no longer games where the Chiefs are overwhelmed by another team's superior talent. In the last five seasons, the Chiefs have captured 20 spots in the Pro Bowl all-star game, representing nine different players. New fans enjoy a football team capable of winning every time it steps on the field. And for long-time fans, the gnawing fear that some horrible misfortune will eventually snatch defeat from the jaws of victory slowly is being dispatched.

With a change on offense and a host of new players, the 1993 season was frequently an emotional roller coaster, with tremendous highs (come-from-behind victories over Pittsburgh and Houston in the playoffs) and shattering lows (disturbing regular season losses to Chicago and Minnesota.) The ride ended with the AFC Championship Game loss to the Buffalo Bills, a heartbeat away from the Super Bowl.

From the time he took over operation of the team, Peterson said he did not want the Chiefs to be a meteor, flashing across the NFL sky for a few bright moments only to crash to earth with a thud and a fizzle. He wanted to build a franchise that would be among the league's best year after year.

The goal of the organization, its president-general manager, and head coach has never changed: a Super Bowl championship.

"We fell one game short," Peterson told the players on the team's plane flight home from the AFC Championship Game defeat in Buffalo. "That means we must return and work even harder in 1994.

"But that does not diminish the work and efforts you put into the 1993 season. We took another step forward, a giant step."

In the pages ahead, the rebuilding of the Chiefs will be explained in detail. For the first time, Peterson, Schottenheimer and their staffs reveal the strategies, philosophies and ideals that returned the Chiefs to respectability. Heeding Santayana's advice, the story is told against the backdrop of the past, in order to reveal the depth of the problems and the measures taken to make sure there is no repeating of the 1970-80s history.

As the Chiefs head into the 1994 season, a solid foundation has been built under the team, one that should withstand the rumblings of a football earthquake called NFL free agency.

The days of ineptitude, empty seats and revolving doors are over. Now, around the NFL it has become: Hail to the Chiefs!

CHAPTER ONE

DREAMS DIE IN BUFFALO

Football knows no silence quite like the locker room of a team that has just lost a game in the playoffs.

There is such finality to defeat in the postseason. The struggle to reach the NFL's 12-team tournament is long and arduous, requiring such huge investments of time, capital and sweat, that no one dares imagine it will end with disappointment. Yet, 11 of those teams must suffer the silence in order to crown a champion.

On this January day in western New York, the locker-room quiet was broken only by the banging of helmets and shoulder pads tossed into equipment bags. When a single shower was turned on, it was like the roar of Niagara piercing the silence. Conversations did not have words, but came in looks, hugs, handshakes. A vacant stare here, a chin stuck in the chest there, an angry glare, tears — all spoke volumes.

The Kansas City Chiefs had just stepped off the field at Rich Stadium. Across the tunnel, the Buffalo Bills were celebrating a 30-13 victory in the American Football Conference Championship Game. The Bills would be making their fourth consecutive trip to the Super Bowl, a remarkable feat soon lost in yet another title-game defeat.

As Chiefs players peeled away the equipment that protected them from the violence of the game, the realization that the 1993 football season had ended was a concept understood by only a few in the room. The Super Bowl chase had begun in the July heat of training camp in Wisconsin and was carried through the turn of seasons from summer to fall and finally to winter. Over six months, a rhythm had been established with preparation, game, rest, preparation, game, rest . . . week after week, month after month. It was a pattern that brought comfort to the football soul, especially when a team was able to push into the month of January, which meant the playoffs and the chase for the holiest football Grail, the Vince Lombardi Trophy. As Joe Montana said, the worst part of losing in the playoffs was ". . . they tell you to go home. There's no more football. All you can do is watch. I like to watch, but I love to play."

How incredible the postseason had been for the Chiefs. A heart-stopping come-from-behind victory in overtime against the Pittsburgh Steelers seemed to light a fuse on the Kansas City fans. They exploded the next week when as heavy underdogs, the Chiefs became the only AFC team to win a game on the road in the playoffs, beating the Houston Oilers 28-20 at the Astrodome.

Chiefs fans greeted the team's return flight from Houston with a spontaneous celebration that nearly shut down Kansas City International Airport. Traffic backed up for miles on the access road to the terminals as an estimated 8,000 fans jammed Terminal A, cheering their heroes as they disembarked and made their way through the happy throng.

The days leading up to the Chiefs' AFC title meeting with the Bills was a magical time. There never had been a moment when the city spent a whole week looking forward to a sporting event. In 1985, the Kansas City Royals won the World Series, but there had been no anticipation of that feat. The Royals were down 3-2 in the best-of-seven series when they arrived back home from St. Louis for the final two games. They were seemingly on their way to defeat in Game Six before a questionable call by umpire Don Denkinger gave them new life, and eventually the victory. The next day, the Royals won Game Seven and wild celebrations erupted around the area. When the Chiefs won Super Bowl 4, the team spent the entire week in New Orleans preparing for the game and Kansas City missed out on a lot of excitement.

This time was different. Everyone in the city seemed to limit their wardrobes to red and gold. The radio airwaves were filled with special songs written for the occasion, including the Schottenheimer Polka:

> Whosenheimer, Whatsenheimer, Schottenheimer Polka
> Marty's game plan is the baddest, that's no joka'
> No go fixing notta thing if it's not broka'
> Whosenheimer, Whatsenheimer, Schottenheimer Polka

Signs honoring the Chiefs popped up everywhere and one suburban office building rearranged a Christmas lighting display so it spelled out Chiefs across 15 stories of windows.

When the Bills announced that some 20,000 tickets were available for the game, it sparked a mobilization of Chiefs fans. Charter airplane flights were arranged and sold out so quickly that more flights had to be added. A small army of Kansas City followers invaded snowy Buffalo by plane, bus and car.

The Chiefs arrived in Buffalo Friday evening with TV cameras and reporters recording every move made by the players. A Saturday morning team meeting was the most emotional of the season as player after player stood up and talked about how much the season had meant to them. Marcus Allen spoke of manhood, fortitude and a total belief in his teammates. He told them it did not matter where the game was played, whether on the field or in a stadium parking lot; they had invested too much to turn back now. Joe Montana spoke as well, in a style few had heard from him during his first season in Kansas City. He told his teammates that the successes he already had experienced no longer mattered to him. He was here with them, and that was the most important thing in the world to him.

There was so much emotion surrounding the game, so much baggage being carried by individual players, the franchise, the city; everyone had waited so long for this chance. Suddenly, the season was over. That dreaded silence took hold in Kansas City's tap rooms, living rooms, indeed any room where the faithful had gathered to watch the game. The scene was no different in the Chiefs' locker room. No time to decompress either, as the horde of media came running through the door, seeking explanations.

Kevin Ross stood in front of his locker, his uniform and pads littered at his feet, and talked in a whisper. For 10 seasons he wore a Chiefs uniform. He had gone through so many of the bad times, so much of the controversy. Ross had seen a lot of talent around him go to waste due to front office and coaching ineptitude. He had come so close to chasing all those ghosts away, but now the chance was gone, and Ross knew he would not wear a Chiefs uniform again.

Derrick Thomas was bent over at the waist, throwing clothes into a garment bag and trying to ignore the television cameras and reporters waiting to speak with him. He had spent most of the second half standing next to defensive coordinator Dave Adolph on the sidelines, playing only in obvious passing situations. There were not many of those, since Buffalo kept the football on the ground with the running of Thurman Thomas, trying to eat up as much time as possible on the clock. As he packed, Thomas catalogued his thoughts, trying to think of things to say that would mask his feelings. All he wanted was to get on the bus and hide his anger from prying eyes.

Dave Krieg dressed slowly, something unusual for him. Typically he was the first Chiefs player out of the locker room after games, showering in seconds, dressing in a flash, seemingly in a rush to get somewhere else. Now there was nowhere else to go. As happened so many times in the 1993 season, Krieg was forced into the AFC championship game when Montana suffered a concussion. He performed admirably, taking the team to its only touchdown, but he was unable to overcome the first-half problems that put the Chiefs into a bind. It was the second time Krieg had gotten this close to the Super Bowl. It was the second time he left carrying disappointment in his overnight bag.

Willie Davis dressed quickly, trying to drive away the frustration in the same manner he drove defensive backs crazy — with speed. It had been a postseason of ups and downs for Davis, and the title game continued this trend. He caught five passes against the Bills, but dropped a couple of throws as well. He progressed so far in four years, but now it did not seem to matter.

In a room off to the side of the main locker room, Joe Montana sat on a table and tried to deal with the ache bouncing back and forth inside his head. His helmet had bounced off the rock-hard artificial surface of Rich Stadium in the third quarter, a pile of Bills stacked up around him. He immediately grabbed his face mask with both hands in an attempt to stop the spinning, trying hard to remain on the functioning side of consciousness. He said later that everything had gone white. The rest of his season was spent sitting on the bench, trying hard to decipher the moving figures in front of him. At first, he was not sure where he was. When his senses returned, the ramifications of the game made his head hurt even more.

Marty Schottenheimer was off in the interview room, a host of microphones in front of him, explaining to the media what happened to his team. He had come off the field and spoken briefly and quietly to his players, asking them to see through their disappointment, to remember a terrific 1993 season. It had been such a fun year for Schottenheimer, the most enjoyable of his career, but there were no magic words to lessen the hurt — he knew that. Schottenheimer had been there before with the Cleveland Browns, twice losing in far more devastating fashion than what happened to the Chiefs. Experience taught him the only good that came from losing the AFC Championship Game was remembering the pain.

Marcus Allen found himself standing in front of the media as well. There was no remorse in his voice as he gave credit to the Buffalo Bills, all the while deflecting inquiries about what the 1993 season meant to him. If the media was not already aware that it had been one of the most enjoyable seasons of his football career, he was not about to divulge that information now — not with so many dreams shattered in the locker room next door. However, for the first time in years, Allen's disappointment over a season's end was cut short by his optimism about the future.

Outside the locker room, Carl Peterson stood with a group of friends who flew in for the game from around the country. Although he tried hard to wear a smile, the defeat would linger with him for a long time. Once before, he had been with a team that had made it all the way to the Super Bowl. But his Philadelphia Eagles ended up losing Super Bowl 15 to the Oakland Raiders, leaving a wound that never quite healed. He sported two championship rings from the United States Football League; those were meaningful because he built from scratch the Phila-

delphia/Baltimore Stars franchise. All the same, they were not
Super Bowl rings.

Jonathan Hayes was already sitting in one of the four buses
that would take the Chiefs traveling party back to the Buffalo
Airport and a return flight to Kansas City. He chose the back seat,
directly behind former teammate Deron Cherry where in whis-
pers he talked of his disappointment. Like Ross, Albert Lewis,
John Alt and Nick Lowery, Hayes had been through many tough
times with the Chiefs. And now, as the buses pulled away from
Rich Stadium, he closed his eyes and tried to let sleep soothe the
frustration.

Just a few hours earlier, the Chiefs had walked out of that
Rich Stadium locker room, and down the long tunnel to the
playing field, confident of their ability to pull off an upset. The
Las Vegas oddsmakers installed the Bills as three-point favorites
and while that line wavered a few times, it held up through
kickoff. Certainly, there was no question that the Chiefs were the
sentimental favorite. After two years of inactivity, Montana was
leading another team deep into the playoffs. And over in the
NFC, the San Francisco 49ers were still playing, setting up the
possibility of a dream matchup: the Chiefs led by Montana
against the 49ers with Steve Young. In fact, the questions and
clamor surrounding Montana reached the point where the Bills
became convinced they were the underdog, and they bristled as
the spotlight landed on the Chiefs.

Two months earlier, the Chiefs experienced little trouble
beating the Bills at Arrowhead Stadium, 23-7, in one of their most
complete performances of the season. The offense had domi-
nated the ball, and the defense limited running back Thurman
Thomas to just 25 yards rushing and 69 yards in total offense.

But the AFC title game was miles away from the friendly
confines of Arrowhead Stadium. The Bills were 7-0 at Rich
Stadium in postseason play, and the Buffalo crowd rivaled
Kansas City's for the volume of noise they could create, making
it impossible for offenses to call audibles. Two years earlier, the
Chiefs were soundly trounced in the second round of the playoffs
there, 37-14.

There were two big differences this time: Joe Montana and
Marcus Allen. Acquired through trade and free agency deals,
these grizzled veterans helped the Chiefs, both on and off the

field. To be sure, they were not as dominating as they were in the primes of their careers, but Montana and Allen still could play the game. Their peers had taken notice, electing them to the AFC squad for the Pro Bowl.

The game began with a cold mist falling from clouds that hovered low, almost touching the Rich Stadium light standards. It made for the worst possible weather scenario for the Chiefs' short-passing offense: cold, wet and windy.

Just as he had done in postseason victories over Pittsburgh and Houston, Montana threw the ball poorly at the start and was 0-for-5 before hitting tight end Keith Cash for 11 yards. Even that first completion was tipped by a linebacker. At the end of the first quarter, Montana had three completions and eight incompletions. For a man who has reserved a spot for himself in the Hall of Fame due to his accuracy (a 63 percent lifetime completion percentage), it was a horrendous beginning.

The Chiefs trailed 7-6, but that situation was nothing new for them. Against Houston, they were down by 10 points at the end of the first 15 minutes. Against Pittsburgh, they carried a 10-point deficit into the half-time locker room. Over the 1993 season, they had learned how to come from behind; it was Montana who taught them. However, two disturbing patterns had already begun, and ultimately they would destroy the Chiefs' chances for victory.

Twice in the first quarter, the Chiefs had the ball inside the Buffalo 20-yard line, and twice they had to settle for Nick Lowery field goals. That played right into the Bills' "bend-but-don't-break" defensive strategy. Buffalo finished the 1993 regular season ranked 27th in the fewest yards allowed, but fifth in fewest points allowed. Bills defensive coordinator Walt Corey loved to frustrate opposing offenses in the scoring zone. "We'll give 'em all the three-pointers they want," Corey said.

But the biggest problem for Kansas City was on defense. The Chiefs opened the game with their 42 unit, a scheme that worked in the past against the Bills three wide-receiver aline-ment. The defensive line of Neil Smith, Derrick Thomas, Joe Phillips and Dan Saleaumua remained intact. Outside linebacker Lonnie Marts was on the field, but inside backers Tracy Rogers and Tracy Simien were removed, making way for extra defensive backs, totaling six in all: Albert Lewis, Jay Taylor, Kevin Ross,

Bruce Pickens, Martin Bayless and Charles Mincy. Bayless basically played a linebacker position, giving the Chiefs more speed to cover Thurman Thomas out of the backfield.

But after the first quarter, Thomas already had 33 yards rushing on seven carries, including a 12-yard touchdown run when the Bills caught the Chiefs in a blitz. Quarterback Jim Kelly correctly read Bayless' charge, and with Bayless and Marts rushing the passer, only Mincy was left when Thomas broke through the line of scrimmage. Mincy missed on the tackle — like a matador handling an angry bull — and Thomas rolled into the end zone.

From previous meetings between these teams, Kansas City knew that if Thomas was held under 100 yards rushing, Buffalo had a hard time staying in the game. As prolific a passer as Jim Kelly was, Thomas was the key to stopping the Bills, not only as a runner, but as a receiver. Some members of the Chiefs defense thought Thomas was the most dangerous multi-purpose back in the NFL.

The Bills offensive coaching staff had made an adjustment in blocking assignments after the November game. Tackle John Fina was instructed to brush the defensive end on his side (usually Derrick Thomas) and then go after Bayless. In the past, Bayless was able to plug holes that popped open on the defensive front, limiting the running room for Thurman Thomas. Now he had to deal with a 300-pound blocker.

In the second quarter, the Bills and Chiefs snapped the ball 45 times. Two of those plays shot daggers through the Chiefs and their Super Bowl dreams.

Just after the quarter began, Buffalo had the ball first-and-10 on their own 41-yard line. Working out of the no-huddle offense, Kelly called Thomas' number, this time with a counter-play. Thomas took one step to his right, then turned back to his left. Kelly slammed the ball into his stomach. Guard John Davis and tackle Howard Ballard pulled from their spots on the right side of the line and ran towards the left, as Thomas jumped in behind them.

Davis blocked Derrick Thomas, while Ballard found Bayless. Left guard Glen Parker handled Saleaumua by standing him straight up and pushing him out of the way, while Fina moved downfall, searching for Marts.

Thurman Thomas hit the line of scrimmage, and it looked like the play was stopped for a short gain. Derrick Thomas fought off his block and took a shot at the tackle. Bayless slipped around Ballard's girth and was able to stick out an arm as well.

It would be 33 yards later before Thomas finally was hauled down by the Chiefs defense. Four plays later, Thomas scored on a 3-yard touchdown run. Add to that a pair of Steve Christie field goals, and Buffalo managed a 20-6 lead with less than two minutes in the half.

The Chiefs had minus-10 yards of offense in the second quarter when they took over at their own 20-yard line. But, as frequently happens with Montana, something finally clicked into place. He completed four consecutive throws for 9, 7, 12 and 16 yards. Another completion of 31 yards to Todd McNair moved Kansas City to the Buffalo 5-yard line with 25 seconds to play in the half.

After an incompletion, Montana found the play he wanted. Fullback Kimble Anders lined up in the backfield, ran to the right, hesitated and then cut back to the middle. Montana found him all alone at the 2-yard line. It would have been a touchdown. It should have been a touchdown.

It was a disaster. Anders watched the ball until it was just inches away, and then turned his eyes to find the end zone. As he did, the ball bounced off his hands and into the end zone where Buffalo strong safety Henry Jones grabbed the interception. The first half ended seconds later, and the Bills still had a 14-point lead.

There would be no Montana miracles on this day. He left the field with more than 13 minutes to play in the third quarter, unsteady on his feet and not quite sure of his name after he was tackled by Bruce Smith, Jeff Wright and Phil Hansen. Krieg came in and moved the Chiefs on a 14-play, 90-yard touchdown drive as Marcus Allen scored on a 1-yard run. That made the score 20-13.

But the Chiefs had given up too much. The running of Thurman Thomas and all of the missed opportunities in the first half could not be overcome. Thomas had 57 yards on 13 carries in the second half. That certainly was a better defensive effort than the 129 yards on 20 carries he had in the first half. The Chiefs switched from the 42 to their normal 43 alinement, with one change: Darren Mickell replaced Derrick Thomas at defensive end. D.T. was used only to rush the passer.

"I'm not a coach, so I just have to do what I'm told," Thomas said. "I'm very disappointed. I should have had the opportunity to play more. It's difficult to stand on the sidelines and watch things happen and know that I might have been able to do something about it . . . . It's something I don't want to get into. It would create unnecessary animosity."

After the game, Schottenheimer gave credit to the Bills and tried to explain the thinking that led to placing one of his best defensive players on the sidelines for most of the second half.

"The issue today was that upfront, they did a job on us," said Schottenheimer. "We made a decision that putting a bigger player on the field was necessary, and we felt the best thing to do was put Darren Mickell in for Derrick . . . . We make every decision based on what is best for the team."

Later, Schottenheimer would say the Chiefs fell one game short of the Super Bowl. But that game was not the loss in Buffalo. It was an earlier game, a regular-season defeat that had cost Kansas City the home-field advantage in the playoffs, like losing at home to Chicago or falling on their face the day they clinched the division title in Minnesota.

"It was one game during the regular season that we failed to win that would have kept us in a position to play here, rather than go to Buffalo," said Schottenheimer. "The record speaks very clearly, nobody has beaten Buffalo in Buffalo in a playoff game.

"The solution is very simple: don't go 7-1 at home; go 8-0. Don't go 4-4 on the road; go 5-3."

Kimble Anders dressed quickly after the game and sat in front of his locker, waiting for questions from the media. Anders had made a significant contribution in 1993, as the new offense fit his running and receiving skills. He had even come out of his shell and, while he was still the quietest player in the Chiefs' locker room, his conversations were more frequent and his shy smile more evident during the season.

"I saw it well and looked it in. I felt like it was slick against my gloves. I really can't say what happened," Anders said over and over again, as wave after wave of reporters washed over him.

Teammates consoled him as best they could, and Allen whispered something in his ear that made him smile. But the pain that showed in his eyes never disappeared.

"The enlightening thing about it is we realize that we are a good team and that we can come back and do this again," Allen said. "I would say that they should be proud of everything they have accomplished, and I think that taste in our mouth should bring us back next year."

Schottenheimer tried to stress the success of the 1993 season.

"There's a frustration and a disappointment that goes with any defeat, especially one that ends your season," said the head coach. "Yet, I think they would be doing themselves a great disservice as players and as people if they were to walk out of here with their heads down. We had a very good season, albeit not what we were after."

That did little to console Montana.

"It's more disappointing to lose this game than to not have made the playoffs at all," said Montana. "If you don't make the playoffs, you can just sort of write the whole thing off. We thought we had done some things pretty well. We had played some pretty tight games near the end, and we felt we had played well enough to advance.

"Then, they came out and played better than we did."

About two hours after the game, the Chiefs boarded their America West Airlines charter flight back to Kansas City. It was dark, and snow was blowing across the icy tarmac, making the scene at the Buffalo Airport seem more like Ice Station Zebra.

Off to the side, center Tim Grunhard stood by himself. At the start of the playoffs, Grunhard had begun growing a beard. He planned to shave it off in the locker room at the Super Bowl. But as he stood watching his teammates board the plane, he was clean shaven.

"I've only felt like this once before," Grunhard said. "That was the day my father died.

"Damn that Chicago game, damn that Minnesota game. That just killed us."

Someone suggested to Grunhard that he remember the hurt so that the next time his team was struggling towards another poor regular-season performance, he could remind them of the pain of losing in Buffalo.

"I'll never forget," Grunhard said. "Never. Not until . . . " His words trailed off in the wind and snow.

Earlier in the locker room, assistant coach Al Saunders talked about what happened that day in Buffalo. "It's a bitch growing up," Saunders said. "You've got to learn the hard way."

The Chiefs had grown up in 1993, and it had been anything but easy.

CHAPTER TWO

THE DEATH OF "MARTY BALL"

The outcome of the AFC Championship Game in Buffalo was disappointing, yet as Marty Schottenheimer counseled, there was an underlying sense of achievement throughout the franchise. The results were not good enough to reach the Super Bowl, but the team seemed headed in the right direction.

The same could not be said for the year before, in the moments after the Chiefs loss to San Diego 17-0 in the first round of the 1992 playoffs.

After the game, in the cramped visitors locker room at Jack Murphy Stadium, the obvious disappointment among the Chiefs was overshadowed by anger. That day, the defense received no help from the offense, reflecting a pattern established during the regular season, one that left most of the players merely happy to make the playoffs, and with little confidence it would lead to anything memorable. The offensive performance against the Chargers proved the doubters' feelings.

Veteran cornerback Kevin Ross seemed the most upset after the game. He vowed that if changes were not made in the Chiefs' offensive attack before the start of the 1993 season, he would not return to the team. Ross said he would rather retire than go through another season with an offense that relied so heavily on a conservative running game.

"When you get zero, you have to make changes," said Ross. "We have a good team, with talent, but we don't utilize what we have. We obviously have to make changes."

Ross spoke for many members of the team that day. What he and other players did not know was that someone else agreed with their view: Marty Schottenheimer.

The Chiefs' head coach decided long before the postseason shutout that his offense needed a significant overhaul. In 1992, Kansas City's offensive yardage total ranked 25th out of 28 teams. They scored just 29 offensive touchdowns, an average of less than two a game. In eight of the 17 games played that season, they scored 21 points or less, and won just one of those games.

Since leaving Cleveland and coming to the Chiefs in 1989, Schottenheimer offense relied on the running game. It was called "Smash Mouth" by some, "Marty Ball" by most. There was no question of its emphasis: heavy on running between the tackles and a lot of play-action in the passing game. The idea was to make no mistakes on offense, rely on a stout defense, and then in the second half of games grind it out with the running attack, wearing down opponents and escaping with victory.

From 1989 through 1991, few teams ran the ball better than the Chiefs. They always finished among the top ten teams in rushing yardage. In that span, no other team ran the ball more times than the Chiefs, and it produced 1,000-yard rushers each year. Christian Okoye led the NFL with 1,480 yards in 1989, Barry Word totaled 1,015 yards in 1990, and Okoye followed with 1,031 yards in 1991.

As with any scheme, there were weaknesses in "Marty Ball," and they became very apparent in the 1991 season. Opposing defenses began crowding the line of scrimmage, bringing eight, sometimes nine players up to stop the run. And when the Chiefs defense could not keep opponents off the scoreboard, it was nearly impossible for the Chiefs to stage a comeback with a passing game so reliant on the play-action pass. They simply did not have the ability to change gears and go from a running emphasis to passing in a moment's notice.

Plus, the Chiefs' touchdown production dropped:

	Total Points	Offensive Touchdowns	Total games/ Games with 21 points or less
1989	318	32	16/11
1990	385	35	17/8
1991	346	36	18/13
1992	348	29	17/8

In preparation for the 1992 season, the Chiefs worked on several new elements for "Marty Ball." Schottenheimer still wanted to rely on the running game, but with a different approach. He started the changes by switching quarterbacks. Steve DeBerg was out, Dave Krieg was in. DeBerg had been the Chiefs starter since 1988, although Schottenheimer benched him numerous times in their three seasons together. Schottenheimer admired DeBerg's toughness, but was driven to distraction by the quarterback's penchant for making the wrong play at the wrong time.

Krieg played 12 seasons with the Seattle Seahawks and was better known for setting an NFL record for career fumbles than for his solid, sometimes spectacular passing. Krieg had one thing DeBerg did not: mobility. The Chiefs signed Krieg to a two-year contract as a Plan B free agent.

Schottenheimer wanted diversity in his attack and he wanted that to come through motions and shifts. Because of his background as a defensive coach, he understood how hard it was to decipher an opponent's offense when players were moving around and lining up in different formations on each play. By adding more dimensions and options, Schottenheimer felt opposing safeties would be forced away from the line and back to their normal stations. Plus, the shifting and motion would create mismatches that could be exploited by the offense. Schottenheimer sought ways to allow receivers room to run after making catches.

"The problem I had with our offense was every catch we made, we had our receiver facing the ball," said Schottenheimer. "We had our backs to the defensive backs, so as soon as you caught the ball, you were hit and went down. There was not a chance for our receivers to run with the ball. Now, unless you have a big, physically strong receiver like Jerry Rice, the big plays only come when a defensive back makes a mistake and your receiver beats him deep. I wanted to do something where you could catch the ball running vertically, creating lanes that could turn a short throw into a big yardage play."

Offensive coordinator Joe Pendry was charged with making sure these new elements were part of the offense. During the off-season program, mini-camps, and early in training camp, the Chiefs worked hard on implementing the changes. But as the 1992 season began, the additions began to disappear and the Chiefs' offense did not look much different than previous seasons. The play calling tended toward the predictable, in part because the offense was struggling as Krieg learned a new system.

"We knew it would start slowly," said Schottenheimer. "David was trying to catch up to everyone else. That's a hard thing to do, especially when it's your trigger-man trying to make up ground."

What disturbed the head coach more than anything was the way the changes slowly drifted out of the game plans. Schottenheimer does not create the offensive game plan each week. He is consulted, but the real work of creating an attack for each opponent is done by the offensive coaching staff.

"When you hire people to do a job, you let them do the job," said Schottenheimer. "You give them whatever assistance is necessary in the form of resources and personnel and then allow them to work. Joe Pendry's position was well taken way back in the off-season when we started working on these changes. He said, 'I don't want to coach something that I'm not familiar with.' I told him, 'I wouldn't do that, it wouldn't be right.' My thought was that as it unfolded during the off-season and training camp, he would become comfortable with it."

Pendry never did become "comfortable with it." His reluctance to implement the changes and the poor offensive play came to a head in Denver with the help of an old Schottenheimer nemesis, John Elway.

It was Sunday, October 4, 1992, and on this warm, cloudy day, with a breeze blowing off the nearby Rocky Mountains, the Chiefs found themselves in control of the game. They were putting together one of their best offensive performances of the season and held a 13-point, fourth-quarter lead, seemingly on their way to their first victory over the Broncos at Mile High Stadium since 1982.

With five minutes to play, Broncos fans were leaving the stadium in bunches. Despite Elway's penchant for late heroics, traffic jams were building on the streets and in the parking lots. The Chiefs also believed this game belonged to them.

"No way he was bringing them back," remembered Ross. "We had it."

Not quite. Elway had them. Again.

Thanks to several key Chiefs blunders, Elway was able to throw two touchdown passes in the final two minutes. Denver won the game 20-19. It was the 30th comeback victory of Elway's career.

As the Chiefs filed into their locker room under the erector-set stands of Mile High, shock masked the face of every player and coach. Distress glazed their eyes. Cleats hitting the concrete floor was the only sound that pierced the silence of frustration and embarrassment.

Schottenheimer walked off the field, jaw set, eyes clear. He had seen this happen many times before, perhaps more than any human being should be asked to endure over a coaching career. Elway did it twice to Schottenheimer's Cleveland teams in the 1986 and 1987 AFC Championship Games. In 1990 and 1991, the Chiefs held fourth-quarter leads in Denver, but had been unable to pull out a victory.

Schottenheimer had been an NFL head coach since the middle of the 1984 season, and through that visit to Mile High, his record against the rest of the NFL was 78-46-1, a career-winning percentage of .628. Yet against the Broncos and Elway, his record was 1-9, a winning percentage of .100.

He spoke quietly to his team, checked on injured players with the medical staff and finally headed for the coaches dressing room. Only then did his personal frustration show itself. He slammed the door to the room so hard behind him, some thought it would come off its hinges.

On the flight home and the next day in reviewing tape of the game, Schottenheimer was convinced something needed to change. There were a handful of key mistakes in Denver, with contributions from the offense, defense and special teams. What upset him the most was the offense. The play calling in the fourth quarter was more conservative than Rush Limbaugh. The Chiefs ran on all seven first-down plays in the final period when they had the lead, and Krieg threw only in obvious passing situations. Although they finished the game with an almost five-minute edge in time of possession, they went three plays and punted two of the last three times they had the ball.

Giving Elway those opportunities proved to be football suicide.

"Those guys (Denver) were standing on the sidelines, down 13 points late in the fourth quarter and they knew they were going to win the game," said Schottenheimer. "But that wasn't the problem. Our problem was our guys were on our sideline, and they knew Denver was going to win the game.

"We had to do something to change that mentality."

Schottenheimer's first instinct was to make immediate changes in the offense, demanding that the motions and shifts become a major part of the weekly game plan.

"As the head coach, I had two options," explained Schottenheimer. "I could have mandated that we were going to do the things we had practiced in the off-season and early in training camp. I could have told them (the offensive staff) I didn't care if they were comfortable, that they had to do it the best way they could because that's what I wanted. That was one option.

"The alternative was to go on and do the things your staff is familiar and comfortable with, and make changes after the season was over."

By "changes" Schottenheimer meant a shuffling of his offensive coaching staff and probably a new coordinator. After talking it over with Carl Peterson, the head coach decided that mandating change five weeks into the season would cause more problems than it solved. The Chiefs would emphasize "Marty Ball," and if everybody stayed healthy, and if they made a couple of breaks for themselves, the offense could take them into the playoffs and possibly beyond.

"My concern was, if I became a dictator on this thing, we would have coaches working with something they didn't believe in," said Schottenheimer. "That was going to be obvious to the players, and we probably would not have even made the play-offs."

The decision to stick with "Marty Ball" did not end the Chiefs' offensive woes. Krieg improved as the season progressed, and by November, he was the only consistent part of the attack. Schottenheimer began a running-back roulette as he tried to find the ball carrier with the hot hand. Okoye, Word and Harvey Williams were all given chances. From one game to the next . . . heck, one half to the next, there was no clue who would be the featured back that day. Over 17 games that season, all three backs had starting assignments, and they traded the leading rusher role on almost a weekly basis.

The indecision at running back and the problems with the direction of the entire offense eventually became apparent to the players.

"When I reflect back on it, what was going on with the offense and the offensive staff, I think the players could sense that," Schottenheimer said. "There was a lot of pressure on some coaches during the year and that's not something you can always hide. I'm sure I did not always cover my feelings as well as I should.

"But a feeling had permeated the players that there were problems."

Schottenheimer has called the 1992 season one of his toughest as a head coach. He knew in early October that once the season ended, he would be making a change at offensive coordinator.

"It was not Joe Pendry's fault; it was my fault," said Schottenheimer. "I think Joe's a helluva good football coach, and the things he's been involved with, he has been very, very successful. It was my fault for trying to implement something he was not comfortable with doing.

"I thought our football team needed to do things differently."

Some head coaches change their staffs every year, often in an attempt to save their own skin with the owner, fans or media. That, however, is not Marty Schottenheimer's way. He parted company with the Cleveland Browns after the 1988 season, when majority owner Art Modell asked him to make changes on his coaching staff.

In four full seasons as head coach of the Browns, Schottenheimer's staff of assistants had been remarkably stable with only five changes, most of those the result of assistants moving on to head coaching or coordinator jobs. Eight coaches were with him the entire four years. Schottenheimer came up through the NFL assistant coaching ranks and understood the pressures and sacrifices made by the staff. He was loyal— sometimes to a fault— if one was to believe Modell.

In Kansas City, only three coaches left his staff in three years: defensive coordinator Bill Cowher was named head coach of the Pittsburgh Steelers, secondary coach Tony Dungy left to become defensive coordinator of the Minnesota Vikings, and offensive assistant Jim Erkenbeck left to join the Los Angeles Rams, where he was going to have a bigger part in the game plan. Schottenheimer did not want any of them to leave the Chiefs.

In this case, he knew changes were a must, but that did not make it any easier when he called in Pendry, offensive line coach Howard Mudd, and running backs coach Bruce Arians, and fired them the day after the San Diego postseason game.

"You're talking about people that had been through a lot with us," said Schottenheimer. "It was not enjoyable or satisfying. It was necessary. I knew the direction I wanted to go."

Even before he made the changes, Schottenheimer talked with the man who would take over the offense.

Paul Hackett spent 23 years in coaching, going all the way back to his first days on the sidelines at his alma mater, the University of California-Davis. Through stops at California-Berkeley and Southern California in the college ranks, and Cleveland, San Francisco and Dallas in the NFL, Hackett coached only one position: quarterback. In fact, it was the only position he played in high school and college. Even when he became a head coach at the University of Pittsburgh in December 1989, Hackett still coached the quarterbacks.

"I was never as interested in the hitting part of the game as I was in the passing, the ways to fool people, the sense of spacing, throwing, spreading people out, that's been the theme of what I've done over the years," said Hackett. "For me, the thrill has a lot to do with strategies, the X's and O's, the teaching of how you go about doing things as you attack and put together game plans. I've been very fortunate because quarterbacks are naturally inquisitive, and they are naturally interested in why you do things, and the little things that exist in their game. That's always been great fun for me. Maybe it is as close as I can get to still be playing. It's taking what you know and giving it to someone else, and watching them take it to greater heights with their physical ability."

Hackett is the type of coach who lays awake at night, mentally drawing diagrams on the bedroom ceiling as he searches for new ways to move the ball. He is an intense competitor, a stickler for fundamentals with his quarterbacks.

During his stop in Cleveland (1981-82), Hackett worked with Schottenheimer on Sam Rutigliano's staff. When Hackett went to Pitt in 1989, Schottenheimer — a graduate of Pitt, Class of 1965 — made some phone calls. They stayed in touch over the years.

Hackett had been considered one of those up-and-coming assistant coaches in the NFL ranks while with the 49ers (1983-85). He was there when San Francisco won Super Bowl 19. When candidates for head coaching jobs were mentioned, his name seemed to be near the top of everybody's list. Part of the reason he left San Francisco and joined the Dallas Cowboys for the 1986 season were the rumblings that Tom Landry was going to retire soon as the Cowboys head coach. People in the Dallas organization such as general manager Tex Schramm were talking about Hackett as a possible replacement for Landry.

"I left San Francisco at a real high point, both for the 49ers and for myself," said Hackett. "I went to Dallas because it was a new horizon, a new opportunity. I had great admiration for Tom Landry, Tex Schramm and that organization. I felt it was the right move for me at that time. There was a sense that maybe Tom would be towards the end of his career, and there were rumblings with ownership. It was an opportunity to coach an offense I knew, to mix it with what Tom had been successful with. It was a great learning experience for me."

Tom Landry, however, did not retire. He was fired. Jerry Jones bought the franchise and dumped Landry in April of 1989, replacing him with his old college football teammate at the University of Arkansas, Jimmy Johnson.

Hackett landed at the University of Pittsburgh, where he coached quarterbacks on Mike Gottfried's staff. But in December of 1989, Gottfried resigned under pressure, and Hackett was named interim head coach for the John Hancock Sun Bowl, a 31-

28 victory over Texas A&M University. Eventually, the interim was removed from the title, and Hackett became the leader of a Pitt program that faced some major problems.

There were developing stories about some of the actions by assistants on Gottfried's staff, the type of activity that usually brought NCAA investigators to campus. The school's booster club, the Golden Panthers, was having problems as well, with an internal investigation of its financial records. Then, the two men who hired Hackett — Chancellor Wesley Posvar and athletic director Edward Bozik — both resigned. A new group of leaders took over, with J. Dennis O'Connor as chancellor and Oval Jaynes as athletic director, and their agenda was different than Hackett's.

Had the Panthers won enough football games, Hackett probably could have survived the off-field turmoil. But Pitt went 3-7-1 in 1990, 6-5 in 1991 and 3-9 in 1992. They were never a factor for a bowl game.

Under pressure from all sides, Hackett resigned in November 1992, before the Panthers' final game of the season in Hawaii.

"College football is an interesting phenomenon right now," said Hackett. "In the late 1970s, when I was at USC, it was totally different than it is in the 1990s, because of the involvement of the college presidents. The things that went on at the University of Pittsburgh from an academic standpoint were different from the historic Pitt approach. I felt I had the ideals and philosophies that were in keeping with the administration and the athletic director. But when all the changes were made, with a new athletic director and a new president, we were not speaking the same language, if you will."

Schottenheimer considered several people for the offensive coordinator's position. Lindy Infante was available. Infante was fired after the 1991 season as head coach of the Green Bay Packers, and he was on Schottenheimer's staff in Cleveland. They remained good friends, and Infante's offensive philosophy matched what Schottenheimer was trying to do with the Chiefs.

"What I wanted was to get receivers in a position where they can catch the ball in the seams and run vertically with it because it obviously produces more yardage," said Schottenheimer. "We were doing some of that in '92, but ultimately we didn't get it done. Within the framework of this type of offense, you can create possible mismatches and you can get people running wide open because somebody, through shifting or motion, fails to cover that guy. It puts a lot of pressure on the defense, as they try to sort out the possibilities.

"I was not looking for an aerial assault-type offense, where the ball is launched down the field all the time. I wanted a possession, high-percentage type of passing game."

The man to do that was Hackett, and his appointment was announced on January 13, 1993, less than two weeks after the postseason disaster in San Diego. Upon his introduction, Hackett used all the words and phrases the Kansas City fans wanted to hear — "wide open", "multi-dimensional" and "split-back" — while promising that the offense would have a lot of motion and shifting.

"We will be a ball-control, passing team," said Hackett. "This system is about getting the ball to people in space and letting them be successful. It's not about power running; it's not going to be deep passing. It is based on the use of many different looks. You won't see us doing the same thing over and over again. It uses a variety of ways to attack a defense, both with the use of formations and the use of multiple plays.

"The nice thing about this offense is we will always be creating, we will always come up with new ideas," Hackett continued. "We are never going to be afraid to try new ideas because we are not waiting for something to happen. We are going to make something happen."

Schottenheimer was very happy that Hackett was coming to Kansas City.

"No. 1, Paul Hackett is an outstanding football coach and No. 2 he has a familiarity with a system that I thought was very, very efficient, with multiple formations and shifts, which I think are very, very important," said Schottenheimer. "And there was a third reason, and it was as important as the first two: he is an outstanding quarterbacks coach. He has excellent ability to teach, coach and instruct that particular position."

With the addition of Hackett, the Chiefs took a 180-degree turn in offensive philosophy. The new scheme eschewed the power game, relying on the short, possession-type passing that Schottenheimer felt pressured defenses into making mistakes. "It's not that this offense is all that unusual or that unpredictable," said Hackett. "It's just that it is so different than what the Chiefs did; it is so magnified."

Whether it is called the San Francisco offense or West Coast offense, Bill Walsh made it work with the 49ers, winning three Super Bowls before resigning after the 1988 season. The next year, San Francisco won another title with George Seifert as head coach. The 49ers were the unquestioned team of the 1980s, and Walsh was dubbed a football genius for making the offense work so well with quarterback Joe Montana.

Like most in the coaching profession, Walsh borrowed from the different offenses to which he was exposed as he rose through the ranks and studied the game. He was influenced by Clark Shaughnessy's man-in-motion offense created in the 1940s at Stanford and with the Chicago Bears. Walsh's offense featured a lot of ball-handling by the quarterback, and this came from Delaware's winged-T offense under Dave Nelson. The biggest influence came during the one season when Walsh worked with the Oakland Raiders (1966). Raiders managing general partner Al Davis' offensive concepts came from his stint as an assistant coach for Sid Gillman of the Chargers in the early 1960s. With the Raiders, Walsh learned the multi-dimensional passing game, with its emphasis on throwing to the backs and tight ends.

During time as an assistant coach under Paul Brown with the Cincinnati Bengals (1968-75), Walsh refined his offensive thoughts even more and learned the importance of preparation and planning. By coming up with an alternative for every situation imaginable, Walsh learned there was very little that defenses could do to surprise him.

The key to the Walsh offense is the short passing game, or the "nickel and dime" attack as it was called by detractors. Walsh's thinking became: Why have a running play that gains 3 or 4 yards, when a safe, short pass gains 6 or 7 yards? In its purest form, this offense might not put a lot of points on the scoreboard, but it dominates possession time, racking up first downs and keeping the opponent's offense off the field.

The short passing game works with timed passes and precise patterns. This is achieved through hours of practice with specific situations and quick releases by the quarterback. Sometimes the ball is thrown to a spot on the field, with the quarterback aware that this is where the receiver will end up.

It is a scheme that demands rhythmic passing by the quarterback. When the passer drops back to throw, he begins running through the list of possible receivers; usually four, sometimes all five eligible players are involved in the play. He checks short first, allowing the deeper patterns to develop before looking long. The whole time, the clock is ticking in his head . . . one . . . two . . . three . . . and if he sees nothing available, he dumps it off to his alternate receiver — usually the running back — on a short pattern in what is nothing more than an extended handoff.

The offense tries to create pass coverage mismatches through shifting and motion, hoping the opposing defense overreacts and leaves an area of the field vulnerable. If the defense is playing in man-to-man coverage, this motion can create situations where a linebacker is forced to cover a speedy wide receiver or running back. If the defense is in zone coverage, moving a player across the formation can overload one area, forcing adjustments by the defense that can be exploited elsewhere.

"I came into this offense in 1983, and there had been a lot that went on during Bill Walsh's coaching career," said Hackett. "There was a Sid Gillman influence, a Paul Brown influence. Bill had worked with Kenny Anderson in Cincinnati, and that was probably the basis of what I know in this offense.

"Bill Walsh was an absolutely superb teacher. He could go to the board and get you into this offense like nobody else. And he had a mind for creativity. It was those elements, combined with Joe Montana's skills, that over 10 years developed this offense, and sent it out in various other forms. There's Sam Wyche in Tampa, Mike Holmgrem in Green Bay, Denny Green in Minnesota. We all took a piece of what was happening there, expanded and refined it."

Walsh's offensive style relies completely on the skills of the quarterback, and was designed around the talents of Montana.

"Every offense does not run on the quarterback," said Hackett. "The quarterback is always the driver of the car, but the car may be designed so that he only compliments the running game.

"Our offense starts with the quarterback's skills. We design a system that is going to enhance the quarterback's ability to be successful. All of this is based on the short passing game. It's not the I-formation, running the ball, although that doesn't mean we wouldn't use the I-formation. But we are never going to start with a running back or a wide receiver or a tight end. We start with quarterback. We are going to construct around this person in every way possible, to take advantage of his abilities."

In January of 1993, the No. 1 question became:

Who was going to play quarterback for the Kansas City Chiefs?

CHAPTER THREE

THE IDEA OF JOE

Valentine's Day 1993.

The Westin Hotel.

Indianapolis, Indiana.

That was the date and location when the Kansas City Chiefs first seriously discussed the possibility of acquiring Joe Montana.

On a day reserved for lovers, Chiefs vice-president of player personnel Lynn Stiles' thoughts were not of hearts and flowers, but of the quarterback many people believe is the greatest to play the game. February 14 was the day when Stiles first said out loud what he had been thinking for several weeks: instead of trying to cram the Chiefs' new offense down the throat of Dave Krieg, why not acquire the man who helped create the attack and turn it into one of the most successful schemes in pro football history?

Montana's name already was being thrown around by radio talk show callers in Kansas City. General Manager Carl Peterson's mail was encouraging the Chiefs' interest in Montana or San Francisco's other quarterback, Steve Young. The common belief around the National Football League was the 49ers could not keep both Montana, who was coming back from two years of inactivity because of elbow problems, and Young, who stepped into the job and led the NFL in passing efficiency. Public speculation reached a point where the Kansas City Star ran a story on

February 12, mentioning the talk of Montana, Young and the Chiefs.

On Valentine's Day, the front office and coaching staffs of the Chiefs were in Indianapolis, attending an exercise known as the Scouting Combine workout sessions. Each February, 300 to 400 players from the college ranks who will be available for the spring NFL draft are brought to Indy, where they undergo every test imaginable, from physical to mental — even emotional. It is one of the most significant moments of the annual talent evaluation process, and it brings all the league's general managers, head coaches and personnel people together in an intense week of work.

The Chiefs entourage had been in Indianapolis for several days, and phoned home with their Valentine's Day apologies to wives and significant others. Holidays, birthdays, anniversaries, school plays — they take a back seat when there is work to be done in the NFL. After a long day of meetings and player interviews, most of the Chiefs group retired to the lobby bar at the Westin for a before-bedtime beverage. As they sat and chatted, Stiles began building for Peterson the scenario of Joe Montana's availability.

As Stiles talked, Peterson did not jump out of his chair with excitement. These "what if" discussions happen all the time in the world of professional football, and 99 percent of them never become more than conversations.

"Carl's first reaction — and I'll never forget it — was, 'He's a 49er, he is still under contract,'" said Stiles. "And that was true. But I just asked in the vein of what if? What would it take to get him, what would we give up to get him, what are the possibilities? Would the 49ers at least consider a possible trade?"

Said Peterson: "I guess that night in Indianapolis is when we first really talked about Joe Montana. His name came up several times before in conversations, but it was never seriously discussed. During the course of a season, you talk about a lot of players, do a lot of 'what if . . .' talking. When we hired Paul Hackett as offensive coordinator, the conversation included a discussion of Joe. But I don't think anyone took it seriously."

Stiles took it seriously. Before joining the Chiefs, Stiles was an assistant coach with San Francisco for five years (1987-1991), taking part in two of the 49ers' Super Bowl victories. Because of his connections, Stiles knew something Peterson did not: the 49ers' starting quarterback was not going to be Joe Montana, even if his injured elbow was healed. It was going to be Steve Young.

"Obviously, I had a little more insight into what was going on than most people," said Stiles. "And it wasn't just the knowledge of Joe's elbow injury, but knowledge about the status of Steve Young and the thought process that was transpiring there with the 49ers. George Seifert and I have known each other for a long time. We went to college together (University of Utah); at one time we were roommates. So I could talk with George and be right up front, and I felt he was with me. He was committed to Steve Young."

Stiles also knew there was no way Montana was going to be the backup for Young in San Francisco, or any place. Montana did not like Young and had a hard time concealing his feelings. Theirs was termed a "working relationship." In the summer of 1992, Montana was quoted as saying about Young: ". . . He's on my team, but as far as I'm concerned, he's part of the opposition. He wants what I have."

Montana has never said publicly what Young did to upset him. He has hinted that Young said and did some things behind the scenes that Montana felt were unprofessional. Montana also sensed the 49ers organization treated Young differently. Almost from the time he was acquired in a 1987 trade with Tampa Bay, Young was given 50 percent of the offensive snaps in practice. Most backup quarterbacks are lucky to get 25 percent. The Montana-Young rivalry was also fueled by the San Francisco media and fans, all aware of Montana's contributions, but wondering if Young was not a better option because he was five years younger and without a lengthy history of injury. And, their frosty relationship could simply have been two very competitive people fighting over playing time.

Throughout his career, Montana did not make a habit of feuding with the other 49ers quarterbacks. In fact, he was a very good friend of San Francisco's third quarterback, Steve Bono, and they frequently played golf together. Had Bono been the starter — and at one point when Young was injured in 1991, Bono directed the 49ers to a 5-1 record before he too, was injured — it would not have been so bad for Montana.

Stiles knew all of this.

"What I tried to get across to everyone that night in Indianapolis was Joe Montana was not going to be on the sidelines with the San Francisco 49ers, carrying a clipboard," Stiles said. "I knew there was no way that was going to happen. That is not his style. If he is able to play football, he's going to be playing, not watching.

"Marty had already made the moves on the coaching staff, bringing in Paul, and the San Francisco offense. And that's all well and good, but coaches coach, they don't play. To be able to go get the trigger man who made it all possible just seemed like the reasonable thing to do."

Hackett owned his own Super Bowl ring from his time as an assistant coach with San Francisco. Although he did not work with Stiles, he went through very similar experiences.

"We had, in a sense, been in the huddle with him," said Hackett. "We understood the impact he can have on a team, not simply as a talent, but because of the kind of player and person that he is. Once you've had a chance to be around him, you don't forget the experience."

Hackett had been away from the 49ers for eight years, and while he talked regularly with Montana, he was not as informed about the situation in San Francisco as Stiles.

"I did not know Steve Young; he came after I left," said Hackett. "I did not have a full appreciation for the team and the organization, where it was going and what their plans were. I did not have a clue in what direction they were gravitating. But there was no question that if Joe Montana was going to leave San Francisco, we needed to find a way to be involved."

Until that Valentine's Day conversation, the Chiefs spent more time talking about Young and Bono, who both were scheduled to be free agents. Montana had one more year on his contract with the 49ers, although there was some dispute over the terms.

Peterson and head coach Marty Schottenheimer were not unhappy with the 1992 performance of Krieg. He carried the Chiefs to the playoffs with a strong effort in the second half of the season, and the step backwards in '92 was blamed on many things and people, but not Krieg. The only reason the quarterback position was discussed was the new offense being installed by Hackett. The Bill Walsh-system is built completely around the quarterback and Peterson and Schottenheimer knew it might take time for the offense to perform at a successful level under Krieg. He would be learning his third offensive system in three years, and one significantly different than the "Marty Ball" scheme of the previous season.

"We were talking about starting from scratch," said Schottenheimer. "It was going to be difficult for just about any quarterback to learn enough about this offense to get it up and running the way we needed. David had not been exposed to an offense like this one."

So, while Stiles was building the case for Montana with Peterson, Hackett worked on Schottenheimer. He found a willing listener.

"Paul did not have to do much convincing with me," said Schottenheimer. "I liked the idea from the time it was first seriously discussed. I saw Joe as a guy who could make a difference — and make it quickly — with our team.

"My feeling is you always have an open mind about things you don't know. As an example, I was a bit reluctant with the Barry Word situation when we signed him in 1990. He had been out of football. He had a strike against him with the drug policy (Word had been imprisoned on cocaine charges while at the University of Virginia). But (pro personnel director) Mark Hatley was very persistent. He kept coming back and selling me on the idea of signing Barry. And despite how it ended (Word was traded in September of 1993), I think signing Barry worked out well for us.

"It was pretty clear he was going to leave San Francisco. If that was the case, then I certainly wanted to consider the possibility (of a trade), and consider it seriously."

Added Hackett:

"Marty was always fascinated by the idea of Joe from the very beginning. I don't know how serious he was, but he was always asking, talking about Joe. We had open-ended discussions about the offense and the position.

"This system is good enough that we can use the base, and then depending on who the quarterback is, we could develop the priorities and emphasis areas. But I always came back to one thing: this offense was developed for this one person's skills —

Joe Montana. If this person was available, it seemed silly not to make an attempt to get him."

Hackett had a close relationship with Montana and stayed in touch even after he left San Francisco.

"I had talked with Joe on a regular basis, especially during that last season (1992), when he had such a tough time and couldn't get on the field," said Hackett, who at the time was at the University of Pittsburgh. "He was frustrated, and he was always saying, 'Something has to happen, something has to happen.' But he never said anything about leaving.

"The day Marty offered me the job, before I had even given him an answer, I called Joe. We talked about him coming here then, but that was only kidding. Neither one of us took it seriously. But at some point, we did start to discuss the possibility a little more seriously."

The major question, however, was not whether the Chiefs wanted Montana, or Montana wanted the Chiefs. It was: Could Joe Montana still play? Could he perform at the same level that over the 14 previous seasons guaranteed his admission to the Pro Football Hall of Fame once his career was over?

Under every criteria established for judging quarterbacks, Joseph Clifford Montana, Jr., is considered the best to play the game of professional football. Arguments can be made for the greatness of Johnny Unitas and Otto Graham. Quarterbacks like Bart Starr and Fran Tarkenton will be mentioned by some, and old timers will point to Sid Luckman and Sammy Baugh.

But Montana's career overshadows all of them.

STATISTICS: Montana ranks among the NFL's all-time leaders in career passing yards, attempts and completions. Only Tarkenton, Unitas and Dan Marino have thrown more touchdown passes. In the league's complicated quarterback rating system, he is the highest-rated passer in history.

CHAMPIONSHIPS: Montana was part of four Super Bowl championships with San Francisco. The only quarterback to start in more victorious NFL title games is Starr, who played in five with the Green Bay Packers. Terry Bradshaw was also on four Super Bowl winners with the Pittsburgh Steelers.

CLUTCH PERFORMANCES: Look up clutch in the NFL dictionary and it says, "See Joe Montana." Going into the 1993 season, he had directed 26 fourth-quarter comebacks to victory. A couple of those ranked among the most famous clutch plays in NFL history.

On January 10, 1982, in the National Football Conference Championship Game at Candlestick Park, Montana faced third-and-three at the Dallas 6-yard line with one minute to play and the 49ers trailing by six points. Scrambling out of the pocket and under heavy pressure, he found wide receiver Dwight Clark in the end zone for a touchdown pass that sent the 49ers to their first Super Bowl. San Francisco 28, Dallas 27. In San Francisco, they call it "The Catch."

On January 22, 1989, in Super Bowl 23 at Joe Robbie Stadium in Miami, Montana faced a 92-yard drive with just over three minutes to play in the game. The 49ers needed a touchdown to beat the Cincinnati Bengals. Over the next 11 plays, Montana led the San Francisco offense down the field, finally connecting with wide receiver John Taylor on a 10-yard touchdown pass with 34 seconds remaining. San Francisco 20, Cincinnati 16. It is still considered the most exciting finish in Super Bowl history.

That was the Montana who San Francisco came to love, NFL teams feared and the rest of America admired. But by the start of the 1993 season, he would be 37 years old. NFL history is littered with great quarterbacks, past their prime, who were traded in hopes of reviving their careers. None had worked out very well.

In 1961, San Francisco traded 34-year-old Y.A. Tittle to the New York Giants. Tittle played for four more seasons and appeared in three NFL title games, losing twice to Green Bay (1961, 1962) and once to Chicago (1963). In those first three seasons, he was among the league leaders in passing, but in that final 1964 season, when he was 37 years old, Tittle threw 22 interceptions, and the Giants finished the season 2-10-2.

Johnny Unitas was 40 years old when the Baltimore Colts traded him after 17 seasons to the San Diego Chargers in 1973. The Chargers went 2-11-1 and Unitas sat on the bench behind Dan Fouts and Wayne Clark. He retired after that season.

Joe Namath was 34 years old in 1977 when the New York Jets traded him to the Los Angeles Rams, ending a 12-season association. Namath played one season for the Rams, who finished 10-4 as he sat on the bench behind starting quarterback Pat Haden.

No matter how remarkable the achievements of football players, they are made of mere human flesh, and after years of being abused by the game, the body sometimes says "Enough."

On August 13, 1991, Montana lofted a 40-yard pass in a drill at the 49ers' training camp in Rocklin, California, and felt something tear in his right elbow. Six weeks of rest followed before Montana threw the football again. When he came back, he tossed some short passes with no problem, but the first time he tried to throw long, there was more tearing and more pain. The common flexor tendon was completely torn away from his right elbow. This tendon controls the rolling motion of the wrist and hand, and rest could not cure the injury.

Surgery was performed on October 9, as holes were drilled in Montana's elbow, and the tendon was reattached to the bone. It was believed to have been the first time the procedure had been done on a football player, let alone a quarterback.

The rehabilitation period caused more problems than the surgery. Montana had undergone procedures on his elbow before, including the removal of a bursa sac in 1988. He had countless shots of cortisone over the years to help him through other injuries to that joint. And Montana was a fast healer, and always seemed to defy the medical assessment of team doctors. He shocked everyone in 1986 after major surgery on his back. A ruptured disk was removed, and his spinal column was widened, which led to serious doubts about whether he would play again. When Montana left the hospital, he was able to move around only with the use of a walker. Eight weeks later, Montana threw three touchdown passes against the St. Louis Cardinals, stunning even long-time teammates and friends who thought they had seen everything. It was the greatest comeback of his career.

However, the elbow injury would prove much harder to overcome, and nobody knew that better than Terry Bradshaw. Growing up in western Pennsylvania, Montana followed Bradshaw's storied career with the Pittsburgh Steelers through four Super Bowl titles, including a 1983 elbow injury. Bradshaw underwent surgery on the elbow and then tried to come back too quickly in the rehabilitation process. The elbow never responded to continued treatment and his career was over.

A similar scenario happened to Montana. Five weeks after his surgery, the brace was removed from his arm, and he started throwing the football; this happened far faster than anyone thought possible. But the elbow was not healed and the setbacks piled up in 1992 for Montana:

APRIL: The 49ers said he looked good throwing the football in limited work during a mini-camp before the NFL draft.

MAY: Minor surgery was performed to remove scar tissue in the elbow.

JULY: As training camp opened, Montana was held to a rigid throwing schedule, working in just one practice a day, with every pass charted by an assistant coach. He threw 40 passes one day, 60 the next.

AUGUST: Montana again experienced pain in the elbow while throwing and his practice work was stopped, leading to a visit with noted orthopedic surgeon Dr. Frank Jobe in Los Angeles. Dr. Jobe told him there was nothing seriously wrong, and prescribed more rest. Montana took more cortisone shots and acupuncture therapy. Before the regular-season opener, he was placed on the 49ers' injured-reserve list, knocking him out of any chance to play in the first four games of the season.

SEPTEMBER: Another minor surgery was performed to clean out debris in the elbow. This procedure, however, would become a major moment in the story of Montana's elbow. While trying to relieve pressure on a nerve near the tendon, the surgeon accidentally nipped the nerve itself, causing the little finger and part of the ring finger on Montana's right hand to become numb and weak.

OCTOBER: Montana began throwing again, but still experienced numbness in his right hand.

"There is so much uncertainty with a nerve," said Montana. "I was wondering if it would come back completely, if it did, when would it come back completely, and how long would it take. I was more scared of the nerve than the original injury."

NOVEMBER: The nerve slowly came around, and Montana was finally taken off the injured-reserve list and added to the 49ers' practice squad. He began throwing regularly in practice with no physical problems.

DECEMBER: Despite Montana's efforts and pleas to be placed on the active roster, George Seifert did not make him eligible until the final game of the year. It was December 28, a Monday night affair at Candlestick Park against the Detroit Lions. The 49ers already had wrapped up home-field advantage through the NFC playoffs. That made it a meaningless game in the standings.

Meaningless, that is, for everyone but Joe Montana.

"I knew at mid-season (1992) that the chances of me being able to stay in San Francisco were not good," Montana said. "Making the attempt to come back, and the things I had to go through, all these little stages and checks I had to go through, which somehow were delayed every time I was ready, it became apparent they weren't going to let it happen.

"That last game was important for me to show that I could still perform. It was probably the most pressure I ever played under, knowing it meant my career."

Before an emotional Candlestick crowd and a national-television audience, Montana started the second half against the Lions with a standing ovation ringing in his ears. He looked like the same calm, cool Montana, completing 15 of 21 passes for 126 yards and touchdown passes of 9 yards to tight end Brent Jones and 8 yards to running back Amp Lee. He also scrambled three times for 28 yards in San Francisco's 24-6 victory. After 23 months of watching, it was an impressive performance — another classic Montana comeback.

"I was traveling cross-country at the time with my son in a car," Stiles recalled. "We listened to the game on the radio, and I can remember that when he went on the field to start the second half and the crowd roared, I got goosebumps.

"Joe Montana could put together a performance like that with his elbow held together by a paper clip," Stiles added. "What he did that night really didn't show anyone how stable and strong his elbow really was. But I knew some people with the 49ers who were catching balls thrown by Joe Montana in practice, and I knew from them that there was nothing wrong with his elbow."

Some six weeks after Montana's return to the field, Peterson remembered walking back to his hotel room in Indianapolis after his conversation with Stiles. More and more his thoughts turned toward Montana.

"There was still so much we didn't know," said Peterson. "But Lynn seemed to have a pretty good handle on the situation.

It did not seem farfetched that Joe Montana would be somewhere other than San Francisco in 1992. If that was going to happen, we needed to be involved. I did not know if it was possible to make a deal, whether it would ultimately make sense for us, but Lynn convinced me we had to investigate."

Despite his own feelings, Paul Hackett was not so sure Joe Montana would ever wear a uniform other than that of the San Francisco 49ers.

"I felt for the longest time that there was no way it would ever happen," said Hackett. "Joe Montana leave San Francisco! A guy with his magnitude and what he meant to the community out there. I had experienced it. I knew how those people felt about him. I knew how Ed DeBartolo, the 49ers owner, felt about him.

"Now, Lynn felt they weren't going to have a choice, that he was too big in the game of football for them to make him stay. That may or may not have been true. But I just couldn't believe they were going to let this thing happen, no matter how much Joe wanted it."

Stiles returned home from Indianapolis, found a picture of Montana, and put it up behind the desk in his Arrowhead Stadium office.

"It got to be a joke with the scouts," Stiles said. "They didn't know how this thing would play out.

"None of us did."

CHAPTER FOUR

CHASING A LEGEND

Joe Montana a free agent?

For a while, the Kansas City Chiefs thought it might be possible.

Montana signed a contract with the San Francisco 49ers in 1990 that reportedly was to pay him a total of $13 million over four seasons ($4 million in 1990, $3.5 million in 1991, $3 million in 1992 and $2.5 million in 1993). As a signing bonus, the 49ers paid Montana his salary for the final year of the contract — $2.5 million — in 1990. The contract language indicated his salary for the '93 season would be negotiated between the parties.

By the time Montana reached the final year of the contract, he had a different attorney representing him, Peter Johnson. After reading the contract, Johnson pointed out what he thought was ambiguous language about the last year of the deal. He told the 49ers that in his opinion Montana had fulfilled the contract terms.

The 49ers thought otherwise, and asked the National Football League office to rule on the validity of Montana's contract.

"There was a real question about his contract status and naturally that was going to affect what happened with him," said Paul Hackett. "It certainly makes a difference if you are signing a player as a free agent, compared to having to pull together a trade."

Said general manager Carl Peterson: "If Joe Montana was a free agent, then it was a whole new ball game. A very complicated situation would then become very uncomplicated."

On March 9, 1993, NFL Commissioner Paul Tagliabue ruled Montana's contract with San Francisco was valid, and his rights remained with the 49ers.

"I talked with Joe after the league ruled on his status, and the conversation turned toward the possibility of a deal," said Hackett. "I told Joe that wasn't my area. I could express how much we were interested, but when you start talking about deals, that's the responsibility of Carl and Marty. Once it became a deal-making situation, from that point on, I really kind of stepped out of the situation."

Montana received assurances from every level of the 49ers organization that he would be allowed to investigate his options around the league. But, once his contract status was clarified, all Montana could do was wait; San Francisco was not going to do anything about his situation until it knew the status of Steve Young and Steve Bono, who were both free agents.

The 49ers solved half the problem in February by naming Young the team's franchise player. Under the new collective bargaining agreement between the NFL owners and players, this special designation effectively removed a player from the free-agent market. There were two options for a team dealing with a franchise player: 1) guarantee him at least the average salary of the five highest-paid players at his position, or 2) allow the player to seek offers from other teams. But if he signed with a new club, the compensation in return was a pair of first-round draft choices. The 49ers selected the first option (Young eventually signed a contract in July that made him the highest paid player in NFL history: five years, $26.5 million. Dallas quarterback Troy Aikman would top that, with his eight-year, $50 million deal signed in December).

Bono became the next hurdle between Montana and freedom from the 49ers. There were some in the San Francisco organization who thought Bono should have been the team's starting quarterback in 1991 instead of Young. When injuries forced Young to the bench that season, Bono stepped in and performed at a very high level before suffering his own knee injury. In 1992, Young remained healthy and Bono spent his time on the bench.

The Chiefs talked seriously about the possibility of signing Bono. Peterson, Schottenheimer and Hackett studied the list of 29 quarterbacks that were in some form of free agency (21 unrestricted, eight restricted). The new offense required a specific style at quarterback, and as they went through the list, names were quickly eliminated until only Bono and Steve Beuerlein were left. Beuerlein was with the Dallas Cowboys as Troy Aikman's backup, and had previously played for the Los Angeles Raiders.

Beuerlein was the first to visit Kansas City, touring the facilities at Arrowhead Stadium on Monday, March 15. He eventually signed a three-year, $7.5 million contract with the Phoenix Cardinals. Bono visited Kansas City on Friday, April 2 with then-Los Angeles Rams running back Robert Delpino.

"We were interested because Bono had kicked our tail running that offense out there," Peterson said, remembering a 28-14 San Francisco victory in 1991 over the Chiefs, where Bono threw three touchdown passes. "But by that time, the key for us really was whether we could get the master — Montana. Could we get the guy who did the original painting?

"We hoped having Bono in and beginning discussions with him would force San Francisco's hand. The 49ers were not going to do anything until Bono signed a new contract. If they didn't get him signed, Joe probably wasn't going to be available. It was a log jam and it could have stayed that way until August."

Said Hackett: "We were very honest with Steve. We told him if there was a chance to get Joe Montana, we would have to consider that. He was very high in our thoughts, but I think by then everyone had decided to see the situation with Joe through, to see if he would actually be available."

Peterson knew Montana was very interested in the Chiefs. By NFL rules, the parties could not contact each other without permission from the 49ers. But there were ways around that without breaking the regulations, i.e., Hackett's regular conversations with Montana that had been going on for years. And, while the Chiefs did not hold discussions with Peter Johnson, Montana's primary agent at the International Management Group (IMG), they were in regular contact with Tom Condon, who also worked for IMG.

A former Chiefs player who spent 11 seasons with the team, Condon heads IMG's pro football division. Headquartered in

Kansas City, he is a regular visitor to Chiefs functions and annually negotiates several contracts with the team. He also happened to be the agent for Beuerlein.

There was little doubt in Montana's camp that Kansas City was a viable option for their man.

"I think from the moment they hired Paul Hackett, I felt Kansas City was where Joe would end up," said Johnson. "It just seemed too perfect a situation. The Chiefs needed a quarterback, and Joe needed a place to play. Plus, Hackett was coming in with the offense that Joe knew. It all made sense."

The only thing stopping the process was the status of Bono. Peterson tried to break the log jam, making a contract offer to Bono and his agent Ralph Cindrich during the April 2 visit. It took less than 24 hours for the 49ers to hear about the Chiefs' offer. San Francisco president Carmen Policy immediately called Bono with a counter-offer that he accepted two days later.

"It was a slam dunk," said Peterson of the 49ers' offer to pay Bono $5.1 million over three seasons. "Steve Bono had to make a decision. It was an awful lot of money, and he was comfortable out there, his family liked living there. His decision to stay did not surprise anyone."

The details on Bono's new deal were completed and announced on Tuesday, April 6. One of the first people Bono called with the news was his good friend Joe Montana. And the first thing Montana did was call Peter Johnson, who then called the 49ers. With Young and Bono locked in, it was time for the team to back up its promise to allow Montana to investigate other opportunities. Policy gave his permission, and Johnson immediately called Carl Peterson. The next day, Wednesday, April 7, Montana made his first visit to Kansas City.

When word leaked out that possibly the greatest quarterback in the history of the game was headed to Kansas City and was interested in playing for the Chiefs, it caught the community by surprise. This was no longer simply the fantasy talk of radio call-in shows. This was the real deal. Television stations shifted into overdrive, and crews were stationed at Kansas City International Airport, monitoring every flight coming in from the west coast. Stories popped up on the front page of the *Kansas City Star* — not the sports section, but page No. 1 of the entire newspaper. Rumors started that Montana already had picked out a home in

Kansas City, and his children were secretly enrolled in a private school.

Montana was the subject of discussion not only on sports radio shows and in sports bars, but over the coffee pot at the office, in lines at the supermarket and in the waiting rooms of doctors and dentists. Calls started pouring into the Chiefs offices from fans who wanted to help in the process. They had ideas, places for the team to take Montana, houses for sale in their neighborhood, recommendations on everything from pediatricians to dry cleaners.

In the face of this emotional response, Peterson had to remain the pragmatic general manager. A top-notch quarterback is the hardest thing to come by in pro football. That is why so many mistakes are made by NFL teams trying to land the next great passer. About the only way to claim the top quarterback prospect in the NFL draft is to finish with one of the worst records in the league, and thus a higher spot in the selection order. Trading a quarterback in the prime of his career is unheard of in the NFL. History shows the harder a team tries to fill the void at quarterback, the more it seems to create problems for itself because it ignores other positions on the team.

Just ask any long-time Chiefs fans. Len Dawson ended his 19-season Hall of Fame career in 1975, and nearly 20 years later the Chiefs were still trying to replace him. In that time frame, they tried selecting quarterbacks in the first round of the NFL draft like Steve Fuller (1979) and Todd Blackledge (1983). They used second-round selections on Mike Elkins (1989) and Matt Blundin (1992). They went out and signed the top quarterbacks from other leagues, such as Tony Adams of the World Football League (1975) and Tom Clements of the Canadian Football League (1980). They made trades for quarterbacks Steve DeBerg (1988) and Steve Pelluer (1989). They signed free agent quarterbacks Ron Jaworski (1989) and David Krieg (1992).

But from 1976 through the 1992 season, 13 different quarterbacks started games for the Chiefs, sometimes with dubious results:

Quarterback	Seasons As Starter	Record As Starter
Mike Livingston	1976-79	11-32
Tony Adams	1977-78	1- 4
Steve Fuller	1979-82	8-15
Bill Kenney	1980-88	34-43
Todd Blackledge	1983-87	13-12
Frank Seurer	1987	0- 2
Matt Stevens	1987	0- 2
Doug Hudson	1987	0- 1
Steve DeBerg	1988-91	34-20
Ron Jaworski	1989	1- 2
Steve Pelluer	1989	1-1-1
Mark Vlasic	1991	0-1
Dave Krieg	1992	10-7

None of these quarterbacks were considered among the best in the game. Bill Kenney went to the Pro Bowl in 1983 as an injury replacement after a 4,348-yard passing season. From 1976 through 1992, 22 quarterbacks were on the Chiefs roster for at least one game, and 10 different quarterbacks were drafted.

Peterson knew all about the history. He had seen it as a competitor while with the Philadelphia Eagles. In the United States Football League, Blackledge had been a territorial draft choice of Peterson's Philadelphia Stars. Peterson participated himself, drafting Elkins and Blundin, trading for Pelluer and signing Jaworski and Krieg. Elkins and Pelluer were major disappointments that Peterson could not forget were part of his record.

"We had failed previously on the selection of some quarterbacks that people in our organization had pushed for very hard," said Peterson. "None were able to keep Steve DeBerg out of the starting lineup. Somehow DeBerg kept resurrecting himself. We made the move with David Krieg, but that was really not much of a gamble.

"What I did not want to happen is another situation like Steve Pelluer. We gave up third-round (1990) and fourth-round (1991) draft choices for Steve Pelluer (in a trade with Dallas) and he contributed very little to our team. For me, it wasn't so much Joe Montana's past and his abilities. These were obvious. It came down to what was the best deal for the Kansas City Chiefs organization. That's where I have to begin and end my thoughts.

"When Peter Johnson called, I told them we were interested in meeting with Joe, but only under certain conditions. The thing we couldn't forget was we were talking about a guy who was going to be 37 years old in the 1993 season. He had been out of football for two years and was coming off major surgery to his elbow.

"Anybody making a deal for Joe was going to have to work out a contract with him. My speech to them was, if Joe was willing to take less compensation than what I knew some other teams would offer him and if the 49ers were willing to take less compensation than I knew other teams would offer them, then we were interested in beginning discussions.

"They didn't hesitate. They were still interested, so we set up the first visit."

At the same time the visit to Kansas City was arranged, Montana and Johnson were talking with the Phoenix Cardinals, the New Orleans Saints and the Tampa Bay Buccaneers. All three teams expressed an interest in Montana, especially the Cardinals, who not only needed a quarterback, but a franchise savior.

After moving the franchise to the Arizona desert from St. Louis before the 1988 season, owner Bill Bidwill's methods drove off Phoenix football fans. Through the 1992 season, the Cardinals had played 40 home games, and only two drew more than 70,000 spectators in Sun Devil Stadium. In those first five seasons in Arizona, Bidwill's team never won more than seven games or challenged for a spot in the playoffs.

And like the Chiefs, the Cardinals had struggled for years to replace a great quarterback. Jim Hart's last season as the full-time starter was 1980 and in the seasons after his eventual retirement in 1983, many players tried the position. Neil Lomax was the most successful before his career was cut short by a serious hip injury. After Lomax came names like Gary Hogeboom, Timm Rosenbach, Tom Tupa and Chris Chandler. The Cardinals invested a 1987 No. 1 draft choice in Kelly Stouffer, who never played a down for the team. So yes, Phoenix was very interested in Joe Montana and a visit was quickly arranged.

New Orleans, however, was a very different story. Montana and Johnson felt the Saints might provide a great opportunity, but they knew the 49ers would never make a trade with a team in their own division. If New Orleans had been in any other division in football, Joe Montana might be wearing a Saints uniform today.

On April 7th, Montana made it past the television cameras and newspaper photographers at Kansas City International Airport. He dined that night at the Plaza III Restaurant with his agents, Johnson and Condon. The next morning, he had breakfast at the Ritz-Carlton Hotel with Marty Schottenheimer and Paul Hackett. Montana spent the rest of the morning with Schottenheimer before going off to the doctor's office for a complete physical examination. Finally, around 5 p.m. he went to the team's indoor training facility for a workout.

Montana threw passes to scouting department intern Bill Osborne, a former defensive back at the University of Pittsburgh. He threw all the different types of passes that the new offense required, and even tested his arm on some deep balls.

By the time it was over, Montana had worked up a sweat.

"It wasn't a super impressive workout," Peterson said. "He's never had a gun of an arm. He doesn't have a tight spiral. He has that tight wobble of his. If you stand behind him and he throws the ball, for an instant you are saying to yourself, 'Where is he throwing it?' And then all of a sudden, the receiver is there, catching the ball. His timing, his anticipation are really the thing that he has done better than anybody in the league and maybe in the history of the game."

Said Stiles: "He went back, he planted those feet, that ball came out of there, it had a little flutter on it and Carl asked me, 'Does he throw the same kind of ball he did a couple years ago?' I told him that ball has always looked that way. He is not at his best until game time. But the workout showed that there was nothing wrong with his elbow, or his arm."

Said Schottenheimer: "It was a good workout, but Joe Montana's never going to look great until he's in a game; the competition drives him. It was enough of a workout to show everyone that he could still throw."

The next morning — Friday, April 9 — Montana was off to Phoenix. He met with the Cardinals owner Bill Bidwill, general manager Larry Wilson and head coach Joe Bugel. He did not work out for the Cardinals, and was flying back to San Francisco by the end of the day.

"I had kind of stepped out of the thing with Joe, but once Phoenix got involved, I became involved more, re-involved I guess you could say," said Hackett. "It was not one of those things where I was talking to him all the time. He knew how I felt and I knew how he felt; we didn't have to keep grinding on it. I just called as a friend and we talked about the situations available to him.

"Hey, I still did not think he was going to leave San Francisco. I thought it was all fantasy."

Tampa Bay became a non-factor because they were not a talented enough team to protect Montana and give him what he wanted most — a fifth Super Bowl ring. Montana called Detroit coach Wayne Fontes to see if the Lions might be interested in talking about a deal. The next day Detroit announced it would not get involved in the chase for Montana.

That left Kansas City and Phoenix. The two teams went in very different directions after Montana's first visit with them.

The Cardinals made Montana a huge contract offer, reportedly three years for $15 million, including $8 million in salary and bonuses the first year. Also, they immediately called the 49ers and began working on a trade, offering the 20th selection in the first round of the draft in exchange for Montana. Ironically, this pick was one the Cardinals were awarded by the NFL after San Francisco signed away Phoenix safety Tim McDonald. Designated the Cardinals' franchise player, McDonald was part of the NFL players' anti-trust lawsuit seeking free agency. As part of the settlement he was able to move without impediment.

Peterson decided the important thing was finding out if an economically feasible deal could be worked out with Montana. Peterson and Johnson held several discussions about a contract by phone, and as happens in most negotiations, both parties were feeling their way, trying to discover what was important to the other side.

On Thursday, April 15th, Montana was back on the road. Tired of waiting, ready to make a decision, Montana wanted it all done by the weekend. With his wife Jennifer, he flew first to Phoenix. As they stepped off the plane at Sky Harbor International Airport they were greeted by the now ubiquitous horde of media. A billboard on the airport access road read: "Arizona: a great place to live and play. The Cardinals welcome Joe Montana." The Montanas met with U.S. Senator Dennis DeConcini. They talked with Bill Bidwill. Joe spent time with head coach Joe Bugel and offensive coordinator Jerry Rhome, while Jennifer was given a tour of Phoenix. Eventually, Montana would go through a light workout, throwing about 30 passes to a group of Cardinals wide receivers, as Bidwill, Bugel and general manager Larry Wilson watched.

Part of the conversation that day may have taken the Cardinals out of any chance of acquiring Montana. As he met with Bidwill, Montana asked who would coordinate the Phoenix offense; the owner had promised to implement the Walsh scheme if Montana joined the Cardinals.

"Bidwill said something like, well Joe, you'll coordinate the offense," said Peterson. "They wanted him to be the offensive coordinator and the quarterback! Joe's a smart guy. He knew that something like that wasn't going to work."

The next day, the Montanas were to visit Kansas City. Rather than have them arrive in the morning, the Chiefs arranged for a private jet to pick them up in Phoenix. The Montanas arrived late on the evening of April 15 at Kansas City's Downtown Airport, greeted again by television cameras, reporters and even a few fans. The Montanas were then whisked off to the Hyatt Regency Hotel in Crown Center, where they were registered under Jennifer's maiden name, Wallace.

"We wanted to give them a chance to get to Kansas City and get a good night's sleep," said Peterson. "And we wanted to spend that whole next day with them. We were recruiting, and we wanted to make it as attractive and easy as possible for them."

On Friday, April 16, the Chiefs put a day-long, full-court press on the Montanas. Joe spent the morning at the stadium with Marty Schottenheimer and Paul Hackett, while Pat Schottenheimer and Elizabeth Hackett showed Jennifer around the city and its neighborhoods. They all met together at Hallbrook Country Club for lunch, and the group also included the Chiefs executive vice president Tim Connolly, Lynn Stiles' wife Marigene, and K.O. Stohbehn, a member of the school board in the Blue Valley district. Then, it was back to the stadium with Marty

Schottenheimer for more discussions with Peterson and the coaching staff.

It was the first exposure to Jennifer Montana for Peterson and Schottenheimer, and they quickly realized she was going to play a big part in any decision.

"She asked very pointed questions," said Peterson. "And not just about homes and schools. She wanted to know about the football team; she wanted to know who was going to protect her husband. She wanted to know what direction we were going to take the team, what kind of defense was going to be around to help us succeed on the field."

Added Schottenheimer: "She made it very plain she would want what was best for Joe, and she wanted to know why we would be right. She asked good questions."

After meeting at the stadium, the Montanas went to Hackett's home in Overland Park. That's when the offensive coordinator got quite a shock.

"It was at my house that I realized he was going to leave San Francisco," said Hackett. "That's when I realized it was really going to happen. He had worked it out in his own mind and that part was over. It's one thing to say, as he had, that it was time to get out, to make a change. But now, I felt for the first time that Joe had made a decision. At that point, I wasn't sure if he was going to go to Phoenix or come with us, because the Phoenix offer was dramatically different, a lot more money.

"But I remember driving to dinner that night, saying to myself, 'I'll be damned. He's really going to do it. He's really going to leave San Francisco.'"

After the Montanas left Arrowhead, Peterson held a meeting with Schottenheimer and Stiles. The head coach wanted to make a move.

"Basically, Carl's feeling was that we couldn't do anything right then," said Schottenheimer. "I felt differently. I felt it was time to make a move, to pull the trigger. After the meeting, I went back to my office and stewed on that for awhile. I talked with Lynn; I talked with Tim Connolly. I was convinced that at some point we had to seize the moment.

"So I went down and talked to Carl again."

Schottenheimer went to Peterson's Country Club Plaza condominium and again pushed his point.

"I was standing in the doorway of Carl's bathroom while he was standing in front of the mirror shaving," Schottenheimer said. "I just felt it was time, that we had gone too far to let this thing slide much longer."

Peterson, however, did not view the evening as a make-or-break situation.

"The purpose of this trip and the dinner we had scheduled was not to walk out of there with an agreement," said Peterson. "This was just another step in the recruiting process."

The Chiefs reserved a private upstairs room at Starker's Restaurant on the Country Club Plaza for dinner that night. Those attending were Joe and Jennifer Montana, Marty and Pat Schottenheimer, Carl Peterson and his girl friend Lori Larson, Tim and Kathy Connolly, assistant general manager Denny and Carmen Thum, and Paul and Elizabeth Hackett. Chiefs owner Lamar Hunt flew up from Dallas just for the evening. With the Montanas were Peter Johnson and Tom Condon of IMG. Lynn and Marigene Stiles arrived late.

Part of the group met at Peterson's condo, including the Montanas and Hunt. It was a warm spring night in Kansas City, and Connolly remembers walking the four or five blocks to the restaurant.

"Lamar and Joe were walking together, talking about the 1979 Cotton Bowl," said Connolly. "I think Lamar's been to every Cotton Bowl in the last 40 years, and this was the famous one where Joe was sick and came back on the field and led Notre Dame to victory in the last few minutes against Houston.

"I was walking behind them, and it was fun watching the reaction of people coming the other way. They would look at Joe, and then after they passed him, they would stop and look again. By then, I would be right next to them, and I would say, 'Yep, that's him.' And all these people got so excited; they just couldn't believe what they were seeing."

Once everyone got to Starker's, Lori Larson worked on the seating. "We wanted Joe and Jennifer to get a chance to spend time talking with Lamar, so we had Jennifer sit right next to him in the middle of the table," Larson said. "Joe was real close to Lamar, too."

Hunt made the trip from Dallas at the urging of Peterson.

"They had been in Phoenix the day before, and from everything we understood, it had not been a good visit down there with Bill Bidwill and his people," said Peterson. "That's why I wanted to have Lamar at this dinner. I knew they had met Bidwill, and I thought it was important for our owner to be there, to talk with Joe.

"I think they really appreciated that. Jennifer spent a lot of time showing Lamar pictures of their kids. She's into antiques, and she had been up in Lamar's suite in the stadium earlier and saw all the antiques he has up there, and they talked at length about antiques."

Connolly was seated next to Peter Johnson at one end of the table. He knew his head coach was anxious to pull the trigger on a deal. But he was shocked when he found out during the appetizer that apparently Johnson was also ready for serious contract talks.

"He never came right out and said anything," said Connolly. "But I've negotiated enough contracts to read between the lines of what he was saying. I could sense that they were prepared to work out a deal. I got excited."

Johnson, however, says he was not in a hurry to make a deal, but that he sensed the Chiefs wanted to move forward. "I got the impression they wanted to do a deal with Joe that night," said Johnson.

Connolly had arranged for a private jet to take the Montanas back to San Francisco that night. It was fueled and waiting at the Downtown Airport for a scheduled 9:30 departure. But Connolly kept calling and pushing back the time as the dinner dragged on. Finally, near 11 o'clock, the dinner seemed to be breaking up.

"I remember walking down the stairs with Lamar, and the valets had brought up all the cars, and they were sitting in front of the restaurant with the motors running," said Hackett. "This night was over. Joe and Jennifer were supposedly going to the Airport.

"But, all of a sudden something was happening upstairs."

Just what happened as everyone was leaving the dining room remains hazy. This much is clear: Peter Johnson grabbed Carl Peterson's arm and asked, "Do you think there's some way we can get this thing done tonight?"

"I said sure, let's talk some more," Peterson remembered. "So everybody went into the bar, and Denny Thum and I went back upstairs with Peter Johnson, Tom Condon, Joe and Jennifer."

Johnson said:

"Late in the dinner, I went off to the side and talked with Joe and Jennifer. We talked about the pros and cons of both Kansas City and Phoenix. But Joe had already made his decision; he wanted Kansas City. They were comfortable with the people who were in that room. I was really trying to slow them down at this point. There was no reason to make a decision that night. But Joe said he had made his decision."

While the Montanas waited in an anteroom, the negotiations kicked into high gear in the private dining room. Connolly joined the discussion as napkins, the tablecloth, slips of paper in people's pockets became doodle pads, as both sides worked with the numbers.

"We had discussed a lot of parameters up to that point, length of contract, injury protections, playing time bonuses and so forth, but that's when it really got down to how much in salary, how much in a signing bonus, reporting bonus, workout bonus, etc.," said Peterson.

Schottenheimer was sitting with the Montanas.

"First Denny would walk in, and then Joe would go over to the other room and come back," said Schottenheimer. "It was back and forth quite a few times."

Downstairs, the rest of the party sat and waited in the bar.

"I had not gotten a chance to know Lamar, so we sat in the bar and talked," said Hackett. "There was a musical group there playing, but I don't think too many people were listening. Eventually, some people got tired of waiting and went home."

Stiles was waiting downstairs with Hackett and Hunt, watching for any sign of action.

"I'll never forget this; it was 11:45 and there was a break upstairs," said Stiles. "I went up to Carl, and I said, 'You see my watch?' It was one of those with the date and the time, and it was April the 16th. That's four, 16. That's four Super Bowls with number 16 (Montana). I told Carl, 'We are in luck. We are going to get him.'"

The clock struck midnight, however, ushering in April 17, and still everyone waited. Busboys and waiters began to get impatient as the negotiations continued. Everyone else in the restaurant had left. The only people remaining were those with the Chiefs party.

"Oh, that was a long wait," said Hackett. "I couldn't go anywhere because I was supposed to give Joe and Jennifer a ride."

Piece by piece, the contract fell into place. Johnson wanted $1 million more than the Chiefs had offered, so the package would be closer to the Phoenix proposal. Peterson wanted assurances that the negotiations were going to produce a trade and not a late change of mind from Montana.

"Finally, Peter Johnson left the room to speak with Joe and Jennifer," said Peterson. "I was confident that what we had hammered out was a good deal for the Chiefs, and I thought it was a good deal for Joe. I wasn't sure what was going to happen if they turned it down.

"He walked back in and said, 'You've got a deal.'"

Joe and Jennifer Montana walked down the steps from the private dining room right over to Lamar Hunt and thanked him for the chance to become part of the Kansas City Chiefs. Everybody returned to the dining room, and champagne was served all around.

Only half the hard work was done; there was still a trade to be worked out with San Francisco. But from that moment, Joe Montana considered himself a member of the Kansas City Chiefs.

"It really did not hit me until we cracked open the champagne, and Joe stood up to make a toast," said Peterson. "He's a very modest guy who doesn't say a lot, but he got up and toasted Lamar Hunt, and said he couldn't be more pleased to be part of the Chiefs family.

"Now, we hadn't done the trade yet; we hadn't signed any contracts. This thing was far from being over, but in Joe Montana's mind, he was now part of the Chiefs. He was giving his word on it, and he turned out to be a man of his word."

Connolly said: "Joe stood up and said, 'Here's to Lamar Hunt and here's to a fifth Super Bowl.' It sent chills down your back. I'll never forget that moment."

Hackett was not surprised a deal was completed, not after realizing earlier in the afternoon that Montana had made up his mind to leave San Francisco.

"I felt very strongly that between Phoenix and Kansas City, clearly Kansas City was the choice for Joe," said Hackett. "I didn't have to express it, although I did. I felt given time, he would feel that way. Now, I didn't realize he would feel that way in eight hours. I was surprised it unfolded as fast as it did.

"Lamar, Marty and Carl, they were flying. It had worked. It had been a fantasy for so long, and it worked out."

What had turned the tide? After two months of speculation, negotiations and recruiting, why had this thing come together in a matter of hours, with people writing on restaurant tablecloths to get it done?

"I'd like to think it was our recruitment of him, the fact they felt comfortable with the people here," said Peterson. "Jennifer had been out earlier in the day, and had looked at homes, and got a chance to see the community. Joe obviously liked the fact that Paul Hackett was here, with an offense he knew.

"Phoenix was talking about more money than we were willing to pay him, but obviously we had a better team than they did. We had been in the playoffs for three straight seasons, and we had one of the NFL's top defenses. I give Joe and his people a lot of credit because they were willing to base his contract on performance and we were protected from injury."

The deal Montana signed with the Chiefs turned out to be pretty straightforward. It was for three years, for a total of $10 million, with $4.2 million paid in the first year.

Various media reports have said the entire contract is guaranteed, meaning Montana would receive $10 million even if he suffered an injury and could not play a down for the Chiefs. Other reports said the guarantee was only for the first two years.

In reality, the only portion of the $10 million that was guaranteed was the $750,000 signing bonus.

On the HBO program "Inside the NFL," *New York Daily News* sportswriter Gary Myers said Montana's contract had a $1 million bonus if the Chiefs won the Super Bowl. He later amended that by saying the total was $750,000.

In reality, Montana has a Super Bowl bonus in the contract of $500,000. But he receives that extra money only if he plays in at least 70 percent of the offensive plays during the regular season and playoffs. (Had the Chiefs won Super Bowl 28, Montana would not have received this bonus. In 19 regular and postseason games, he played in 60 percent of the offensive snaps.)

Now that a contract was struck, everyone's attention turned toward San Francisco.

CHAPTER FIVE

THE DAY
SAN FRANCISCO CRIED

Tim Connolly walked down the aisle of the Overland Park movie theater and grabbed a pair of seats for him and his wife. As they sat down, Connolly was shocked to find Marty and Pat Schottenheimer sitting directly in front of them.

It was the day after Joe Montana toasted his new life as a member of the Kansas City Chiefs.

"Marty had the biggest grin on his face," said Connolly. "And this was not some comedy movie we were there to see. He just couldn't stop smiling about Joe."

Lynn Stiles also was excited about Montana agreeing to contract terms. It had been two months since he first brought up Montana's name in Indianapolis. After all those weeks of looking at the picture of Montana posted behind his desk, Stiles realized he now would have the chance to look at the real thing every day.

Stiles' fervor, however, quickly was tempered when he found out that Montana was not heading home to San Francisco, but instead was going to Youngstown, Ohio to meet with the 49ers owner Edward DeBartolo, Jr.

Youngstown is the home of the Edward J. DeBartolo Corporation, a real estate development company that specializes in building and managing shopping malls. It was started by Edward DeBartolo, Sr., and his son Edward, Jr. is now the chief executive officer of the company.

"I got scared," Stiles admitted. "Not a lot of people understand the relationship between Ed DeBartolo and Joe Montana. It's like father and son, brother and brother; it's not a relationship you normally find between owner and player. They were family and treated each other in that manner. These guys had been through a lot together.

"I recall telling Paul Hackett, 'It all sounds well and good, but it's not over because if Eddie DeBartolo wants to give Joe a 20-year contract with the DeBartolo Corporation, he might do that.'

"Once he went to Youngstown, I was very skeptical that it would come out favorably for the Chiefs."

Hackett was not worried; he saw the trip to Youngstown as just the next step in the process.

"My own feeling about Joe was that he would never finalize anything without talking to Eddie DeBartolo," said Hackett. "He may have finalized it in his own mind, and his trip to Youngstown was the logical next move. He had to do it. He had to go talk to him.

"But I had no doubts that he would be part of the Chiefs. When he says something, that's it. He doesn't say very much, but when he does, you can take it to the bank. This guy is a man of his word, totally. It's important to him. He said he was part of the Chiefs; then he was part of the Chiefs."

Before Montana left Kansas City for Youngstown on Saturday morning, April 17, Peterson had a conversation with him.

"I told him that the hard part was still to come," Peterson said. "And I think he understood that better than anyone. We talked about Eddie DeBartolo, and how he would probably end up saying whatever he thought Joe wanted to hear. And I could understand that because of how much Joe had meant to that franchise. I knew it wasn't going to be easy for them to cut the ties. And we talked about how the San Francisco community was going to react, the media and the fans, and the pressure that was going to be on him and the team.

"Joe didn't say much, but I remember him telling me, if they offer me the spot as the No. 1 quarterback, I don't feel I can believe that."

As Montana flew off to meet with DeBartolo, Peterson made his first contact with San Francisco 49ers president Carmen Policy about a possible trade. The talks did not progress very far, as both sides waited to see what happened in Youngstown.

"I talked with Jennifer several times on that Saturday and with Peter Johnson," said Peterson. "I was just checking, making sure Joe was remaining firm in his commitment. They both confirmed that."

All of what happened in Youngstown is unknown because neither Montana nor DeBartolo has talked about the meeting. Considering their relationship, it surely was emotional.

In a sense, Montana and DeBartolo are brothers. Although separated by 10 years, both attended the University of Notre Dame. Both grew up in the same part of the country and were raised with similar values. DeBartolo bought controlling interest in the 49ers in 1977, and two years later, the team drafted Montana, who became the first star of the DeBartolo Era. The owner loved to spend time with his players, and went out of his way to reward them beyond contractual requirements. The 49ers frequently drew the ire of other NFL teams with the little extras their players received from DeBartolo. Of course, the jealousy of other teams may have had more to do with the 49ers' success on the field, with four Super Bowl championships in the 1980s.

A private jet delivered Montana to Youngstown, and he sat down over beer and pizza with DeBartolo. It was then that the owner told his quarterback what Carl Peterson expected and worried about: San Francisco head coach George Seifert had changed his mind and was promoting Montana ahead of Steve Young on the depth chart. Montana was now the 49ers' designated starting quarterback.

That was quite a change of heart by Seifert. Originally, he said Young was the 49ers starter. Later, he amended that by saying Montana could compete for the starting job. Now, as it became clear that Montana was pulling away from the 49ers, Seifert said Montana could go to training camp as the starter. A phone call from the head coach confirmed the change for Montana.

But, as he told Peterson before leaving Kansas City, Montana did not believe what he was hearing from the 49ers. Too much happened in his comeback from the elbow injury; for weeks he tried to get back on the active roster during the 1992 season and Seifert blocked any move, afraid that Montana's return would disrupt the team and Young's status as the leader of the offense.

It was one of the toughest emotional periods of Montana's career. He was healthy and could not get on the field.

"People were saying I would never throw again, that I could never compete, that I can't do this and can't do that," said Montana. "I guess the lesson I learned is that the only ones you can rely on are your close friends and family, and sometimes not even your friends or people you thought were your friends. The only one that might have understood was my father. My wife was bitter and my mom still is bitter about the way things happened . . . I relied on them a lot for my support because let's face it, I didn't get it from anywhere else.

"My family was always saying you have to do what is best for you, what you feel good about."

There were not many who believed it was solely Seifert's decision to offer Montana the starting job.

"I know I didn't believe it," said Peterson. "They were under a lot of pressure — the whole organization. But that wasn't important. The important thing was Joe Montana did not believe it."

On Sunday, April 18th, a DeBartolo Corporation private jet flew the owner and Montana from Youngstown to San Francisco, where they were greeted at the airport by Jennifer Montana, Policy and Seifert. The Montanas returned to their home, promising to give the 49ers an answer the next day on the offer to be the designated starter.

What would Montana do? Despite the clumsiness of the offer, he now seemed to have what he wanted: a chance to be the starting quarterback again for the San Francisco 49ers. He would not have to move, his family life would not be disrupted, and he would not have to learn the habits and patterns of new teammates. Bay Area newspapers reported the story as if Montana's decision already had been made — that he was remaining with the 49ers.

Stiles thought any chance of Montana wearing a Chiefs uniform had pretty much gone out the window.

"I immediately went to Paul Hackett and said, 'You can forget about this one,'" Stiles said. "The one thing that stood in Joe's way of staying in San Francisco was that he didn't feel he was going to get a fair opportunity. That obstacle apparently had been eliminated. "

Marty Schottenheimer had a completely different feeling.

"I did not think Joe Montana would go back on his word," said Schottenheimer. "You have to remember, he was from western Pennsylvania, and I know a lot of people don't understand why that's important, but it is (Schottenheimer was born and raised in western Pennsylvania). From what I knew about Joe before, and what I learned in talking with him, you could see that his background was grounded in some very basic things, and one of those was living up to a promise. Once he said he was part of the Chiefs, I never had any doubt that he had made his decision. He had made a commitment. If you're from western Pennsylvania, you live up to your commitments.

"I knew there would be pressure on Joe, but I also knew that he had put a lot of time and effort into his decision. He's not the type of person that runs around and makes commitments without thinking it through."

Schottenheimer was right. Montana could not walk away from his late-night toast to Lamar Hunt, and he simply did not believe the 49ers were considering him to be the starter again.

"If I take the offer, I would look like an idiot," Montana said. "It would have been, 'He complained until he got the job,' which would not have been the case. I couldn't figure out what 'designated starter' meant anyway."

Peterson talked to Montana that Sunday night.

"All he said to me was, 'I'm a Chief, if you can work the deal out,'" Peterson remembered.

Said Johnson: "There was no way that Joe Montana was going to re-sign to play with the 49ers. It just was not going to happen, and it took the 49ers awhile to realize that nothing they did was going to change that."

Over that weekend, newspapers in the San Francisco Bay area and Kansas City television stations reported information about supposed trade discussions between the two teams. But it was not until Monday, April 19 that the Chiefs and 49ers had a substantive conversation about a possible deal. The 49ers had been waiting for Montana's reply before they got serious.

"What people — and especially the media — did not understand was that before I made any trade for Joe Montana, I had to be assured I could do this for the proper dollars," said Peterson. "That's why we approached Joe first, as opposed to Phoenix, which worked out the trade with San Francisco first.

"I don't know if I called Carmen Policy, or he called me," Peterson continued "At that point, it really did not matter. We had talked before about other things, but we did not talk specifically about Joe Montana. Carmen immediately mentioned Derrick Thomas as part of the deal. There had been a time when they really wanted Derrick and we had told them we were not interested in trading him. I think Carmen said it this time somewhat facetiously, but I quickly let him know that wasn't going to be possible, under any circumstances.

"I told him that if there was someone on our team that he liked, and we felt we could give them up in the trade, then we would look at that."

Peterson also let Policy know that even though the 49ers already had an offer of a No. 1 draft choice from Phoenix, the Chiefs were not going to make an even one-for-one swap, Montana in exchange for a first-round pick.

"Carmen took the stance that I would, that the market price had been set," Peterson said. "But there was no way that was going to happen. I could not in good conscience do that to this franchise. It would not have been a fair trade."

The Chiefs were not unwilling to give up a first-round draft choice in a deal. However, there would have to be something else coming from San Francisco besides Montana.

"I told Carmen that I wanted a second-round pick coming back," said Peterson. "I then told Lynn Stiles to go through the 49ers' roster and highlight some players who might be able to help our team."

At the end of the 1992 season, the Chiefs felt one of their top priorities was finding a big, physical player for the free safety position. Deron Cherry retired after the 1991 season, and second-year man Charles Mincy stepped into the starting job. But Mincy was not physical enough for Schottenheimer, who believes the position needs to be filled by an aggressive, hard-hitting tackler.

"We felt we needed to get a big safety," said Stiles. "And we were looking at the college draft as the way to fill that bill. But as the negotiations continued, we knew that we were not going to have a No. 1 draft choice, and we had already used our No. 2 in the supplemental draft on Darren Mickell. Our chances of getting the kind of safety we wanted weren't good at that point."

Stiles coached special teams with the 49ers, and during the 1990 season he was very impressed by a young rookie covering kicks for the New York Giants, an unknown safety from Stephen F. Austin University named David Whitmore.

"We played them twice that season, and we couldn't block him," said Stiles. "We highlighted him, put together some special things for him, and we didn't stop him. When his name came up on the Plan B free agency plan after that season, I told George Seifert that David Whitmore was a guy we wanted to bring to the San Francisco 49ers. We brought him in, worked him out and we liked him. He was a bit of a project, but he had the size, speed and hitting ability to play safety. So we signed him, and I coached him with the special teams. Ray Rhodes coached him in the secondary, and he liked him. We knew it would be a matter of time, but he was going to perform."

In 1992, his second season with San Francisco, Whitmore started 12 games at strong safety, finished fifth in tackles with 62, and added one interception and two forced fumbles. But in the free agent market, the 49ers signed Tim McDonald away from Phoenix. The year before, they drafted Dana Hall out of the University of Washington in the first round. McDonald and Hall were going to be the starters.

"I told Carmen that because of the signing of McDonald, they were going to have an unhappy safety on their hands with Whitmore," said Peterson. "And he was perceptive enough to understand that, so he said fine, we'll trade you Joe and David for the No. 1 pick.

"I still wanted more."

Peterson wanted the second-round draft choice as well. An exasperated Policy ended the conversation and announced the trade talks were going nowhere.

A press conference was held on Monday afternoon, April 19, in San Francisco. Montana released a statement earlier in the day, turning down the team's offer to be the designated starting quarterback and renewing his request to be traded to the Chiefs. Policy and Seifert faced a San Francisco media contingent that was just coming to the realization that Montana was not going to return to the 49ers. It led to some tough questioning, as Seifert had to explain his waffling on the quarterback position and Policy tried to deflect some of the heat away from the organization. Across the Bay Area, the perception was building that the 49ers were making a mess of the situation. Others speculated that the offer was made to Montana as an attempt to get the team off the hook, to make it look like the quarterback was rejecting San Francisco, rather than being forced out by the 49ers.

San Francisco football fans were beginning to panic. Steve Young had little or no following among the 49ers faithful. Montana was the man, and now it looked like he was history. Radio talk shows were filled with angry voices. Some blamed the 49ers. Some were upset with Montana. All were scared that he was really going to leave the Bay Area.

Montana heard none of this. On Monday afternoon, Montana went to a small airport near his home in Atherton. He had just begun taking flying lessons and he wanted to get up in the air, away from the phone calls and questions. He wanted to concentrate on something other than the Chiefs, 49ers and football. He spent a restful couple of hours practicing takeoffs and landings.

Policy called Peterson back and re-opened talks. He offered a fourth-round pick in the package. Peterson clung to his demand for the second-round choice. Again, Policy publicly said the talks between the teams were stalemated, and he accused Peterson of trying to steal the quarterback.

Peter Johnson got involved. When Policy made a show of cutting off talks, Johnson got on the phone with both sides. He reminded Policy of the team's promise to Montana that they would make a deal. He reminded Peterson that this was a very emotional and trying time for the 49ers.

The Chiefs wanted a No. 2 draft choice; the 49ers were offering a No. 4. The obvious compromise was a No. 3. It would take several more phone calls before the deal was struck: Joe Montana, David Whitmore and the 49ers third-round selection in the 1994 NFL draft for the Chiefs' first-round selection in the 1993 draft.

When the deal finally was announced Tuesday evening, April 20, it caused a juxtaposition of emotions in San Francisco and Kansas City. In the Bay Area, it was as if a member of the family was moving out of the house for the first time. Callers to the radio talk shows became even more livid, unable to comprehend how a civic treasure like Montana could be traded away, and to no less than a God-forsaken place than Kansas City. It was as if somebody had stolen the famed cable cars that climbed halfway to the stars. Montana was San Francisco and San Francisco was Montana. A No. 1 draft pick was nice, but it was not Joe. Brian Fry, a 12-year-old Montana fanatic was filmed by a Bay Area television station in his bedroom, Montana posters all over the wall, tears streaming down his face, inconsolable because his hero was leaving the 49ers.

The reaction to the trade was national in scope. On the NBC Evening News, Tom Brokaw ended his broadcast with: "San Francisco still will have the Golden Gate Bridge, cable cars, Fishermen's Wharf, North Beach, and the best marriage of city, sea and sky in America. But it will no longer have Joe Montana."

Sports Illustrated carried the story on the cover of that week's edition, complete with a picture of Montana, wearing all four of his Super Bowl rings and the headline: "Kansas City, Here I Come."

In Kansas City, the reaction was as if the entire city had just hit a lottery jackpot. The phones at Arrowhead Stadium rang off the hook, with people trying to buy tickets to what already was a sold-out 1993 season. Within days, the Chiefs' waiting list for season tickets effectively doubled. Fans called with available housing and suggestions for the new arrivals; it was as if the entire community became a welcome wagon for the Montanas.

Kansas Citians and residents of similar cities like Buffalo, Cleveland, Milwaukee, Indianapolis, Pittsburgh, and Cincinnati often suffer from an inferiority complex. While their city may be a great place to live, they constantly hear real or imagined put-downs from people on either coast. These slights tend to illicit emotional responses in the face of hard truths, and the citizens of these cities are always on guard with their provincialism.

So imagine the community feeling when one of the civic treasures of San Francisco decided he was moving to the Mid-west. Some of the folks in Kansas City quickly decided Montana was joining them because it was a great place to live and raise a family. It was supposedly a civic booster shot to the Midwestern way of life.

Just one problem, however: Montana was moving to play for the Chiefs, not because he wanted to live in Kansas City. Listen to the words of Peter Johnson, who said during Montana's first trip to Phoenix: "He's going to go where he feels he has the best opportunity to win. It's not the sun. It's not the grass. It's not the turf. It's not the community. This guy would play in

Alaska if he thought he could get to the Super Bowl. That's all he cares about."

Montana decided on Kansas City for these reasons:

1)   A chance to be the starting quarterback on a winning football team, and thus have . . .
2)   A chance to return to the Super Bowl.
3)   The opportunity to play in an offensive system familiar to him.
4)   The chance to work with an offensive coordinator he knew and liked in Paul Hackett.
5)   A chance to play with a team that had a defense considered among the league's better units.

And finally . . .

6)   A place where he and his family could live comfortably.

Montana would have asked for a trade to Cleveland, Green Bay, New York, Los Angeles or Miami if he thought he could match those first three conditions. Montana is paid millions to play football, and with that kind of salary, a comfortable life for a family can be found anywhere. Every city in the country has good schools and nice neighborhoods. Montana was coming to play for the Chiefs. Ultimately, the Montanas would find Kansas City a nice place to live. But their home still was going to be San Francisco.

And now there was the little matter of saying goodbye. On Wednesday, April 21st, before the largest media gathering San Francisco had seen in some time, a press conference was held at the 49ers offices in Santa Clara. Montana, flanked by DeBartolo, Policy and Seifert said his goodbyes. It was carried live on both radio and television in San Francisco and Kansas City.

Policy spoke first.

"Everyone cried for some simple solution, some immediate conclusion, some type of closure that would satisfy everyone," said the president of the 49ers. "We couldn't provide that. We tried. We stumbled. We were clumsy. Yes, we were passionate. Yes, we were emotional. We couldn't provide what everyone was looking for. The truth of the matter is if we could reverse it today, we would throw another curve ball at you."

Montana answered questions from the Bay Area media, specifically on why he did not accept the team's offer to be the designated starting quarterback.

"No matter what would have happened going into training camp, who was No. 1 or what, it would have been a chaotic camp and probably the biggest disruption," said Montana. "This takes a lot of pressure off the whole organization in dealing with the situation.

"This gives me an opportunity to play and compete, and gives the 49ers an opportunity to improve for the future."

When DeBartolo spoke, his words made it plain how he felt about Montana.

"I don't think I'll ever have a relationship with anybody with this organization, no matter how long I own this team ... like I have with Joe," said DeBartolo. "It transcends football. It is personal. It is with his family.

"It's a deep, sad, personal loss for me. I would have done anything in my power to do something about it."

Montana had one last goodbye for the San Francisco fans.

"I'll miss the fans, miss going into Candlestick and playing before all the 49ers faithful," he said. "I'll miss the guys in the locker room, the camaraderie and friendships I've made over the years. I'll miss all the people involved in this organization. They've been good to me over the years and we've had some great times and great memories that are impossible to replace."

That night, Joe and Jennifer Montana, along with three of their four children, flew to Kansas City. On Thursday, April 22, it was time to say hello to the people of their new home.

"On behalf of Jennifer and the rest of our family, we would like to say it is a pleasure to be here and finally have this thing over and done," Montana told a packed news conference in the Chiefs' team meeting room on the ground floor of Arrowhead Stadium. "We look forward to getting settled in, and I know my old buddy upstairs, Paul Hackett, can't wait to get a hold of me. I look forward to being a part of another great organization and hopefully can step in and contribute right away and continue the winning success that this organization has had in the past.

"I had 14 wonderful years back in San Francisco. It's something I will never forget. We had some great times, and I look forward to more great times here."

Flanked on this day by Jennifer, Carl Peterson and Marty Schottenheimer, Montana fielded questions for 40 minutes.

Question: Do you feel like you have something to prove?

Montana: "I think every player has to go out like they have something to prove, not just myself. I think everybody on the team does. If everybody doesn't have that approach, you won't have success as a team."

Question: Are you glad all this is over?

Montana: "Up until now, it has really been no football at all. I'm really looking forward to getting back into something that I have loved for so many years, and get the opportunity to participate again."

Question: Do you still have the Joe Montana skills after being out for two years?

Montana: "One of the things that makes me feel confident is the last year that I played was probably the best numbers year that I had . . . I was actually ready to come back to the team earlier than was approved . . . I think they know that I was ready before, too.

"There is a big desire to get back and prove that I can still play, not only to everyone else, but to satisfy myself."

Question: Mainly from outside of the organization, the expectations of you have included, "He is going to take us to the Super Bowl, he is going to teach everybody the system, he is going to groom young quarterbacks and bring everybody's concentration level up" . . . How many of these expectations are reasonable, how many of these hats can you wear? How much of this can you do?

Montana: "The way I approach it is not wearing hats. I wear one hat — the helmet — and that's it. I go out there and do the best that I possibly can in the way I've gone about it for years. It doesn't seem like there needs to be a lot of carry-over here; they've been pretty successful. I'm just going to try to fit in . . . it's not just one person who is elevating that feeling; I think everybody gets a better feeling about themselves and strives to be a little bit better (when winning)."

The press conference ended, Montana changed into workout clothing and took part in the Chiefs' off-season training program that was going on in the team's indoor practice facility. Normally, these twice-weekly affairs draw one or two members of the media. On this day, however, there were four television cameras, four photographers and a host of reporters from newspapers, television and radio stations. Every move Montana made was recorded as he went through drills with Hackett and the offense.

After the workout, Montana returned to Arrowhead. He changed clothes again and returned his workout gear to equipment manager Mike Davidson. Montana sat in Davidson's office and talked about what number he would wear with the Chiefs.

This had become one of the big questions in the days after the trade. Montana had made the No. 16 famous in San Francisco. But the Chiefs had their own famous No. 16, quarterback Len Dawson. The number was retired after Dawson left the team in 1975, and there was speculation the Chiefs would ask Dawson to unretire No. 16 for Montana.

That was not on Montana's mind as he talked with Davidson. He didn't care what number he wore, he just wanted to play. And he certainly had no plans to ask for No. 16. Ultimately, Joe Montana settled on No. 19. It was the number he wore playing peewee football back in western Pennsylvania.

A new city, a new team, a new number . . . and soon, Joe Montana would have yet another new teammate.

CHAPTER SIX

ESCAPING AL DAVIS' DOGHOUSE

As soon as the National Football League released the list of unrestricted free agents in February of 1993, Marty Schottenheimer zeroed in on one name.

With a new offensive scheme being installed, Schottenheimer knew the Chiefs would have to overhaul their running backs corps. Despite all the attention that is focused on wide receivers like Jerry Rice and John Taylor in the San Francisco offense, the backs are the engine that push the Bill Walsh-style attack. The short passing game is really nothing more than an extended handoff, and besides running ability, the backs also must catch the football and block. In the 1985 season, Roger Craig of the 49ers had 1,000 yards rushing and 1,000 yards receiving — the only running back in NFL history to accomplish that feat.

Christian Okoye and Barry Word were talented runners, and each had enjoyed 1,000-yard seasons. But Okoye and Word never were asked to be complete backs, and there were doubts about their ability to catch and block. Plus, Word was a restricted free agent, and considering the way things had gone in 1992 with the revolving door at running back, it did not seem likely there would be a quick resolution to his contract situation.

"Plain and simple, I felt it was going to be very difficult for Christian Okoye and Barry Word to function in this offense," Schottenheimer said.

The running back who seemed the best fit for the offense was Todd McNair, but he was also a restricted free agent, and early contract discussions convinced the Chiefs that difficult negotiations were ahead. Harvey Williams had the running and receiving skills, but after two seasons he had been an inconsistent performer who was prone to nagging injuries and had shown no affinity for making a block.

On the lookout for a complete running back, Schottenheimer saw one free agent he thought was perfect for the offense. This guy could run, block and was an especially good receiver. This multi-talented back also played for the Chiefs' most-hated rivals, the Los Angeles Raiders; he had been very effective in games against the Chiefs and Schottenheimer knew that signing him would not only strengthen his roster, but hurt the silver and black.

So the Chiefs put a full-court press on Los Angeles Raiders running back . . .

Steve Smith.

That's right, Steve Smith. Not Marcus Allen . . . Steve Smith.

"I don't think I've ever seen the head coach so focused on getting one guy as he was on Steve Smith," Carl Peterson said. "From the first time we talked about the players available, he was the guy Marty always talked about. I've never seen him recruit a player like that in my life, ever."

How Marcus Allen ended up playing with the Chiefs and becoming their most valuable player in 1993 — and how Smith went on to a subpar season with the Raiders — is one of the most interesting off-field stories of the NFL's 1993 season.

And even though the guy he wanted never made it to Kansas City, Schottenheimer was the driving force behind Allen eventually wearing a Chiefs uniform.

"I was the only guy that wanted Marcus," said Schottenheimer. "I had to convince a lot of people that we needed to sign him."

Said personnel man Lynn Stiles: "We did not view ourselves as much of a player with Marcus at all. Marty had a much better feel for Marcus than anybody else, maybe anybody else in the National Football League, including the Los Angeles Raiders."

And while Schottenheimer admits he was interested in Smith, he said signing Allen was one of his prime objectives.

"I wanted both of them," Schottenheimer said with a smile.

The courtship of Steve Smith began in early March. A 6-1, 235-pound product of Penn State, Smith has never posted big rushing or receiving numbers. His best season was 1989, with 611 yards of total offense, 471 yards on the ground. His best receiving season was 1988 when he caught 26 passes for 299 yards and six touchdowns.

Smith's blocking skills excited Schottenheimer. The Chiefs had not been able to find a blocker at the fullback position to replace Bill Jones, who was released midway through the 1992 season. Smith was as good a blocker as Jones and a much better all-around talent.

As a member of the NFL's Competition Committee, Schottenheimer spends several weeks each year in meetings to discuss possible rules changes that will be put before the NFL owners at the league's annual spring meeting in the third week of March. The 1993 spring meeting was in Palm Springs, so Schottenheimer spent almost three weeks in the desert, attending NFL meetings and playing golf. One night, Smith and his wife were invited to Palm Springs to join Marty and Pat Schottenheimer, along with Carl Peterson and his girl friend Lori Larson for dinner.

The Smiths had just returned from a trip to Africa and brought with them pictures of the vacation.

"They didn't just bring a couple pictures, they brought two huge photo albums full of pictures from the trip," Peterson remembered. "You know what it's like looking at pictures of somebody's vacation. If it's your vacation, you can sit there all day and remember what a great time you had. If it is somebody else's vacation, after about four or five pictures, your mind starts to wander.

"But Marty sat there and looked at all the pictures."

After the NFL meetings, Smith flew into Kansas City, where he looked over the city, met with the offensive coaching staff, checked in with the Chiefs' doctors and spent even more time with Schottenheimer. While this was going on, Peterson was in touch with Smith's agent, Tony Agnone, and the Chiefs felt a deal could be worked out.

Smith left Kansas City and within a week re-signed with the Raiders.

What happened?

Peterson and Schottenheimer say they changed their minds late in the game. Smith said publicly he did not really want to leave Los Angeles and was happy with the offer made by Raiders managing general partner Al Davis.

As sometimes happens in the world of recruiting, a full-court press had not produced results. The Chiefs still did not have the kind of fullback they needed for their new offense, and what was left in the free agent market did not excite them. Chicago's Brad Muster made a visit, but the Chiefs were only marginally interested in the Stanford product.

Schottenheimer decided to turn his attention to Steve Smith's teammate on the Raiders — Marcus Allen.

After six years of feuding with Davis, there was no question Marcus Allen wanted the opportunity to play somewhere else in 1993. The problems between the two had reached a point where Allen could not keep them out of his mind.

"Over six years I don't think I went into a game without thinking about what was going on, instead of clearly thinking about the game and the game alone," Allen said. "I wouldn't want anyone to go through what I went through."

But Allen's frustration seldom showed itself publicly; he preferred not to make waves. That changed in 1992.

The first volley came near mid-season. Allen had agreed to become part of anti-trust litigation filed against the NFL, seeking free agency for the league's players. In November of 1992, a court date for Allen's suit was set for June 1, 1993.

The same afternoon the court date was announced, the Raiders demoted him to third-team status, with duties only on third down and short-yardage situations.

"It is typical of the way the Raiders operate," Allen said then. "In the morning I got my case on the calendar. I come back later that day and they tell me they're demoting me . . . no one has gone through what I've gone through. Sometimes I feel like they keep me here just to torture me."

Then on December 14, Allen fired a major shot at Al Davis. During a taped interview at halftime of the Raiders-Dolphins Monday Night Football game broadcast on ABC, Allen spoke publicly about his problems for the first time. The self-control that kept him quiet for so many years no longer could hold back the frustration and anger.

Speaking with Al Michaels, Allen was asked if he felt Davis had a personal vendetta against him.

"No question about it," Allen said. "Absolutely. He told me he was going to get me. We've had conversations. I don't know for what reasons, but he told me he was going to get me. He has done that. He has tried to ruin the later part of my career, tried to devalue me, trying to stop me from going to the Hall of Fame.

"... What do you think of a guy who has attempted to ruin your career . . . this is what I've wanted to do since I was eight years old, and this very thing has been taken away from me and not, I don't think, for a business reason, but a personal reason."

Allen went on to say he respected coach Art Shell, but that Davis pulled the strings with the Raiders and decided who did and did not receive playing time. Allen said it was Davis who told Shell to bench him.

As he sat in the locker room that night at Joe Robbie Stadium, knowing the interview was airing across the country, Allen had even more trouble thinking about football.

"I knew the shit was about to hit the fan," Allen said. "I really couldn't think about the second-half plan."

Recriminations flew immediately. Shell blasted back, calling Allen a liar and saying the decision to bench Allen was not made by Davis, but by him. Davis called Allen a cancer on the team, something he had done several times before. The only support for Allen came from his Raiders teammates. They understood the situation, and ended up voting him the team's most valuable player for 1992, despite his lack of playing time.

"Al Davis has problems with players who aren't afraid of him, who aren't afraid of showing their manhood," said Reggie McElroy, an offensive lineman who spent two years with the Raiders and ended up signing with the Chiefs as a free agent for the 1993 season. "He likes to challenge the manhood of players.

"Everybody in the locker room knew that the way they were treating Marcus Allen was wrong. Here was a guy who had given everything to the Raiders organization. He had played great football, and he had performed in all situations, even when he was hurt.

"But Marcus was his own man."

Tight end Mike Dyal spent several seasons with the Raiders before signing with the Chiefs as a Plan B free agent in 1992.

He said there was no doubt where the feelings of the locker room fell in the battle between Davis and Allen.

"I think the way the Raiders treated Marcus hurt that team for a couple of years," Dyal said. "You see this happening to someone like Marcus Allen, a guy who would do anything for the team, and you know that it can happen to anyone. You try to stay focused, but it's just something else that makes it harder to do."

What started the feud between Davis and Allen is known only by the participants, and quite possibly only by Davis himself. The Raiders managing general partner seldom speaks to the media and when he does, it is usually only with those he considers sympathetic to the Raiders' cause. Thus, he grants few interviews. Allen has said very little about the details, preferring, he said, to save it all for his own book.

"I know some of the stories, some I've seen, some I've heard Marcus tell," said Dyal. "I won't repeat them because it's not my place. Just what I know, it is unbelievable what he had to put up with."

There are several theories as to why Allen and Davis had their falling out:

THEORY A: Davis never wanted Allen to begin with.

Allen was the Raiders' first-round draft choice in 1982. The NFL draft came at a very memorable time in Davis' life, as he was attempting to move the Raiders from Oakland to Los Angeles. It was a time of lawsuits, depositions and threats against Davis by both the city of Oakland and the NFL. In fact on May 7, 1982, just 11 days after the draft, a U.S. District Court jury found for the Raiders and against the NFL on two anti-trust charges. That opened the doors for the team's move to the Los Angeles Coliseum.

Theory A says Davis was so wrapped up in other problems that he really did not pay much attention to preparations for the NFL draft and went along with selecting Allen because that is what his personnel people suggested. Unlike previous No. 1 choices, Davis had little personal investment in Allen.

Plus, Davis never sought great halfbacks for his team. His offense was built on the vertical passing game, with dump-offs to the tight end. The running game was designed around the fullback, not the halfback. While Allen had played fullback for several years at the University of Southern California, he won the 1981 Heisman Trophy and set major college rushing records playing the halfback position.

This theory puts forth the idea that Allen's success rubbed Davis the wrong way because it did not fit the historical picture created by the man most often compared to movie villain Darth Vader.

THEORY B: Davis hated Allen because he was successful and wanted to be paid more money.

Over the years, the Raiders have developed an image of being the home for wayward football players. While most teams shy away from players who find themselves in trouble with the law or possess hard-to-deal-with personalities, Davis welcomes them. Once they join the Raiders and show they can perform, the team allows their eccentricities.

This also allows Davis to maintain a lower payroll; many of these players are just happy still to be in pro football and they are willing to play for less than many others with similar skills. Plus, in the mid-1980s, the Raiders were annual participants in the playoffs, and that meant an extra paycheck at the end of each season.

Some long-time Raiders observers say Allen was the most prominent player to challenge Davis on money. After Allen won the NFL's Most Valuable Player award in 1985, they locked up in a bitter contract dispute. Davis felt Allen should take less money to play with the Raiders. Allen was not swayed by silver and black loyalties and wanted to be compensated as the league's best player.

In his last four seasons with the Raiders, Allen signed nothing but one-year contracts, all for the same salary: $1.1 million. He was annually a training-camp holdout and, for his last four years with the team, never attended mini-camp practices.

THEORY C: Davis could not intimidate Allen and that upset him.

One statement Davis has made for years illuminates what makes this man tick: "I would rather be feared than respected."

In Marcus Allen, Davis ran into a man who was not afraid of him. Whether over contracts, Allen's desire to receive more carries in the Raiders offense or other problems, Davis was unable to intimidate his running back. Each dispute widened the gulf, as Davis kept finding his bluster had no effect on Allen.

This personal conflict came despite the fact that the rest of the organization enjoyed having Allen around. Teammates spoke highly of him and former head coach Tom Flores had nothing but good things to say about Allen. In fact, friends of Flores believe one of the reasons he retired as the Raiders head coach after the 1987 season was that he had grown tired of dealing with Davis and situations like the one with Allen.

And there is another possibility . . .

THEORY D: All of the above.

No matter the reasons, the feud was a problem for the Raiders. Davis was constantly searching for a running back to take the focus away from Allen. That is why the Raiders selected another Heisman Trophy winner in the 1987 draft — Bo Jackson.

The Tampa Bay Buccaneers made Jackson the first pick overall in the 1986 draft. But Jackson did not want to play with the Bucs, and instead signed a contract with the Kansas City Royals baseball team. He spent most of the 1986 baseball season in the minor leagues. In 1987, he joined the Royals on a full-time basis, becoming a starting outfielder.

Davis was enthralled with Jackson's remarkable combination of size and speed. Since he did not sign with Tampa Bay, Jackson's name went back into the draft pool and the Raiders selected Jackson in the seventh round. Jackson announced several weeks later that he was going to play both baseball and football. He called football his "hobby." Jackson joined the Raiders midway through the 1987 season, beginning a four-year pattern where Allen was the featured back for the first half of the schedule, until the baseball season ended. Then, Allen moved to fullback and blocked for Jackson, who became the No. 1 running back.

But successive visits by the Raiders to Arrowhead Stadium in 1987 and 1988 revealed the differences between Allen and Jackson as football players.

On Sunday, December 13, 1987, Jackson made his first visit to Kansas City wearing the Raiders' silver and black colors instead of the blue and white of the baseball Royals. He carried the ball three times for a single yard before Chiefs defensive lineman Bill Maas twisted Jackson's ankle on a tackle, and Jackson had to leave the game. He limped off to catcalls from the fans and never returned. The Chiefs won that game 16-10.

The next season, the Raiders returned to Kansas City on Sunday, October 16, and Jackson stayed healthy, carrying 21 times against the Chiefs. Allen, however, had a cut on his right hand and a wrist injury that made holding the ball — and especially catching it — next to impossible. Rather than miss the game, Allen wore a glove to protect the injuries and spent most of the afternoon blocking. He finished with 11 carries and made a great one-handed catch that Arrowhead Stadium veterans still talk about. The Raiders won that game 27-17.

Despite his abilities and toughness, Allen's impact on the Raiders offense shrunk with Jackson around. In 1989, Allen missed eight games with a knee injury and ended up touching the ball just 89 times. When he returned for a full 16-game schedule in 1990, his total of carries and catches jumped to 194, but that was far below the average of 297 per season he recorded in his first seven seasons in the NFL.

Allen missed eight more games in 1991 with a knee-ligament injury and touched the ball just 78 times. In 1992, he dressed for all 16 games, but never started and had only 67 rushing attempts and 28 catches. He was used exclusively as a third-down back in '92, playing behind another Davis acquisition — Eric Dickerson.

Before the dawn of the NFL's new free agency system, there was little that Allen could do about his situation. His contracts expired and he carried the tag "free agent," but no team bid on his services under the old system because the compensation was too high; a franchise that wanted Allen had to give up a pair of first-round draft choices to the Raiders. From the time it was established in 1977, through its death with the new system in 1992, just two players switched teams under the old format.

That's why Allen was one of the first NFL players to sue the league for free agency. Eventually, all those suits were settled in a Minneapolis courtroom as a new labor agreement was pounded out between owners and players. In this system, players with five years of experience in the NFL could become unrestricted free agents, unencumbered by any compensation rules.

The new system, combined with that half-time interview, punched Allen's ticket out of Raidersland. But where would he go? Media speculation centered on two teams, the San Diego Chargers and the Miami Dolphins. Supposedly, Allen would only play where it was warm and only on a natural grass surface. Born and raised in San Diego, with his entire college and pro careers played in Los Angeles, Allen was viewed as a warm-weather player. Plus, he had been a frequent and vocal critic of artificial turf, blaming his knee injury at the start of the 1991 season on the plastic surface of the Astrodome.

That speculation showed how little the media knew about Marcus Allen. Ultimately, he seriously considered five teams: Seattle, Green Bay, Washington, Atlanta, and Kansas City. He signed with the Chiefs, a cold-weather team with an artificial-turf field, although the Chiefs are scheduled to play the 1994 season on a new, natural grass surface.

During the same time he was in Palm Springs for league meetings and was recruiting Steve Smith, Schottenheimer also was talking with Allen. They met at the Frank Sinatra Celebrity Golf Classic on Friday, March 5. Along with his wife Pat, the head coach had breakfast with Marcus and his then-fiancee Kathyrn (Marcus and Kathryn Allen were married before the start of the 1993 season).

"I have never made a secret of my respect for Marcus," said Schottenheimer. "I think he's one of the most talented players I've ever seen, and as good a player as he is, he's a better person."

No one had to convince Carl Peterson of Allen's talents.

"It had been so refreshing to see him standing on the sidelines for a few years next to Art Shell," Peterson said. "Scoring touchdowns, inside the 20-yard line, there was nobody better. The first few years we were here, you knew he was going to get the ball inside the 20, and we still couldn't stop him. He was still scoring touchdowns."

But there were still questions that had to be asked about Allen. He was 33, and few running backs have been able to sustain their skills at that age. With nearly three years of inactivity, did he still have all the skills that made him Marcus Allen?

"I remember having dinner with Lamar at the owners meetings and telling him about Marcus, why I thought he would be a great addition to the team," Schottenheimer said. "Lamar was very noncommittal. He was worried about his age and the fact he'd barely played for a couple of years. A lot of people were worried about that."

Schottenheimer was not worried. He sensed Allen was one of those special players with a combination of physical skills and mental determination that allowed him to achieve seemingly improbable goals. Plus, Schottenheimer correctly gauged Allen's desire to prove Al Davis wrong and cement his spot in NFL history.

Allen visited Kansas City on March 30, along with offensive lineman Dave Richards, safety Tim McDonald, and wide receiver Mike Sherrard. In public comments then, he gave no indication where he might play in 1993.

After that, the phone calls started. Nearly once a week Schottenheimer would call Allen; throughout April and May the message was always very simple: We want you.

"Marty was very persistent," Allen said. "He was the guy that really said, 'We want you, we want you to be part of this team, part of this organization and we think you can make a difference.' And that's what I wanted to hear."

Said Schottenheimer: "I don't know that I said anything that made that much of a difference. It was a situation where we had a lot going for us, with the new offense, the addition of Paul Hackett (who coached at Southern Cal when Allen was there), Joe Montana and our success in recent years. There were questions he had about some things like the weather and the turf. I tried to answer them."

Despite the phone calls, Allen was not going to rush into anything. Finally free of the Raiders' bonds, he wanted to take his time with this decision, one he hoped was the last of his career.

"With some of the free agents, you get the impression they want to sign quickly," said Peterson. "Either through things they say or things their representative says, it becomes plain they want to make a decision. About 90 percent of the free agents last year did that, signing before the draft. They looked on it as if they didn't sign, then teams would draft a player at their position and the opportunity or money would be gone.

"With others, you sense that they aren't in a hurry, that they are going to take their time. That was the case with Marcus . . . he was not going to be rushed into any decision. I respected that; it's one of the things that makes Marcus Allen the person he is.

"So it wasn't that we weren't interested, because we were. But we stayed at a distance, and so did he for some time. We just had to handle it in a different manner than we did with other players."

Even Joe Montana got into the act.

"Joe called me right after he was traded, and I told him I would call him back," Allen said. "And I didn't call him back for a couple of weeks. I was still in my thinking process and I didn't want him to influence that. But obviously it did. I would be a blatant liar if I said that wasn't a factor. When you have a chance to play with a guy like him and the possibility of what the Chiefs could become, I wanted to be part of it."

As with Montana, Peterson had to consider the financial aspects of the deal; the Chiefs were not going to be able to throw big money at Allen.

"He received offers for more money, a lot more money," said Peterson. "That was just something we couldn't do. And we didn't view him as being the feature back. He was going to be the third-down back. He was going to get more playing time than he had at the Raiders but he wasn't going to be the back who handled 65 or 70 percent of the offense."

From the beginning of their discussions, Schottenheimer told Allen he would not be the starter. The Chiefs viewed Harvey Williams as the back who would get the bulk of the carries. They wanted Allen to spell Williams and catch some passes out of the backfield. Allen would play some fullback, but in goal-line situations he would become the No. 1 man.

"All I told Marty was I wanted the opportunity to play," said Allen. "He was very honest with me; that this (third-down back) is what he wanted. But in the back of my mind, I felt I wanted to participate a little bit more, and if I got the opportunity I could contribute a great deal more."

Around the Chiefs there is no question who sold Allen on Kansas City.

"Give Marty credit. We weren't really a factor in Marcus' thinking, and he wasn't really a factor in ours," said Peterson. "But Marty was able to convince both sides that it was best for both parties, and he was right."

Added Lynn Stiles:

"He had a real sense of where Marcus was coming from. He had always admired Marcus as a football player. The key was, did he have any juice left? He had visited with Marcus on several occasions and was reasonably convinced that he did. Thank goodness that he did."

What secrets did Schottenheimer have on Allen?

"We had Marcus in the Pro Bowl and I had gotten a chance to be around him every day and see him interact with other players," said Schottenheimer, who coached the American Conference team in the Pro Bowl after the 1986 and 1987 seasons. "His demeanor was impressive and the other players respected him.

"I remember one day in Hawaii, we had a practice scheduled and I told the players to bring their helmets. Well, they were grumbling because the NFC team wasn't even practicing, so I show up to get the bus for practice and (assistant coach) Dave Redding comes over and says, 'Coach we've got a problem: the players don't have their helmets.'

"A couple players — Marcus and Hanford Dixon— got together and everybody 'forgot' their helmets. I got on the bus and said, 'Gentlemen, no helmets today' and we went off to practice."

Schottenheimer sought the assessment of others on Allen. He talked with his good friend, Tom Flores. He also talked with a pair of assistant coaches on his staff, defensive coordinator Dave Adolph and offensive line coach Alex Gibbs, who once had been assistants with the Raiders.

But the overriding reason for Schottenheimer's interest was Allen himself.

"I would have to say the single most significant factor in the whole thing was the way Marcus Allen conducted himself as it related to his role with the Raiders," said Schottenheimer. "He was the marquee player, so to speak, on the team and that may have been the reason for the fall-out between him and Al. Then Bo would come in or Eric Dickerson would come in and Marcus would move to the fullback spot. Despite the fact he would have every reason to balk at that, he never said a word, never did anything but went on about his business and performed in a winning fashion."

On the question of Allen's skills, Schottenheimer said he never considered them deficient because of the inactivity with the Raiders.

"There was no evidence that Marcus Allen was anything but a talented player," said Schottenheimer. "Even in the games where he spent most of his time standing next to Art Shell, when they put him in the game, he played like crazy. He was obviously a guy who took good care of himself, and wasn't off abusing his body off the field."

On Wednesday, June 9, the Chiefs announced the signing of Marcus Allen to a series of three one-year contracts. The news caught many people in the NFL and Kansas City by surprise, since it came with no warning, fanfare or tour of cities like the situation with Montana. At the time, the movie *Jurassic Park* was in the theaters and some joked that Arrowhead Stadium was becoming a home for football dinosaurs, with a 37-year-old Montana and a 33-year-old Allen.

Schottenheimer was off on a cruise in Alaska and missed the announcement of Allen's contract. But there was no doubting his influence on the proceedings.

"I wanted Marcus Allen for three reasons," said Schottenheimer. "One, we needed him to perform on the field, but just as importantly we needed him to be a presence in the locker room. And, I felt he could be a positive influence for some of the younger players.

"Marcus Allen is a professional."

CHAPTER SEVEN

"SCARED MEN CAN'T WIN"

Head east on Interstate 94 from the twin cities of Minneapolis and St. Paul, and cross the picturesque St. Croix River into Wisconsin. Grab the third exit, Route 35, and head south on a road that winds through plush farm fields and past the occasional dairy farm. Don't miss Avey's Taxidermy and Cheese Shop on the east side of the highway, and keep an eye out for all sorts of little critters scurrying from one side to the other.

In just a few minutes the road rolls into River Falls, Wisconsin.

On the banks of the Kinnickinnic River, this town of 10,000 or so is a little slice of Americana. It is Mayberry and Green Acres rolled into one. Visitors strolling Main Street joke that Norman Rockwell did not pass away; he moved to River Falls because it reminded him of his previous works. This is small-town living at its best. Children ride everywhere on bicycles, and car doors do not have to be locked every time a stop is made for shopping. Four cheeseburgers at Mary's Cafe are $2.50, and you can see a first-run movie, buy a large popcorn and a large drink for less than $5. On a summer's evening, ballfields are full of kids playing baseball and adults playing softball, everyone swatting at mosquitoes seemingly big enough to carry away a small dog.

Downtown St. Paul is 40 miles away, but River Falls seems like a world away from city life.

Since 1991, the Kansas City Chiefs have held training camp at the University of Wisconsin-River Falls. For four weeks every summer, the folks of this quiet hamlet find million-dollar football players strolling their streets, drinking in their bars and ordering pizza at Luigi's.

The Chiefs picked River Falls for several reasons. The weather is milder than the oven that is Kansas City in July and August. Other National Football League teams like the Minnesota Vikings and New Orleans Saints have training camps in close proximity, providing practice diversion several times during the camp schedule. And it's a chance to get the players away from familiar surroundings, putting them together in day-to-day life so that the process of creating a team can begin.

Football training camps are unique in sports. Baseball teams go to spring training, spend a week practicing and then begin the rhythm of playing games day after day. Basketball and hockey do likewise in their camps. None of those sports asks of their athletes what football does. The players live in dormitory rooms of cinder block and garish institutional paint jobs. The rooms are the same for Joe Montana and the most obscure veteran. They eat three meals a day in the cafeteria, albeit with a menu significantly better than the choices available to the average college student. They are asked to practice twice a day for a month and attend at least two, sometimes three, meetings every day. Ask any veteran of pro football what he hates most about his job, and he will say training camp. Ask any rookie what he fears most, and he will say training camp.

No sport relies more on its training camp than football simply because of the sheer numbers involved in the game; there are a dozen coaches, with 45 to 50 players on the regular-season roster and another 12 to 15 support personnel who are trying to come together to form a cohesive unit. Something like that does not happen overnight or even in a week of practices. In football, it requires everyone forgetting their real families for awhile and forging a familial relationship with each other.

Each and every NFL franchise begins the season with question marks. Training camp is when the answers start making themselves known and the ramifications become visible to everyone. As the 1993 Chiefs unpacked their bags in River Falls on Thursday, July 15, many questions hovered over the team:

• There were all the new faces, including the marquee names of Joe Montana and Marcus Allen. Safety David Whitmore and cornerback Jay Taylor were acquired in trades, and offensive linemen Danny Villa and Reggie McElroy signed as free agents. There were also five draft choices and four new assistant coaches, including the key positions of offensive coordinator and offensive line coach.

How would they all fit together? Would there be resentment of all the attention directed at Montana?

• A new offense had to be installed. It was so different in style from the previous scheme that no matter how hard some players worked in camp, they would find themselves obsolete in Paul Hackett's new system.

How long would it take for the offense to click? Did the Chiefs have the personnel to make it work?

• There was the switch of All-Pro linebacker Derrick Thomas to defensive end in the 4-3 scheme. It was a move few of his teammates understood or thought necessary.

Would Thomas still be the impact player he had been in the four previous seasons at linebacker? And would Thomas accept no longer being the marquee player now that Montana and Allen were around?

• Harvey Williams had been designated as the featured running back in the offense by head coach Marty Schottenheimer, even though his previous two NFL seasons did not produce results to warrant that honor.

Could Williams handle the assignment? If he could not, who would? At 33, could Marcus Allen be that man?

• Starting jobs were undecided at right guard, right tackle, wide receiver, fullback, both inside linebacker spots and strong safety. There was a new starter at free safety in Whitmore.

Could a team with this many changes in its first unit be considered postseason material?

• Four players were missing because of contractual difficulties, including All-Pro defensive end Neil Smith. Joining him were running backs Barry Word and Todd McNair and safety Charles Mincy. Smith and Mincy were starters in 1992.

How long would the holdouts be away from camp? Since Word and McNair refused to take part in the off-season training program, could they learn the offense fast enough to make any contribution in 1993?

• And what of the team chemistry that had been so wrong in the previous season? Schottenheimer believes the mixing together of the different personalities on the team each year is an important part of the equation for success.

Had the returning players matured? Did they learn anything from the dismal finish to the 1992 season? Did the new faces have the kind of leadership skills that would smooth their transition in the locker room?

There was no question about one thing: the Chiefs' goal was to win the Super Bowl. From the time Schottenheimer was introduced as head coach on January 24, 1989, he never wavered in his belief that anything less than a championship was failure. He went out of his way to emphasize this point.

Certainly, every coach in the NFL wants to win the Super Bowl; there has to be another reason besides money for a person to put up with the pressures and headaches that go with the head coaching job. But few coaches are willing to put themselves on the line so publicly. It leaves no room for maneuvering when times are tough. The average life-span of a head coach over the NFL's 74 seasons is less than 40 games. In today's NFL, that equals 2.5 seasons. That lack of job security keeps many coaches from putting their employment possibilities in such a black-and-white form as "Super Bowl or bust."

Schottenheimer shrugs off the bull's eye he paints on his back each season as part of the price to be paid in his profession.

"I don't believe you can achieve a goal that you don't have," said Schottenheimer. "If you get involved with a large group of people and you set certain intermediate goals, and you realize those goals, you now have to find a way to take that large group of people and focus them on something new.

"Unfortunately, what happens is that there is 50 percent of that large group you can focus. But the other 50 percent are drinking champagne because they got where you set out to go. I think the concept of setting attainable, intermediate goals is good when you are dealing with a small number of people. But when you are dealing with a football team, the goal must be set as high as possible. It is the only approach that makes sense."

Schottenheimer wasted no time focusing on the Super Bowl goal in training camp. On Friday morning, July 16, the Chiefs held their first team meeting of the 1993 season. All 80 players on the camp roster, 13 coaches and assorted others were crammed into the meeting room. Schottenheimer ran through a few housekeeping items, alerting players to changes in the schedule. He went over the disciplinary fine schedule — everything from $200 for throwing a football into the stands to $1,000 for losing a play book, scouting report, or game plan. League policies were discussed, including the upcoming mandatory drug test.

Then, Schottenheimer asked six people to say something: Montana, Allen, Whitmore, Hackett, defensive line coach Tom Pratt and director of college scouting Terry Bradway. They were the only people in the room who had been part of a Super Bowl championship team. Schottenheimer asked them to talk about the experience.

"I've never been to the Super Bowl; I do not have one of those rings," said Schottenheimer. "Here I am, talking about it all the time and there are these other people who have been there. I just thought it might be nice if they shared their thoughts. I didn't warn anybody that it was going to happen. I was curious as to what they would say."

Obviously, the man with the most to contribute was Montana with his four rings from San Francisco in Super Bowls 16, 19, 23 and 24. But he still was feeling his way with his new teammates, learning names and faces. Those inside the room do not remember his comments as being extraordinary or enlightening. Montana does most of his talking on the field with actions, not words.

Whitmore and Bradway's rings were from Super Bowl 25 with the New York Giants. Whitmore talked about how different people always seemed to step forward at crucial points in that season to make the big play. Bradway mentioned the veteran leadership that came through that season for the Giants.

Hackett's ring came from Super Bowl 19 in San Francisco. He mentioned the togetherness of that 49ers squad, its ability to focus and ignore distractions. Pratt was an assistant coach with the Chiefs in their Super Bowl 4 victory over the Minnesota Vikings, and he talked about injuries. Starting quarterback Len Dawson was hurt early in that season, and his replacement Jacky Lee also suffered a major injury. Inexperienced second-year man Mike Livingston stepped in at quarterback and the team rallied around him. "You never know who the hero could be," Pratt told the room.

The most memorable comments belonged to Allen. He had been the Most Valuable Player of Super Bowl 18 in the Raiders victory over the Washington Redskins. Despite his troubles with management, he had always been an inspirational leader in Los Angeles, and Allen immediately hung out his shingle with the Chiefs.

Allen mentioned that the drive to a championship was a test of manhood, an examination of each and every player's character. He talked about being able to look at oneself in the mirror each morning, confident that everything possible was being done to accomplish the goal. He spoke of personal pride, of the importance of how a player is remembered in the history of the game. Allen told his new teammates that when it came time for a player to step forward — elevating his performance at the appropriate part of the game or season — he had to be ready to make the move, sure of his skills and confident in understanding his assignment.

He finished with words that teammates and coaches would repeat many times during the 1993 season:

"Scared men can't win."

"I thought it was a good session, especially with the comments by Marcus," said Schottenheimer.

Outside the meeting room, the media circus surrounding Montana's debut as a member of the Chiefs was beginning to show itself. Reporters from around the country joined an already larger-than-normal contingent of Kansas City media in staking out River Falls. On the bus ride into town, the Chiefs noticed a billboard on Route 35 that read: "Welcome Joe Montana and the Kansas City Chiefs." Club officials cringed when they saw it, and a few players grumbled about the message. "It was like 'Welcome Gladys Knight and the Pips,'" said defensive tackle Joe Phillips. "And we were the Pips."

But Montana was working hard at fitting in with his new teammates. He began building a relationship with Dave Krieg, hoping to avoid the problems he left behind with Steve Young in San Francisco. Montana and Krieg were frequently golfing partners in the few idle moments of camp. Krieg had grown up in Wisconsin, so friends and members of his family were always stopping by River Falls, and sometimes Montana was included in their late night beer runs.

At training table meals, Montana made an effort to sit with different groups — some days the offensive line, other days the defensive backs. There was an early camp battle of pranks with safety Bennie Thompson. During the team's mini-camp in May, Thompson had filled Montana's helmet with shaving cream one day. Montana answered back in River Falls with shaving cream in the safety's helmet. Thompson discovered the shaving cream before going out to practice and was quite proud of not being caught by Montana's prank. He was quite surprised, however, when he put on his gloves and found them full of shaving cream as well.

One day in the team's public relations office, Montana was returning phone calls to the media. Derrick Thomas walked in, sat down and called one unsuspecting reporter and identified himself as Montana. With the real thing sitting next to him, Thomas conducted the interview as if he were Joe Montana. Occasionally, he turned towards the real Joe for little pieces of information. The reporter never knew. "They got a much better story out of Derrick," said Montana.

There was no getting around the fact that the media was there to see Montana. They especially wanted to see if the repaired right elbow could withstand tossing the football.

Saturday morning, July 17, the Chiefs took the field for their first practice of camp. It was a cold, foggy morning, punctuated by an occasional rain shower. The Chiefs wore helmets and no other padding, since there was no physical contact planned for that practice.

All was quiet and normal, with one exception: Montana was not allowed to throw the football. Schottenheimer had decided to limit Montana's throwing in training camp to the afternoon practices. During two-a-day practices, a quarterback can easily throw 100 passes or more. String together a few days like that and even the freshest arm will grow weary.

Montana was no youngster, and he had a surgically-repaired right elbow. Schottenheimer felt it necessary to put Montana on a limited throwing program. Montana did not like the decision, but the head coach was adamant about the plan.

Reaction to this news proved the enormity of Montana Mania. In less than 24 hours, rumors spread through the league that Montana's elbow was not physically sound and would require even more surgery. Calls to the Chiefs public relations staff for confirmation and comment by media around the country began in earnest. Montana called friends with the 49ers that night, and they all told him about the rumors.

"A guy came over to the house to fix a window and asked about it," Montana said.

When Montana finally did throw the football, it was straight and true with the uncanny accuracy that is his trademark. All anyone had to do was watch — and the practices were open to the media and fans — to see it was obvious there were no problems with his elbow. And if there were, then every quarterback should be so lucky as to have a bad elbow like Montana's.

Amidst the growing Montana Mania, the serious work of training camp began, especially with the new offense.

Hackett moved slowly, working on the basics of the scheme, making sure no player was left behind as they received their first taste of the offense. Quarterbacks Dave Krieg and Matt Blundin had been immersed in the scheme since March, but they started with the fundamentals, just like everyone else.

"The base offense we put in was pretty straightforward," Hackett said. "The thing I did from the very beginning — because I felt the team needed to be affected by him right off the bat — was open up the discussion all the time with Joe. I was always asking, 'What do you think Joe, how about this?' And we drew David Krieg into the discussions as well. I tried to use the communication skills that quarterbacks have with their wide receivers to open up the discussion of some of these fundamental things in the offense to everyone.

"The great passing teams all have that communication, a relationship that develops between the passer and the receivers. They come to know the offense and each other so well that words aren't always necessary; everyone knows how the other guy will react. Putting in this new system for the Chiefs, we had none of that."

At times, the process must have been frustrating for Montana; he knew the offense better than anyone, even Hackett. The coach did not have to make the plays work on the field — that was up to the quarterback — and Montana had mastered the intricacies and subtleties of the scheme over 14 seasons. He was reading chapter 28 of a book he helped write while the rest of the Chiefs were still on the table of contents.

So Montana tried to make the most of his one chance a day to throw to his receivers.

"When the timing of this offense gets thrown off, they have to be able to adjust," Montana said. "You're not going to be able to go back five steps, drop and throw the ball smoothly every time. You have to work with them enough so that when we've seen a certain defense so many times, I know what the receiver is going to do against it. When I have to move on the run, I have to know where the receivers are going. They have to learn what I expect of them when a play breaks down."

Said Hackett:

"Joe really is the one who knows the offense, and the people around him have to go to him and say, 'Is this how you want it? Is this the way that play is supposed to be run?' I can cover a lot of ground on the blackboard, but having Joe around means we can cover more ground; we can move along more quickly. It is entirely different hearing it from a coach, compared with hearing it from the guy who is going to be throwing the ball."

Montana rediscovered what a stickler for fundamentals Hackett could be on the practice field.

"Paul doesn't let anything slide," Montana said behind a grin. "He spends a lot of time on details, probably more so than anybody I have been associated with. It's constant. Everything you do is scrutinized from little handoff drills to footwork in passing."

Said Hackett:

"I learned from Bill Walsh that the game at quarterback is played with your feet, not your arm. Watch Joe Montana play; watch the escapability, the throws he makes. That's something you work on and you must have the right fundamentals. That begins with footwork. It's not just realizing you should throw the ball to this spot on the field; it's doing it with the correct foot, the correct body lean and the correct placement of the lead foot as you go to throw. We work on the mind and the fundamentals with the quarterbacks every day of the season."

Hackett's training camp work with all the offensive players was as much mental as physical. With the returning players, he had to change their thinking. In simplistic terms, "Marty Ball" meant power, "Hackett/Montana Ball" was finesse. No longer would the Chiefs run over an opponent. Now, they would try to out-think their foes.

"There was a natural period of uncertainty with the change," said Hackett. "We had the off-season program and mini-camp, but that does not paint the same picture as when you are practicing twice-a-day, meeting all the time, and the clock is ticking towards the start of the season.

"We had to stress all the time that our mindset was different. We all fall into habits; we all get comfortable with one way of doing things. This offense was a contradiction to many of the things they had done in the last four years."

Within the development of the offense was the progress being made by Harvey Williams.

There were already a pair of 1,000-yard rushers on the roster — Christian Okoye and Barry Word — when the Chiefs selected Williams as the 21st choice in the first round of the 1991 NFL draft. When he was healthy at Louisiana State University, Williams was considered one of college football's top running backs. He has the much sought after combination of speed and size (4.5 seconds in the 40-yard dash at 229 pounds). In his first two seasons with the Chiefs, Williams showed flashes of his gifts. It was enough to convince Schottenheimer he possessed the necessary tools to be the team's featured running back.

But Williams carried baggage into the starting role. His practice habits were less than exemplary and his work in the film room, trying to learn the finer points of the game, was inconsistent at best. He had sprinter's speed but a sprinter's problems with muscle pulls in his legs. Off the field, Williams had other problems. In June of 1992, Williams opened a Cajun restaurant in Johnson County, Kansas, called Cafe LeBlanc. He ran into problems with some of the people he hired to run the business, and that led to several confrontations and lawsuits. Williams and his family took over control of the establishment, changing the name to Harvey's Place, and learned just how time-consuming the restaurant business can be. It was more than Williams could handle, and he closed the restaurant in the spring of 1993.

"I didn't sleep well at all from the time we opened until the time we closed," Williams said. "I was always tossing and turning, worrying about things. Once we decided to close, I slept like a baby. It was a load off my mind. It was a successful restaurant, but there is just so much time you have to put in, and I didn't want to deal with that during the season."

There were other problems; Williams and his wife Lorie were arrested by Overland Park police on assault charges in early April. It was part of an altercation with a female friend of Harvey's. The couple patched up their differences, dealt with their legal problems, and Lorie Williams was a frequent training camp visitor to River Falls.

In May, Schottenheimer held a one-on-one meeting with Williams.

"He talked about how important football was to him and how it was important to him to go out this season and do the very, very best that he could," Schottenheimer said. "He had some things going on off the field and he took care of those. He told me football was the most important thing to him and he didn't want any distractions. He said, 'I want to go out and give it a shot to do my best.' That's a sign of maturity."

During their meeting, Schottenheimer told Williams he would be the featured back.

"I was told I was going to be the guy," Williams said in River Falls. "From that point on, I approached every day, every practice in that manner. The job is mine and I plan to keep it. I think this offense is tailor-made for me. It spreads the defense out. That's what I like about it. It's not like it was last year when you had a lot of people on the line of scrimmage. I can catch some passes out in the flats, where a linebacker is going to be covering me. I feel I add more dimensions than Roger Craig or Ricky Watters in San Francisco because I have more speed and I'm a great pass receiver too.

"I don't think there are any questions left unanswered about me. I'm confident in what I can do."

The start of training camp also signaled the official move of Derrick Thomas from linebacker to defensive end. The change was first talked about after the 1992 season. During the team's May mini-camp at Arrowhead Stadium, the defense worked with the new alinement on a test basis.

"Derrick has a unique ability to rush the passer," said Schottenheimer. "To be able to give him the most opportunities to rush the passer, he had to be a down lineman. In this system, you don't rush the passer that often when you are a linebacker — not with four defensive linemen ahead of you. We break it down into three areas: run downs, run or pass downs, and pass downs.

At linebacker, Derrick would rush the passer in only one circumstance, the pass downs. At defensive end, he could rush the passer in two situations, the run or pass plays and the pass downs."

It was part of the continuing evolution of the Chiefs 4-3-4 defense. Through the first three seasons under Schottenheimer, the Chiefs played a 3-4-4 alinement. In that scheme, Thomas was one of the top quarterback sackers in the league; in 53 games in the 3-4 defense, he had 49 sacks.

But the addition early in the 1992 season of massive defensive tackle Joe Phillips forced a change in thinking. Phillips had been released after a contract dispute with the San Diego Chargers and signed with the Chiefs on September 30. It took only a few practice sessions to see that Phillips — standing 6-5 and weighing 300 pounds — could be a force in the middle of the defense. Schottenheimer and his coaching staff felt Phillips was a much better player than any of the team's linebackers, with the exception of Thomas.

The decision was made to change to a 4-3 defense, and the Chiefs started with that alinement against the Dallas Cowboys in the seventh week of the 1992 season. In 11 games with the 4-3, Derrick Thomas had 9.5 sacks, including four in one game and three in another.

In preparation for the 1993 season, Schottenheimer and his staff wanted to get young linebacker Lonnie Marts on the field more often. They said he was a better player than veteran defensive end Leonard Griffin, who was starting in the 4-3. Moving Thomas to end would pull Marts into the lineup and send Griffin to the bench. It also would give Thomas more opportunities to rush the passer. A similar switch from linebacker to defensive end had been done with Chris Doleman by the Minnesota Vikings. Doleman went on to become one of the league's top sackers.

Thomas was skeptical that the change would work for him and made his thoughts known to the coaches and media. But Thomas decided he would keep his mouth shut and try the position. Schottenheimer stressed to him that the Chiefs would have a better defense on the field with him at defensive end and Marts at outside linebacker. Thomas even predicted great success in his new position.

"I keep dreaming about the number 24," Thomas said in training camp. "Twenty-four is the magic number. I can get that many sacks."

The competition was hot to fill the open positions in the starting lineup. At strong safety, 1992 starter Martin Bayless was back, but being challenged by second-year man Doug Terry. At inside linebacker, Tracy Simien, Tracy Rogers, Dino Hackett and Percy Snow were trying to find their spots at the "mike" and "stack" positions. Okoye impressed everyone early in camp with his pass catching, and Kimble Anders was showing significant improvement from 1992, making the starting fullback a tough call.

The biggest question marks were on the right side of the offensive line. Dave Lutz was the starting right guard in 1992 but after he was informed his chances of starting again were slim, he signed as a free agent with the Detroit Lions. Derrick Graham and Rich Baldinger handled the right tackle spot, but both were returning from injuries that required surgery — a knee ligament tear for Graham and a shoulder problem for Baldinger. Free agent signees Villa and McElroy were competing along with rookie draft choice Will Shields and free agent Ricky Siglar.

The Chiefs opened the preseason schedule against the Green Bay Packers in Milwaukee and won easily 29-21, as Krieg and Blundin worked the offense for three touchdowns and two field goals.

Five days later, the Chiefs returned to Kansas City to play a Thursday night game against the Buffalo Bills. It was Joe Montana's first appearance in a Chiefs uniform. He was scheduled to start and play only the first quarter against the Bills. The game was broadcast nationally by the TNT Network and announcer Pat Haden called it "a playoff-like atmosphere" around Arrowhead Stadium that night. There was some debate about whether the offensive or defensive unit would be introduced to the crowd before the game. Schottenheimer wanted to introduce the defense, while everyone else in the organization wanted the offense and Montana to be introduced.

It turned out to be the offense. Public address announcer Dan Roberts said, "At quarterback . . . " and little else could be heard. Arrowhead Stadium had seen very few moments of such pure, unadulterated joy as those seconds when Montana ran from the tunnel and onto the field for the first time as a member of the Chiefs.

So huge was the ovation that it even caught Montana off-guard.

"I don't think words can describe the good feeling you get from that," he said after the game. "It was something I won't forget."

Montana ended up playing in just three possessions and completed six of 11 passes for 97 yards. He was sacked once when a blitzing Cornelius Bennett flew past Anders and took him down. The Chiefs ended up losing the game 30-7.

It was not a vintage Montana performance, but at least he finally had played. He did enough to impress some NFL scouts who were there, including Tim Rooney of the New York Giants, who said: "He looked quick and he looked confident. He threw the ball inside well and he took hits. The big thing is, he looked quick, setting up quick, throwing quick, thinking quick. He didn't seem to hesitate."

Former Chiefs head coach Paul Wiggin, now a scout with the Minnesota Vikings said: "He can still do the one thing and that's the throw in the short-intermediate game. And he made the adjustments. It's all a matter of health, because he's still got it."

Wiggin's assessment would prove to be one of the most prophetic of the 1993 season.

CHAPTER EIGHT

CHANGES IN MARTY

The first weeks of training camp in River Falls were a trying time for Marty Schottenheimer.

As the Chiefs went through their two-a-day practices, Schottenheimer was distracted by a family matter. His only son Brian wanted to leave the University of Kansas and transfer to another college. As a high school quarterback, Brian Schottenheimer led his Blue Valley High School team to a Kansas state championship in 1991. Brian accepted a scholarship to play football at Kansas and, during his freshman year, he took a red-shirt season. He was just days away from reporting to his own training camp with the Jayhawks, who were preparing for a Kickoff Classic meeting with Florida State.

But Brian wanted to transfer, and he waited until the last minute before announcing this decision to his family. Dad already was away in River Falls and heard about it over the phone.

Now, it must be understood that the only thing that means more to Schottenheimer than football is his family. Wife Pat, daughter Kristen, and Brian have sacrificed plenty over the years because the man of the house was a football coach. When the head coach talks about his family, he often has a hard time concealing his emotions; his eyes grow misty and there is a catch in his throat. Marty Schottenheimer is an emotional man, but never more so than when the subject is his children.

And that is how he reacted to Brian's news. The emotional Marty Schottenheimer said there was no way his son was going to leave Kansas.

"It was the western Pennsylvania coming out in me," Schottenheimer said. "I was raised to believe you did not walk away until you completed the task. If you started something, you made sure it was finished."

Schottenheimer has told the story many times of how he quit his high school basketball team during his senior year. He was in a slump and became more and more upset with the way he was playing. Feeling sorry for himself, he left the team.

He left, that is, until his parents found out about his decision. Mr. and Mrs. Martin Edward Schottenheimer, Sr., told him in no uncertain terms that he was not quitting the basketball team. He had made a commitment and he could not walk away until the end of the season. There would be no discussion, no compromise, no whining. He rejoined the team and Ft. Cherry High School went on to win a Pennsylvania state basketball championship that spring. Schottenheimer calls it the greatest thrill of his sporting career.

Brian Schottenheimer was not leaving Kansas because he was in a slump or felt sorry for himself. He was a drop-back quarterback and the Jayhawks ran an option offense that relied on the running game. Looking to the future, Brian wants to become a football coach. He wants to learn more about offenses, specifically the passing attack of someone like Steve Spurrier at the University of Florida.

Dad eventually changed his mind and saw that the change would be better for his son. Brian Schottenheimer transferred to Florida and sat out the 1993 college season. He will be eligible to play for the Gators in 1994.

"He had the thing pretty well figured out," Marty Schottenheimer said. "For every question I had, he had an answer. Once I calmed down, I saw that he was making the right choice. It's like anything else in life — make sure you have all the facts and then make an informed decision."

There are those who believe Marty Schottenheimer is as stubborn, pertinacious, intransigent, unbending and bullheaded as any coach in the National Football League. Did I mention obstinate?

And when it comes to winning football games, he is all of those, and more.

"You know, people told me they had heard my name linked to the jobs in Jacksonville and Charlotte," Schottenheimer said of the new NFL expansion franchises that begin play in 1995. "I had to laugh. Those people did not know me very well. Do you know how many games you would have to lose with those teams? I couldn't stand that. I'd go nuts."

The 1993 football season revealed that while there were times when he could still be the stubborn German from western Pennsylvania, Marty Schottenheimer can change. And he can still win football games.

"I think he did change," said tight end Jonathan Hayes. "The most obvious, and the most important, was the change of offense. It made us a better team. But there were other changes as well."

Cornerback Albert Lewis noticed differences in Schottenheimer.

"I think he's a little bit more, I guess 'mellow' is the word," said Lewis. "It is obvious that he's made a conscious effort to change some things. He doesn't try to make everybody in the same mold anymore. He lets the guys that want to practice hard, practice hard, but he doesn't jump all over somebody that might be dogging it that day. Before, practices were as competitive as games. I think he's gradually learned over the course of the year that he can't do that.

"It used to be always, the bigger the game, we tended to work harder during the week. Not necessarily smarter, but harder. In 1993, we did less of that. I think we practiced smarter."

One man, however, does not think the head coach changed at all. That would be Marty Schottenheimer himself.

"Have I changed or has the perception of me changed?" Schottenheimer asked. "I don't think I've mellowed, backed off or changed my ways. We practiced just as much as we had the year before; we just did it in different ways. I do know this: if things aren't working, you would be a fool not to look at different ways to get to the same place.

"I was born at night, but it wasn't last night."

The comments from Hayes and Lewis indicate there is no question the Chiefs players believed Schottenheimer was different in 1993. And it was far more than changing the offense. They saw the differences in the very first days of training camp.

When the 1992 season ended with the frustrating postseason loss to San Diego, the locker room complaints did not stop with the offense. A number of players complained about the way the team practiced, going all the way back to training camp. They said the Chiefs worked too hard and consequently left some of their energy on the practice field. Several players mentioned this during their end-of-season meetings with the head coach. The two most vocal players were a couple of All-Pros, Neil Smith and Derrick Thomas.

"Man, we were too tired at the end of the year," said Smith. "We practiced too much, did too much hitting. There's nobody on this team afraid of hard work, but you've got to be smart about the work you do."

If there is one thing Martin Edward Schottenheimer, Jr. believes, it is the curative powers of hard work. His working-class roots taught him that a day's work brought a day's wages. If more was desired, one had to work harder. The players' complaints bothered Schottenheimer. He showed them the detailed records he keeps, dating back to his first full-year as head coach with the Cleveland Browns in 1985. The practice logs showed the Chiefs practiced no longer in 1992 than they had in 1990 or 1991.

But this was not a question of reality or hard, cold statistics. It was a question of perception, and that was something that could not be ignored by Schottenheimer.

"I was glad they thought we worked too hard and not that we didn't work hard enough," Schottenheimer said. "We are going to continue to work hard because, without any question, I am of the opinion that preparation and hard work gives you the opportunity to have the small edge needed to be successful in this business.

"Obviously, I had to consider the comments of the players. Whether I agreed with their perception or not, I had to deal with the reality of what they were feeling."

The 1992 season was a step backwards for the Chiefs. Thus, every aspect of Schottenheimer's approach came up for second-guessing. During a cruise through the Alaska islands right before training camp started, Schottenheimer spent a lot of time contemplating the past and the future.

"Listen, I was tired of going to the playoffs and losing," said Schottenheimer. "That's no fun. It's never been any fun. I made a concerted effort to go back and review my career as a coach, both as a head coach and an assistant, to pull out the best ideas and principles that I have been a part of, things that had been good to us in the past. I tried to focus on those aspects."

He spent a long time considering the complaints about practice and eventually, Schottenheimer found a kernel of truth in his players' comments.

"The problem we had in 1992 with guys complaining about working too hard began with the offensive linemen in training camp," said Schottenheimer. "And there was a basis of fact for it. What happened was, John Alt was injured and could not practice. Dave Szott got hurt very early and could not practice. Rich Baldinger was hurt and could not practice. There was a tremendous practice load being placed on a small number of our offensive linemen. I should have been more aware of what was going on.

"So I went to training camp (in 1993) and I changed some things, with the idea that we did not want to leave anything there in Wisconsin."

First, there would be more time off for the players in camp, since Schottenheimer wanted to break up the monotony and physical grind caused by twice-a-day practices. Some of the workouts were restructured, with the idea of getting more done in less time. He also gave the players a number of later curfews. During camp the normal curfew is 11 p.m. But with meetings frequently lasting until 10 or 10:30, it leaves little time for the players to relax. Sometimes an extra hour can do wonders for a player's training camp attitude.

Possibly the most important move Schottenheimer made came in the area of equipment.

Football is a violent game, and players must be protected from its brutality with various forms of padding: helmets, shoulder pads, flak jackets, thigh pads, kidney pads, shin guards, padded gloves for the hands. All of those items can be found in the locker of every football player. On game day, a player uses as much of the equipment as he feels comfortable wearing. His hope is to escape injury or protect an already damaged part of his body.

Because this equipment is heavy and bulky, players do not like to wear a lot of padding while practicing before a game. Some coaches never work their players in full pads, even in training camp. Others require full pads only during camp and not in the regular season. Still others ask their players to wear pads during one, maybe two practices a week.

Schottenheimer was one of those coaches who normally had his players in full pads twice a week. He felt it was especially important with the old "Marty Ball" offense. When the idea is to overpower a defense — pushing forward with a huge offensive line — the amount of practice time where bodies bang into each other tends to increase. It becomes almost imperative for players to wear shoulder pads in that situation just to protect themselves. And what generally happens once players put the pads on is a rise in the intensity level. Sometimes it comes from the players themselves, sometimes the coaches push in that direction, and sometimes it happens imperceptibly. Whatever the case, full pads usually means contact in practice.

Schottenheimer knew the change in offense would mean the Chiefs' practices would change as well from 1992. But with the help of equipment manager Mike Davidson, he made another change to lessen the load. Davidson worked with the Power Athletic Equipment Company in developing a new type of padding that would not be as heavy, but would still provide protection for the players.

What they created were two pieces of padding that fit over the player's shoulders and extend about halfway down his chest and back. The pads are then held together with straps and velcro. Worn under the practice jerseys, this padding provides protection, yet is very lightweight compared to normal shoulder pads. An offensive lineman's shoulder pads can weigh as much as nine pounds. This new padding weighs just one pound. This padding proved so popular with the Chiefs, that teams around the NFL are looking at buying the product for the 1994 season.

"The players would probably tell you it's the greatest thing they've been involved with on this team," Schottenheimer said with a smile. "It allowed us to get in the necessary physical work without wearing shoulder pads."

There was more than simply new equipment. Schottenheimer was more laid back in his approach. About

halfway through training camp, he stopped practice one afternoon and moved the entire squad to a nearby baseball diamond.
It was time for "Home Run Derby." Davidson and assistant
coach Dave Redding threw softballs, and the players tried smash-
ing as many as they could over the outfield fence.

Defensive lineman Tom Sims sang an ear-splitting version
of the national anthem and from there, hilarity prevailed. It was
tough for some of the more muscular linemen to turn and hit the
pitches. Rookie Will Shields fouled one pitch off and it smashed
into the windshield of Carl Peterson's car, drawing hoots from
the veterans. Joe Montana and Marcus Allen had their turns as
well, neither one able to record a home run. Finally, it came down
to rookie Danan Hughes and veteran Martin Bayless, with Hughes
taking the title and the $500 first prize put up by Schottenheimer.
It hardly seemed fair since Hughes spent time in the Milwaukee
Brewers minor-league system and one day hoped to be a two-
sport star like Deion Sanders.

In general, there were more laughs around the Chiefs in
1993.

"Listen, I probably agree with Marty on more things than
I disagree with him," said Hayes. "I know where the guy comes
from because I grew up in the same area of the country. He's got
a lot of pride and he believes in what has gotten him to this point.
It's tough to change, but sometimes there are different ways to
accomplish the same things. I think he was a little more flexible,
a little less rigid."

For Schottenheimer, anything had to be better than 1992.
Remember; he knew in early October that a change would be
made with his offense and coaching staff. Maintaining his enthu-
siasm proved to be a real chore.

"The 1992 season was my second most difficult year, behind only the last year (1988) in Cleveland," said Schottenheimer.
"I'm sure the problems with the offense permeated to the players,
and there just wasn't much anyone could do except ride out the
storm.

"Some players have said that (in 1992) there were guys who
were only interested in making the playoffs, and after that they
didn't really care what happened. I think that's true. It was just
not a good year. We did not go forward the way we wanted. We
did not make progress, and if you aren't making progress in this

business, then you are going backwards. I think everything had become a bit stagnant.

"You know, I'm not so sure that changing things up every couple of years might not be good for a team. I'm not talking about changing coaches. I'm talking about bringing new ideas, new concepts, new faces into the environment. The longer you are around, the less people listen to you. When you first come into a situation, people hang on your every word and they do everything they can because they think you have all the right answers. Then as it goes on, the message gets old and doubts start creeping in. People decide that maybe you weren't the genius they thought you were at the start."

Marty Schottenheimer has never claimed to be a genius when it comes to football. He laughs at the mere idea someone involved in the game could even believe they possess extraordinary mental powers. He loves the strategy of football and enjoys the weekly challenge of preparing a game plan. But as a former linebacker with six seasons in the American Football League, Schottenheimer believes the game depends far more on what is in a player's chest than in his head.

"You can train your players; you put them in situations where they can succeed and then it really comes down to the pride of the individual player," said Schottenheimer. "Will he be beaten? How important is it to him not to be beaten? That's the game in its simple form. Man against man, playing for pride. Who wins?"

There are things Schottenheimer will never change, because they constitute the bedrock of his coaching philosophy:

- He will stay involved in all aspects of the team.
- He and his staff will spend time working on the little things.
- His staff will have as many talented assistants as possible.
- They will not try to plug square pegs into round holes.

The first three really intertwine. Schottenheimer believes in hiring quality coaches and then allowing them to put together the offense, defense and special teams. On game days, it is Paul Hackett who calls the offensive plays; Dave Adolph sets up the defenses and Kurt Schottenheimer aligns the kicking teams. During the week, they all meet with the head coach to go over their plans, and Schottenheimer can mandate any changes he wants.

However, he seldom uses that veto power.

"I think if you look to any organization, whether it is football or business, you have an individual who is responsible to the company," said Schottenheimer. "In this case, with the football team and staff, that guy is me. I've always been a hands-on guy, and I always will be a hands-on guy. People that join this coaching staff know that before they sign on.

"But I don't think in my position you should run roughshod with every concept and idea, that you pull all the strings and make all the decisions. I don't do that, and I don't know any head coach who is smart enough to make every decision in planning and preparation.

"I think you stand back and give guidance and direction. But obviously, the one card you hold in your hand as head coach is — if working together you are unable to get certain things done — you've got to go in a different direction."

Schottenheimer sweats the details, something he learned from two coaching mentors, Bill Arnsparger and Joe Collier.

"Talk to me on Monday night, and there's no way in my mind that we are going to get everything done and communicated by kickoff," said Schottenheimer. "Every week, there are so many things to prepare and get ready for. But somehow, by the time Saturday rolls around, we have covered all the important elements and communicated them to the team.

"I think the big things are nothing more than a bunch of little things. To win a 'big' thing like a division championship, you must win 10 or 11 'little' things during the season. To make a big play work during a game, players have to fulfill their assignments. If enough get the little things done, there is a big play.

"In football, if you forget the little things, then you've got big problems."

There are head coaches in the NFL that will bypass good assistant coaches because they are afraid it will put their own job in jeopardy. Schottenheimer has never been afraid to sign on talented assistants.

"There are no geniuses in this game," said Schottenheimer. "There is not a single coach who can handle everything. If you are going to win, you had better have a darn good coaching staff and some darn talented players. Those two things together can make a lot of people look like geniuses."

Schottenheimer does not believe his job is to motivate professional athletes. Despite this, he spends a great deal of time being a psychologist, trying to create an environment that will bring out the best in individuals and the team itself.

"You must have individuals who want to be successful individually, but are also willing to subordinate their personal goals to the common interest of the group," said Schottenheimer. "That's something that comes from working together, preparing together, sweating together, winning together, losing together, crying together, celebrating together... all those experiences you share as a unit give you an opportunity to blend together in an affirmative way."

A lot of pro football has changed since 1971, the last time Marty Schottenheimer was an active player. But the basic wants and needs of players never change: they always want to play, and they always want to be rewarded in money, recognition, or both. He tries to remember those days when he chafed on the bench of the Buffalo Bills and the Boston Patriots.

"I always thought I should be playing," said Schottenheimer. "I was always better than the other guy. They never gave me a chance. I know all the lines because I used them.

"But you know what? Knowing what I know now, I would not have played me either. I wasn't fast enough. If I could catch you, I would hit you, but I had to catch you first. I understand what a player wants. But I also understand what a coach needs. Sometimes those are two very different things."

Nothing creates more problems for a head coach than asking players and coaches to perform tasks they are not capable of doing.

"A player has to be comfortable; he has to have confidence that he can perform the duties required of him," said Schottenheimer. "If he's uncomfortable, if you are asking him to do things he can't do, he's not going to be able to perform, no matter how physically talented he might be.

"On this level, you can't be hesitant. If the player isn't sure of himself, then as a coach, you aren't going to have confidence in him. If he has problems on the field, the only one you can blame is yourself."

That's what led to players like guard Dave Lutz, tackle Rich Baldinger and running backs Christian Okoye and Barry Word either being released or traded. They were built for the "Marty Ball" offense, not the short-control passing game.

"Clearly, one of the mistakes I made in 1992 was asking for changes in the offense that Joe Pendry was not comfortable with," said Schottenheimer. "I don't blame Joe. I blame myself. I put him into a position where he could not do what he does best."

Whether he really changed or only the perception of him changed, Marty Schottenheimer knows that as bad as the 1992 season was, the 1993 season was completely different.

"I had more enjoyment and more fun coaching this team (1993) than in any other year that I coached," said Schottenheimer. "The new offense, some new players, the excitement that they bring, the way things fell together at the end, the way the team matured from the year before.

"Ultimately, we did not achieve our goal, and that was a disappointment. But the season was a lot of fun."

CHAPTER NINE

CREATING A TEAM

As the preseason days dwindled to just a few, the Chiefs' 1993 roster began falling together. The National Football League allowed its teams to take 80 players to training camp. Two weeks before the first regular-season game, that number was sliced to 60. A week before the opener, the squad limit dropped to 47. Teams could then add six players to their rosters for the regular-season limit of 53.

For Marty Schottenheimer it is always one of the toughest times in any season. As a former player, Schottenheimer has too much respect for those who play the game to take lightly the shattering of dreams.

"We are forced to tell someone they are not good enough, and it is strictly a subjective decision," said Schottenheimer. "We may be dead wrong. These people have worked very hard, given up so much and now we are forced to tell them it was not enough. That's a very hard thing to do."

It became apparent during the preseason games that the new additions to the Chiefs' roster were going to have a big impact on the season. Joe Montana, Marcus Allen and David Whitmore proved early that the Chiefs' confidence in their abilities was well-placed. But some familiar faces were having impressive preseason performances, players like fullback Kimble Anders, tight end Jonathan Hayes, defensive tackle Joe Phillips and linebackers Tracy Rogers and Lonnie Marts.

Frequently lost in the eyes of the fans and media when judging potential improvement in a team are the returning players. In basketball or baseball, the addition of a single player can have such an impact that it changes the fortunes of the entire team. In football, new players can be a catalyst, but they cannot turn around a franchise by themselves.

"People don't often credit the improvement that comes from within," said Schottenheimer. "Take a look at our team in 1993 and look at the strides made by some key players, guys like Willie Davis, Tracy Simien, J.J. Birden, Doug Terry, Lonnie Marts, Kimble Anders, Darren Mickell, Keith Cash. That comes from the players working hard with their coaches, buying into the program we have in place and making a commitment.

"You can't add enough people every off-season to generate as much improvement as you can get from within the team itself."

There was once a time when the NFL's best teams wanted only "pure" rosters, meaning players who had played for no other organizations. The Pittsburgh Steelers and Dallas Cowboys of the 1970s — arguably the two best teams of that decade — prided themselves on not picking up players released by the 26 other teams. The Steelers and Cowboys would re-sign players they already had released without even considering a talent who had spent time elsewhere. It was "my trash is better than your trash" thinking.

One season the Pittsburgh Steelers experienced so many injuries at the tight end position, they signed Jim Mandich, who played previously for the Miami Dolphins. There were people in the Steelers organization who were disappointed Mandich was signed. It was like the judges at the Westminster Dog Show finding out a mongrel was one of the contestants. Each year Dallas would start training camp with 120 to 140 players, many of them undrafted rookies. Other teams had 95 or 100 players. The Cowboys hoped this annual casting call would help them find one or two diamonds in the rough.

NFL teams can have that arrogance about personnel decisions when they enlarge the trophy case almost every year. The Steelers and Cowboys believed they were better at finding talent than the other teams, and for awhile, they were right. In the 1970s Pittsburgh and Dallas won six of the 10 Super Bowls.

But in time, that attitude caught up with both teams. Because their personnel view was so narrow, they missed out on some good players. As the Steelers and Cowboys grew older, they were unable to make enough additions through the draft, and they did not have the knowledge of other players around the league. By 1988, the Steelers were 5-11 and last in the AFC Central Division. In 1989, the Cowboys were 1-15, last in the entire NFL.

When rebuilding a franchise, a general manager cannot be picky about where his players come from. Carl Peterson and his staff have turned over every rock, looked behind every bush, and used every avenue available to find football talent. The Chiefs' roster has draft choices, supplemental draft choices, rookie free agents, veteran free agents cut by other teams, unrestricted free agents, Plan B free agents and players obtained through trades. At any given time, the 50 or so roster spots are divided 50-50 between players who have played only for the Chiefs and those who have played for other organizations.

"You cannot build or rebuild a football team only through the draft," said Peterson. "There was a time when people thought you could, but you've got to be incredibly lucky in your drafting and unlucky on the field because you have to be selecting players early in the draft year-after-year. Even if you hit on a good number of your selections, you must find help from other avenues to fill in the holes."

Before Peterson and Schottenheimer arrived on the scene, the Chiefs made some incredibly bad personnel decisions over the previous 15 seasons. It started with Hank Stram and continued through coaches Paul Wiggin, Marv Levy, John Mackovic and Frank Gansz. The one constant in the player personnel department during that time was general manager Jim Schaaf.

A former lineman at Notre Dame, Schaaf started his career in sports as the public relations director of the Kansas City Athletics under Charles O. Finley. He eventually joined the Chiefs as public relations director, and in 1972 was named assistant general manager. Once Stram was fired, Schaaf became a key player in the talent evaluation process. When Jack Steadman became president of the team in 1977, Schaaf was named general manager.

Whether it was Stram, Schaaf or the other head coaches, the Chiefs put together a string of terrible personnel decisions that doomed the franchise to failure. Once the glory Chiefs of Super Bowl 4 retired, there were few talented bodies to take their places. Here's why:

• In 1972, Stram signed free agent defensive tackle George Seals before the third game of the season. Under NFL rules at the time, the Chiefs had to give up their next available first-round draft choice to Seals' old team, the Chicago Bears. That selection turned out to be the 17th spot in the 1973 draft. Seals played only two seasons with the Chiefs and never started a game. He retired before the 1974 season to take a job on the Chicago Board of Trade.

• At mid-season in 1974, Stram made what has to rank as the worst trade in Chiefs history: defensive tackle Curley Culp and the Chiefs' No. 1 draft choice in 1975 to the Houston Oilers for defensive end John Matuszak.

Matuszak played two seasons with the Chiefs, and at least he became a starter, registering 5.5 sacks in the 1975 season. But Matuszak was gone before the start of the 1976 season, and the "Tooz" would become an NFL legend for his off-the-field behavior with the Oakland/Los Angeles Raiders. His most memorable Kansas City moments came when a) his ex-wife tried to run him down with a car at training camp, b) he was caught in the team's Arrowhead Stadium jacuzzi with this same ex-wife, and c) he missed a preseason game because of an overdose of Valium and vodka that sent him to a hospital emergency room. Only the quick thinking of then-head coach Paul Wiggin saved his life in that instance, as Wiggin pounded on Matuszak's massive chest to keep his heart beating Matuszak died about 10 years later, after fighting drug and alcohol abuse for years.

What happened to that No. 1 choice the Chiefs gave up for Matuszak? With the sixth selection, the Oilers selected linebacker Robert Brazile, who played for 10 seasons and made the Pro Bowl five times.

• Without that No. 1 choice in 1975, the Chiefs needed to make sure their second-round pick was a keeper for Wiggin, who was in his first season. Instead, they selected tight end Elmore Stephens from Kentucky. Just one problem: Stephens had been arrested on manslaughter charges. He never played a down for the Chiefs.

• Marv Levy made the picks in 1981 when the Chiefs used their No. 1 choice to take tight end Willie Scott from South

Carolina. Scott was a big, blocking tight end who helped George Rogers win the Heisman Trophy in 1980. He was a perfect fit for Levy's offensive philosophy, which was built around the running game.

But after the 1982 season, Levy was fired. John Mackovic took over and changed the offense completely, relying on the passing game. Scott had no place in the new system and was traded before the 1986 season.

• Looking for the right passer to run that new offense, Mackovic selected quarterback Todd Blackledge of Penn State in the first round of the 1983 draft. That was the "Year of the Quarterback," with six being selected in the first round. Blackledge was the second quarterback chosen, behind John Elway. The Chiefs by-passed Jim Kelly, Ken O'Brien, Tony Eason and most especially, Dan Marino.

Blackledge is the only one of the six quarterbacks from 1983 who never established himself as a full-time starter. He was traded before the 1988 season.

• Schaaf signed several players away from the United States Football League in the mid-1980s. His prize was running back Ken Lacy, who had a 1,000-yard season as a USFL rookie in 1983 for the Michigan Panthers. Lacy received big money to jump leagues, and Schaaf considered his signing quite a coup.

In what amounted to less than three seasons with the Chiefs, Lacy carried the ball a total of 66 times for 235 yards.

• After raiding the USFL, Schaaf went after the Canadian Football League. In 1984, he signed All-CFL cornerback Kerry Parker to a contract that made Parker the highest paid defensive back on the team. But there was a reason Parker was an All-CFL cornerback — he could not cover NFL receivers.

Parker played one season with the Chiefs and was released.

Certainly, in all those years the Chiefs had some success with players. In 1976, they picked up a pair of third-round draft choices in safety Gary Barbaro and wide receiver Henry Marshall who had long careers. Marshall is still the Chiefs' all-time leading receiver. In 1981, they drafted running back Joe Delaney in the second round, and he had a sensational rookie season. Delaney drowned two years later, trying to save three children in a pond. In 1987, Schaaf took a chance on Christian Okoye in the second round. Born in Nigeria, Okoye had a limited background in football, and despite great physical skills, was considered a gamble.

But for every hit, there seemed to be nine or ten misses. The woeful win-loss record is evidence enough that problems far outnumbered solutions.   There were two major reasons for this poor track record:

1)   Each time the Chiefs changed head coaches, some players became obsolete in the new system. Without the consistency of approach, long-term evaluation of talent became a nearly impossible task.

2) The people making the decisions, specifically Jim Schaaf, did not know how to evaluate football talent.

Under Peterson, the hits have easily outnumbered the misses, although the results of the first five drafts are mixed. The Chiefs missed on No. 1 choice linebacker Percy Snow (1990), who was cut before the start of the 1993 season. Quarterback Mike Elkins was a second-round pick (1989) who was gone two seasons later, after playing in just one NFL game. But Peterson and Schottenheimer hit on some late selections, like running back Todd McNair in the eighth round (1989), fullback Bill Jones in the 12th round (1989) and seventh-round guard Dave Szott (1990).

Where the Chiefs have excelled under Peterson is finding talented players in avenues other than the draft.

Probably the best example was running back Barry Word, who was making phone calls in the telemarketing department of Sprint when pro personnel director Mark Hatley talked Peterson and Schottenheimer into taking a look at him. Word had played two seasons with the New Orleans Saints after a college career at the University of Virginia that was cut short by an arrest and conviction on a cocaine charge. Word spent time in a Virginia prison, but was still drafted in the third round by the Saints in 1986. He left New Orleans after two games of the 1988 season. The Saints later released all rights to him and he missed the entire 1989 season.

After a thorough investigation, the Chiefs decided to give Word a chance, provided he followed certain conditions. He was told the first sign of trouble off the field would mean immediate release. And he was required to take a drug test at a moment's notice, if requested by the team.

In 1990, Word had a 1,000-yard season, stepping in for the injured Christian Okoye. Word battled with Schottenheimer over playing time and Peterson over contracts in his three seasons with the Chiefs, but he never caused a problem off the field.

"My initial reaction when Hat (Mark Hatley) brought up his name was no, I didn't want him around," said Schottenheimer. "But in this business, you must gather all the information you can and then sit down and make a decision."

The Chiefs used a second-round choice in the 1992 NFL supplemental draft to select defensive lineman Darren Mickell, who left the University of Florida because of assorted off-the-field problems. During the 1993 season, Mickell improved enough that the Chiefs thought he would be a major contributor to the defense in the future.

The Plan B free agency system was part of the NFL for four seasons. It was an unsuccessful attempt by the league owners to head off full-scale free agency. Teams were allowed to protect 37 players, with the remaining players free to sign anywhere. The Chiefs made possibly the biggest Plan B steal when they signed Detroit defensive tackle Dan Saleaumua in 1989. With the Lions, Saleaumua could not get on the field because he was playing behind All-Pro Jerry Ball. With the Chiefs, Saleaumua not only earned a starting job, but forced the move of nose tackle Bill Maas to defensive end.

Other Plan B free agents making a contribution on the field in 1993 included quarterback Dave Krieg (from Seattle), tight end Keith Cash (from Pittsburgh) and safety Martin Bayless (from San Diego).

The Chiefs 1993 roster was filled with second and third-chance players; guys who were told they were not good enough, but decided to seek a second opinion. Some would play big roles in the success of the Chiefs season:

• Fullback Kimble Anders was an undrafted rookie free agent when he was released by the Pittsburgh Steelers in the 1990 training camp.

• Wide receiver J.J. Birden was an eighth-round draft choice of the Cleveland Browns in 1988, but spent his rookie season on the injured list with a serious knee problem. He was released by the Browns in 1989 and signed with Dallas. The Cowboys let him go in 1990.

• Kicker Nick Lowery had unsuccessful tryouts with eight NFL teams before landing in Kansas City back in 1980. New

England, the New York Jets, Washington, Cincinnati, Baltimore, New Orleans, Tampa Bay and San Diego all had shots at him.

• Defensive tackle Tim Newton played for the Minnesota Vikings and Tampa Bay Buccaneers for seven seasons before signing with the Chiefs in 1993.

• Linebacker Tracy Simien signed with the Steelers after leaving college. The New Orleans Saints signed him as a Plan B free agent in 1990, but then released him during training camp. He joined the Chiefs later in that season.

Lost in the Montana/Allen Mania were two new faces who played vital roles during the 1993 season for the Chiefs: guard Will Shields and tackle Rick Siglar. They ended up starting 16 games together on the right side of the offensive line.

That Shields was available in the third round of the 1993 draft surprised the hierarchy of the Chiefs.

"We had him slotted in the second round," said vice president of player personnel Lynn Stiles. "To think he would be there in the third round was beyond my imagination."

As the 1993 draft class was being evaluated by NFL scouts, Shields seemed to have several deficiencies. No. 1, he did not have the perfect physical numbers for a guard in today's NFL, standing 6 feet, 2 inches. That is considered small by teams that prefer their guards to be a few inches taller.

No. 2, Shields played at Nebraska, and offensive linemen from that program have trouble making the transition to the NFL. The Cornhuskers do not throw the football very much, so their blockers have limited experience in the passing game. Moreover, they do not tend to be athletic players; rather, they are big, muscled hunks who are built in the renowned Nebraska weight training program.

Stiles and Terry Bradway, the Chiefs' director of college scouting, thought Shields was a cut above the normal Nebraska blockers.

"The thing we had to get over was the stereotypical thinking about Nebraska linemen," said Bradway. "He is so much different than those guys because he is so athletic. He was just what we were looking for in this offense. Had we not changed offenses, we probably would not have been as interested in Will as we were."

Said Stiles:"We talked to the coaches up there about his coachability, his intelligence, his work ethic, and they all raved about him. Maybe you question his height, but he weighs 300 pounds. He has unusual balance and the ability to run and move.

"I think I gave him the ultimate compliment when I said he could be to us what Guy McIntyre has been to the San Francisco 49ers over the years (McIntyre is a 10-year veteran who has played in over 100 games for the 49ers and has been selected to five Pro Bowl games). Except Guy McIntyre weighs 270 pounds and Will Shields weighs 300 pounds.

"When he pulls and blocks on the corner, he can search and destroy. He has unusual capabilities to operate in space. He's also exceptionally bright and a very instinctive football player. ''

Fans normally think of running backs and quarterbacks as being "instinctive" players. How does an offensive lineman show he has a feel for the game?

"Being instinctive on the offensive line is being able to make quick and decisive decisions," said Stiles. "You could see that in Will's play at Nebraska. When the defense ran a stunt, he picked up the right guy or he picked up two guys. He positioned himself properly when making his blocks. He's able to position himself; that's something instinctive.

"In the end, I think I gave him a grade that was equivalent to a first-round pick. I was sold on this guy."

Stiles also was sold on Siglar, which was the reason the Chiefs signed the 6-7, 300-pound tackle.

Siglar spent the better part of four years trying to make it in the NFL with the San Francisco 49ers. Stiles was with the 49ers as an assistant coach for three of those seasons, including 1990 when Siglar played in all 18 regular and postseason games for San Francisco.

"If you look into his background, you are going to find out that the last time he started was in junior college, and that was in 1987," said Stiles. "He did not start at San Jose State and he was a free agent with the Dallas Cowboys before he came with San Francisco. He was always moved around and never was able to settle into one position. He was very insecure in terms of establishing himself as a football player. He had the desire, the athletic ability and the size, but was never really given a chance to settle into a spot.

"We brought him in and the thing we said was 'Put him at one position and leave him there.' The kid came in, dedicated himself in the off-season and worked his tail off. He went to camp at 308 pounds and was bigger and stronger than ever. (Offensive line coach) Alex Gibbs put him at right tackle and did not move him. Even after we signed Reggie McElroy as a free agent, Alex said McElroy would back up Siglar."

That is another part of the personnel equation that is sometimes overlooked: how the players are handled by the coaching staff. Stiles says that in the case of Shields and Siglar, both came out of training camp capable of being starters in the NFL, thanks to Alex Gibbs.

"What really happened here with Will Shields has less to do with the selection process and more to do with an offensive line coach who believed in him and gave him every opportunity to develop," said Stiles. "You've got to take under consideration that he is protecting the right arm of Joe Montana. Shields and Siglar had no NFL starts, so certainly there was concern and a lot of discussion.

"But Alex made it work. He took the right side of our line with essentially two rookie players and said, 'Let's go to the playoffs.'"

Shields and Siglar were two of 19 new faces on the Chiefs' 53-man roster for the regular season. That is a 36 percent rate of change from the previous season. There were new starters at nine positions, compared to the final game of the 1992 regular season, which was a 41 percent change:

December 27, 1992		September 5, 1993
Birden	Wide Receiver	Birden
Alt	Left Tackle	Alt
Szott	Left Guard	Szott
Babb*	Center	Grunhard
Lutz	Right Guard	VILLA/SHIELDS
Baldinger	Right Tackle	SIGLAR
Hayes	Tight End	Hayes
Davis	Wide Receiver	Davis
Krieg	Quarterback	MONTANA
Williams	Halfback	WILLIAMS
McNair	Fullback	ANDERS

December 27, 1992		September 5, 1993
Smith	Left End	Smith
Phillips	Left Tackle	Phillips
Saleaumua	Right Tackle	Saleaumua
Griffin	Right End	THOMAS
Martin	Linebacker	MARTS
Simien	Linebacker	Simien
Thomas	Linebacker	ROGERS
Carter	Left Cornerback	Carter
Ross	Right Cornerback	Ross
Bayless	Strong Safety	TERRY
Mincy	Free Safety	WHITMORE

*Grunhard was the '92 starter, but was injured and did not play.

Part of the turnover obviously was due to the new offense. Part could be explained by the NFL's new free agency plan. And part was the normal rhythm of the NFL, where the average career is less than four seasons.

A knee injury suffered during camp ended Okoye's career with the Chiefs. He was placed on the injured-reserve list, but was then given an injury settlement and released outright. Even though Okoye was the team's all-time leading rusher, there was just no place for him in the new offense.

Same for Word. After missing most of the preseason, Word was traded to the Minnesota Vikings for a fifth-round draft choice in 1994. Also traded before the season opener was Rich Baldinger, who was sent to the New England Patriots.

All the changes with the Chiefs sounded more like a team that finished at the bottom of the standings, rather than one coming off a season in the playoffs. As the start of the regular season approached, the Chiefs still had a host of questions that needed to be answered.

CHAPTER TEN

JOE'S INJURIES

As the Chiefs reported to their Saturday morning meeting at Arrowhead Stadium in preparation for the season opener in Tampa, a familiar and welcome face returned.

The night before, Neil Smith and the Chiefs finally hammered out a four-year contract that made him one of the highest-paid players on the team. Smith missed all of training camp in River Falls, four preseason games, and even the three practices leading up to the game against the Buccaneers.

Most players missing that much time would need at least a week of practice and meetings before the team could even consider using them in a game. Not so with Smith. He signed on Friday evening, was on the Chiefs' plane Saturday and expected to play against the Bucs on Sunday, although he would not start in his familiar spot at left defensive end.

"We aren't paying him all this money to sit and watch," Carl Peterson said with a smile.

The Chiefs got another taste of the growing interest they were generating around the country when they checked into their Tampa hotel. There was a time — and it was not long ago — when, if the Chiefs checked into a hotel on a road trip, their arrival was noticed only by the hotel employees. Occasionally, there might be a few family members waiting, but usually there was never any problem finding a stool in the lobby bar or a table in the restaurant.

But when the Chiefs arrived at the Hyatt Westshore Hotel near the Tampa-St. Petersburg Airport, they were greeted by television cameras and a lobby full of fans, all clapping, cheering and calling out the names of Chiefs players. Hotel employees roped off part of the lobby just so the players could get to their rooms. Only those people with hotel keys were allowed near the elevators.

A good many of those fans were there to see one player in particular, and they were quite disappointed when Joe Montana was whisked in a rear door, through the kitchen and up a back elevator to his room. No less than three security people were stationed around Montana for this trip. That was on top of the normal contingent of security types the Chiefs take on all road games — usually three people.

The team hired Ray Zakovich to help out with security for Montana. Zakovich was with the Secret Service for 20-plus years and was part of several Presidential details. When the shots rang out in Dealey Plaza and killed President John F. Kennedy on November 22, 1963, Zakovich was in the car directly behind the President. After the assassination, Zakovich was assigned to guard Jackie Kennedy and her children, Caroline and John, Jr. He later would end up in Independence, Missouri, working with the detail that guarded former President Harry S. Truman. After Truman died, Zakovich left the Secret Service and opened his own security firm. He was joined on the Tampa trip by his son George.

Besides the Zakovichs, there was another extra security man for Montana. Jim Warren was hired 12 years before by the San Francisco 49ers to help with security on the team's road trips. Warren had become a good friend of Montana and his family, and came to help in Tampa.

The security was a normal part of Montana's life around the stadiums and hotels of the NFL. For him, it began in 1981 when the 49ers made their first run to the Super Bowl. His good looks brought out many female fans who filled hotel lobbies and spent the evening trying to call his room. San Francisco also has more than its share of nut cases and as Montana became more visible, more threatening phone calls and letters were received. From that point on, extra security was a fact of life.

There were several times during the 1993 season when, without the special security, Montana would have been injured by the crush of people attempting to get near him. Once the season started, Montana made very few "announced" appearances in public. Any time he did, however, there was always extra security on hand. When Joe and Jennifer made an appearance on teammate Tim Grunhard's radio show right before the AFC Championship Game, it took six off-duty Kansas City policemen to get him in and out of the restaurant.

Montana's high profile did not make him a recluse by any means. Montana and his family often went out to quiet dinners and movies, sometimes with no security other than Joe's mother and father. On Saturday afternoons, Joe Montana was just another father standing next to a soccer field near his home in Leawood, watching his two daughters kick the ball.

The hubbub surrounding his debut in a Chiefs uniform seemed not to bother Montana. Starting his 15th NFL season, he had seen it all before. He just wanted to get on the field and play.

Incredibly, Montana was not even the oldest starting quarterback in the season opener between the Chiefs and Bucs. Across the field was 39-year-old Steve DeBerg, a familiar face to both Montana and the Chiefs.

DeBerg spent four seasons with the Chiefs, arriving in 1988 via a trade with Tampa Bay. He left Kansas City in 1992 after the Chiefs signed Dave Krieg as a free agent. In four seasons, DeBerg started 54 games for the Chiefs, earning the nickname "Freddy Krueger" for his comeback prowess. Like the monster who kept coming back for more in the "Nightmare on Elm Street" movies, DeBerg was benched several times by Schottenheimer, but always regained the starting job. Schottenheimer went with Ron Jaworksi and Steve Pelluer in 1989, and with Mark Vlasic in 1991. In each case, DeBerg sat on the bench for a week or two until an injury claimed the other quarterback.

It was all part of DeBerg's unique professional career. He was with the 49ers when they drafted Montana out of Notre Dame in 1979. A year later, when San Francisco coach Bill Walsh felt Montana was ready to be the starting quarterback, DeBerg was dealt to Denver. He was the starter there for two seasons until the Broncos acquired John Elway in a trade. Within a year, Denver sent DeBerg to Tampa Bay, where he was supplanted by another No. 1 draft choice — Vinny Testaverde. The Bucs traded DeBerg to Kansas City. Four years later, he re-signed with the Bucs.

The first Chiefs player at Tampa Stadium on this humid game-day morning was Montana. Each and every Sunday that he played, Montana arrived at the stadium some 3 1/2 to 4 hours before kickoff. Many times he was the only player in the locker room, and sometimes he was there for hours before his team-mates arrived and began getting ready for the game.

Montana spent that pre-game time getting last-minute medical treatments. He stretched the muscles in his back and arm. Sometimes, Montana went off exploring the stadium. He walked on the field and watched the cheerleaders go through their pre-game practices. Montana sat and kibitzed with the locker room staff. He read the paper. He signed some autographs. He ... did just about anything that would take his mind off the growing knot in his stomach.

"It's just part of my routine," Montana said. "It helps the nerves."

Nerves? Joe Montana gets nervous? Say it ain't so, Joe!

"Any athlete who tells you he doesn't get nervous is lying," said Montana. "When you don't get nervous, when you don't get that knot in your stomach before a game, I think that's when you know it is time to get out and retire."

He was not ready to retire. Neither was DeBerg.

"I get utter satisfaction out of just studying the game and getting ready to play," DeBerg said. "It's a special thing in my life. I'm sure Joe feels the same way. It's something hard to give up. For most players it is their lifelong dream to do this and once you start doing it, and enjoying it, it is hard to find another job like this."

As Montana walked into the Tampa Stadium locker room and found his cubicle, he discovered a message from DeBerg.

Montana's football shoes were gone. In their place was a pair of old-time football shoes, size 15s. There was a note inside:

"Stop following in my footsteps."

Montana knew immediately it was the handiwork of DeBerg. Less than a year before, the Bucs visited Candlestick Park in San Francisco, and DeBerg arrived in the locker room to find his helmet and shoulder pads missing. DeBerg knew immediately who to blame: Montana.

"We've been doing that kind of stuff to each other for years," laughed DeBerg.

By the end of the game, it was only Montana and the Chiefs who were laughing. Kansas City had little trouble beating the Bucs, 27-3.

And Montana had little trouble picking apart the Tampa Bay defense. On a hot, muggy afternoon, Montana completed his first nine passes, including a 19-yard touchdown throw to Willie Davis. From the broadcast booth, Chiefs play-by-play announcer Kevin Harlan roared after the touchdown, " . . . *this could be the start of something big."*

On this day, a Chiefs offense that had been so inconsistent in the preseason was seemingly unstoppable. Montana threw a 50-yard touchdown pass to wide receiver J.J. Birden, and then a 12-yard flip to running back Marcus Allen. He ended up hitting 14 of his 21 passes for 246 yards, and those numbers could have been even bigger, but Montana left the game late in the third quarter.

Willie Davis considered the Chiefs' performance against Tampa Bay one of the key moments in the season.

"That was a very important game for this team just because it made a statement about being able to play in this offense and being a good supporting cast for Joe," said Davis. "Nobody knew what to expect from the offense and Joe hadn't played in a couple years. After that game, everybody stopped, thought about it and said, 'If we go out and play like this, we can go all the way in this thing.' I think that game is where everybody on this team realized what we had. We might have struggled a lot longer offensively than we did, if we had not started out so strong against Tampa."

But the offense and the Chiefs did not look so strong the next week, as they were shut out by the Houston Oilers 30-0 at the Astrodome. Joe Montana did not play, which started two things: 1) a trend of Montana injuries and 2) a mini-controversy over who controls the Chiefs.

The injury came late in the third quarter against Tampa Bay. Montana was hit by blitzing linebacker Broderick Thomas just as he was releasing a pass to Willie Davis in the end zone. As he was about to hit the ground, Montana twisted his body and put out his right hand to brace himself; he wanted to see if Davis caught the ball for a touchdown. The pass was tipped away at the last instant and all Montana received was a sprained wrist. He did not immediately leave the game. In fact, on the next play he threw a touchdown pass to Marcus Allen.

But when Montana went to the sidelines, his wrist and hand hurt. When team doctors took him into the Buccaneers locker room for x-rays, Peterson held his breath.

"I always have access to a phone that reaches the sidelines and our team doctors," said Peterson, who watches games from the pressbox. "When I called down, they said they didn't think there was a problem, but they just wanted to take x-rays to be sure. The 10 or 15 minutes he was in there seemed like an hour. When he finally came back out, I just couldn't stand it; I had to go down to the sidelines and see for myself."

Montana had a sprained wrist, meaning the joint had been traumatized, but there was no major tendon damage. His right hand was also sore, and the Chiefs' doctors made the decision Montana would not return to the game. Afterwards, with a crowd of fans shouting his name in hopes he would make an appearance for autographs, Montana told the media there were no serious problems with his wrist or hand, and he did not expect it would cost him any playing time. Rest and ice figured to be the cure.

But Montana missed the next game, dressing as the inactive third quarterback, and never stepping on the field against the Oilers. The Chiefs offense was terrible that day, turning the ball over five times and never pushing the ball inside the Houston 25-yard line. The right side of the Chiefs offensive line — Will Shields and Ricky Siglar — were beaten badly by the Oilers veteran defensive linemen Ray Childress and William Fuller.

Would things have been different with Montana? That's impossible to say. But the Chiefs soon learned that getting along without the veteran quarterback was going to be a fact of their lives. The sprained wrist was the first of six injuries Montana suffered through the 1993 season:

INJURY No. 1: sprained wrist in the third quarter of Game No. 1 against Tampa Bay. RESULT: missed the next 71 offensive snaps and one full game.

INJURY No. 2: pulled hamstring in the second quarter of Game No. 4 against the Los Angeles Raiders. RESULT: missed the next 94 offensive snaps and one full game.

INJURY No. 3: pulled hamstring in second quarter of Game No. 7 against Miami. RESULT: missed the next 215 offensive snaps and three full games.

INJURY No. 4: suffered a concussion late in third quarter of Game No. 14 against San Diego. RESULT: missed next two offensive series, total of nine plays, before returning to the game.

INJURY No. 5: bruised ribs late in the first quarter of the postseason game against Pittsburgh. RESULT: missed four offensive plays before returning to the game.

INJURY No. 6: concussion early in third quarter of the postseason game against Buffalo. RESULT: missed the last 40 plays of the game.

The longest stretch during the season where Montana did not have to leave with an injury was the three consecutive games from November 28 against Buffalo through December 12, against Denver. Overall, Montana missed 433 plays during the regular season and postseason. And his absences created a whole new set of statistics for Chiefs fans to follow.

The Chiefs were 10-4 in games Montana started, 3-2 in games Montana did not start, 2-2 in games Montana started but did not finish because of injury, and 2-0 in games Montana started, left with an injury, but then returned before the end of the game.

In the 1992 National Football League season, Dave Krieg did something few quarterbacks are likely to duplicate: he took every offensive snap for the Kansas City Chiefs during 16 regular and one postseason games. On all 960 offensive plays, the man behind the center was Krieg.

Unlike baseball, where every throw of the ball and swing of the bat creates a statistic, the NFL league office does not keep such mundane totals as the number of plays a quarterback participates in during the season. There is no way to determine the last quarterback before Krieg who went the distance — from game No. 1 to game No. 17.

This much is known: in the 1993 season, there was not a single NFL quarterback who was there for every play. During the '93 season, only six starting quarterbacks did not lose their job because of injury or lack of production: Steve Young in San Francisco, John Elway in Denver, Phil Simms of the New York Giants, Jim Kelly in Buffalo, Brett Favre in Green Bay and Boomer

Esiason of the New York Jets. There were 55 different quarter-backs who started at least one game, and six teams were forced to start three different quarterbacks over the season — nearly 20 percent of the league.

So it came as no surprise that Joe Montana did not make it through the 1993 season without injury. The Chiefs did not expect Montana would start 16 regular season games. And while Montana did not say so publicly, it would have been foolhardy for him to believe he could survive the season unscathed by injury. The last season where he had not missed at least one starting assignment was 1983.

But nobody — not Carl Peterson, Marty Schottenheimer or Montana — expected the first injury to come in the season opener.

"The way the season started, I was really wondering if I'd ever stay on the field," Montana said. "It was frustrating."

Said Schottenheimer: "A lot of people talked about how fragile Joe was, but I don't see it that way at all.

"The only really serious injury he had was the pulled hamstring, and that's a tough one to judge on recovery, whether the player is 27 years old or 37 years old. Troy Aikman pulled a hamstring, and he's what — 10 years younger than Joe? (Aikman was 27 by the end of the 1993 season).

"It's an unfortunate fact of life that quarterbacks take a beating in this business."

That kind of punishment is what makes Montana all the more unusual. There were plenty of 30-something quarterbacks around the NFL in 1993. In fact, in two of the first three games he played, Montana was not the oldest starting quarterback on the field. In Tampa, DeBerg was 39, and when the Chiefs faced the Raiders, 38-year-old Vince Evans was the starter for Los Angeles. The average age of the starting quarterbacks in the league at the start of the '93 season was 31.2 years, with 18 of the 28 in their thirties.

Few, however, had a medical injury history as lengthy as Montana's. He came back from an elbow surgery that never had been performed on a football player. Plus, he was able to over-come a serious back injury that many thought would end his career (1986). He also missed time because of a bruised sternum (1985), pulled hamstring (1987), more back problems (1988), elbow, knee and rib injuries (1989) and an injury to his abdomen (1990).

Then came the wrist and hamstring problems of 1993.

"The most frustrating thing was having had to sit and watch for two seasons, and then have playing time taken away because of little nagging injuries," said Montana. "I didn't think I had any hamstrings."

Make no mistake about it: Montana has hamstrings. It is one of the reasons he could dunk a basketball when he was younger. A lot of people do not know that Montana was offered a basketball scholarship to North Carolina State in 1974. That was the time when N.C. State was challenging UCLA's dominance in the world of college basketball. Given the determination, intelligence and athletic ability he has shown throughout his pro football career, it is not too farfetched to believe Montana could have had an NBA career, had he chosen that sport.

Montana's first hamstring injury of 1993 occurred against the Raiders at Arrowhead Stadium. Montana was on the run, scrambling out of bounds, when Los Angeles linebacker Aaron Wallace came up from behind and clipped Montana's heel. That caused the quarterback's leg to straighten and hit the turf in an awkward position. Montana could not put any weight on the leg after he finally got off the ground, and he went to the locker room. He did not return that day.

Questions about Montana's health became part of every conversation between Marty Schottenheimer and the media. The head coach even tried to have some fun with it, showing up for his normal Tuesday press briefing on October 5, wearing a turban and carrying a crystal ball.

"Montana . . . Joe," Schottenheimer said, rubbing the crystal ball.

"Very cloudy . . .

"Some sense of uncertainty . . .

"Percentages are 50-50 . . ."

Schottenheimer pulled off the turban and put away the crystal ball.

"I hope I have made my point," Schottenheimer said. "I don't know. I really don't know (if Montana would play in the next game)."

Hamstrings are notoriously hard to treat because once they are strained, they are far more susceptible to further injury. Whether it happens to a professional athlete or a weekend warrior, a pulled hamstring can feel fine one moment and, all of a sudden, the slightest movement can tweak or re-injure the muscle.

That is what happened to Montana. After suffering the injury against the Raiders, Montana sat out the following game — a Chiefs victory over Cincinnati 17-15. The next week, he played against San Diego, and several times in that game, felt a twinge in the hamstring. But Montana played on and led the Chiefs to a come-from-behind victory.

After a week off, the Chiefs travelled to Miami to play the Dolphins. In the second quarter, Montana scrambled out of the pocket on the natural grass surface at Joe Robbie Stadium, planted his left leg and boom . . . another hamstring pull. This time it was not a re-occurrence of the previous injury, but a pull that was located higher in the back of his leg. This one was much more painful and sent shooting pain into Montana's lower back.

Montana learned a lot about pain on that trip to Miami. In the wee hours of Sunday morning, he started to feel discomfort in his lower back and side. He made several trips to the bathroom in the hotel room he shared with Dave Krieg.

"I was worried about waking David up, so I went in the bathroom and closed the door and sat there," said Montana. "But nothing happened, and the pain just kept getting worse. When I started to urinate blood, I figured it was time to get some help."

In so much pain he could no longer stand, Montana crawled out of the bathroom on his hands and knees. He reached Krieg's bed, grabbed his roommate's leg and started shaking it. Krieg woke up to find Montana writhing on the floor, and quickly called the team doctors. Montana was rushed to a Ft. Lauderdale hospital.

Montana was suffering through the first kidney stone of his life. After everything that had happened to him over the years — all the surgeries, all the pain-killing shots, all the injuries — he was unprepared for this kind of discomfort.

"That was the most painful thing I ever went through," said Montana. "I'd heard about kidney stones, but I never had a problem with them before. They gave me something to cut the pain, but the discomfort was still there. Man, that was something."

Eventually, Montana passed two kidney stones and went back to the team's hotel, where he had a bite to eat. That's when he pronounced himself ready to start that day's game against the Dolphins.

"I get a call in the middle of the night that our quarterback is in total pain," said Peterson. "Then I get a call that he's in the hospital and everything is under control. Then, they call me and tell me he's back in the hotel and feels ready to play.

"That's one tough son of a gun."

A personal note: I have suffered through a pair of kidney stones. There are no words available to explain the pain that consumes your body. Nurses who have had kidney stones and children tell me that passing the stones was more painful than delivering a baby. If that is true, I do not understand how women give birth to more than one child. The pain can last a minute or several hours. After the stone is passed and the pain subsides, all the body wants to do is sleep and recover. That Montana would contemplate playing a football game, let alone actually go out and start against the Dolphins that Sunday, was all the proof I needed about the toughness of this man.

But late in the second quarter, Montana found himself in pain again. He scrambled out of the pocket, planted his left foot and the hamstring went. Montana barely was able to walk off the field. He was taken to the locker room on a cart.

About 90 minutes later, Montana sat in his street clothes in the visitors locker room at Joe Robbie Stadium and tried to get comfortable. Drained by the kidney stone and the pain in his upper leg, Montana could not sit still as he listened to the end of the game on a radio.

"As soon as I straightened the leg, I knew there was a problem," Montana said, between swallows of a soft drink. "There's a lot of pain right now."

NFL quarterbacks learn to live with pain; it is an occupational hazard that comes from the defense's desire to put him out of the game or at least impair his judgement. Frequently, the pain must be forgotten or masked because there are plays to be run, an offense to be led on the field. Len Dawson played 19 seasons of professional football and earned the nickname "Lenny The Cool" because of his demeanor on the field. Part of the "cool" persona of both Montana and Dawson was the ability to handle the pain and still function.

"To be successful in the game of pro football, you have to learn the difference between being injured and being hurt," said

Dawson. "An injury is something major, like a broken bone or a blown knee — something that makes it impossible to function on the field.

"Being hurt is having part of your body bruised or sore; every time you move, you can feel the pain. But you learn to live with that feeling. Every player in the league is hurt during the season. You just have to learn how to handle the pain."

That's one of the reasons Montana arrives so early at the stadium on game days. He must prepare his body for the game. His back has to be ready; his elbow has to be loosened up. After 15 seasons of having his body slammed around the NFL, Montana cannot simply walk into a stadium, change clothes and walk onto the field. Montana is one of those players who can handle the pain because he's had so much practice.

But this hamstring problem, while not as painful as some other injuries, became a real nuisance for Montana and the Chiefs. There were no bye weeks ahead on the Chiefs' schedule to provide some rest. Peterson, Schottenheimer and the team doctors decided Montana would sit for several weeks, maybe a month, until the hamstring was completely recovered.

With Dave Krieg in the starting lineup, the Chiefs and Montana aggressively attacked the injured muscle. Montana took cortisone injections, had electrical stimulation therapy, acupuncture, massage, just about every form of treatment available in modern medicine. Countless suggestions arrived from fans across the country. They had special ointments, pieces of equipment and treatments that they were sure would help Montana.

After two weeks of nothing but treatment and therapy, Montana's hamstring felt much better. He thought he was ready to play on Sunday, November 21 against Chicago. But Schottenheimer told him to wait another week. Montana was unhappy about the decision, but returned to the coaching box where he helped coordinator Paul Hackett with the offense.

Montana was given the go-ahead the next week as the Chiefs prepared to meet Buffalo. His first day back at practice, Montana walked over to his locker and found fake cobwebs plastered to his helmet, courtesy of the equipment staff.

While Montana's helmet grew dusty during three weeks of inactivity, Dave Krieg made giant strides in the Chiefs' new offense. If there was any sort of silver lining to Montana's injury problems, it was the extra time it gave Krieg in practices and games. By the time Montana returned to face the Bills in late November, Krieg's confidence was growing.

"About mid-season, David was playing a lot and I think he really benefitted," said Paul Hackett. "There were times in that stretch where he played OK. The game against the Raiders out in Los Angeles was probably the best. Against Green Bay on Monday night, he was terrible in the first half. There were other times when he still didn't look confident.

"But I think once Joe came back and David had a chance to sit back and think about things, it really left him in a great position. Late in the season, when Joe got dinged a couple of times and had to come out of games, David walked in there, and he was humming. He played excellent football."

Montana's injuries forced Hackett to pull in the offensive reins a bit with Krieg, and that hurt the overall development of the new scheme.

"David's natural skills and his tendencies are a little different than Joe," said Hackett. "David throws the deep ball more often than Joe. He's more confident in that area. So in that case, we did gravitate towards different things when David was in there.

"I don't think our team prepared differently, and I don't think we planned differently or put in different plays when David was playing. I guess it was more my utilization of the offense. Naturally, it was different with David. As my confidence grew in him, he was able to get into the flow of the offense.

"Nobody wanted to see Joe get hurt, but what it did was give us an offense that could work with two quarterbacks. In the NFL today, you had better be able to do that."

For Krieg, the whole scenario of Montana's arrival and his demotion to the second team was a trying time. As soon as the trade was officially announced in April, Krieg walked into Carl Peterson's office and asked, "I guess this means I'm traded." But Peterson and Marty Schottenheimer never had any plans to deal Krieg. By the time he was finished talking with his head coach, Krieg was ready to play.

"He told me exactly what I thought he would tell me," said Schottenheimer. "He told me he was going to try to beat out Joe Montana and keep the No. 1 job. I would not have expected anything else from him."

But Krieg knew there was no way he was going to unseat Montana.

"I would have had to look extremely good and he would have had to look extremely bad," Krieg said at the end of training camp. "And maybe even then, I couldn't have won the starting job. I just didn't want to look bad.

"The thing that kept me going is learning this offense . . . learning that has helped me keep from thinking about a lot of the other things."

At the start of the season, a Krieg mistake was greeted by a chorus of boos from the fans in Arrowhead Stadium. Talk show callers roasted him continuously, calling for the Chiefs to play Matt Blundin instead. There were newspaper stories comparing the Chiefs offensive production when Krieg played against the numbers when Montana was on the field. As with all football comparisons to Montana, Krieg came out second best.

Through it all, Krieg kept his cool. He did not strike back publicly. He did not whine about his demotion. He went about his business of learning the offense. And just as Krieg had done the season before, he improved as the 1993 season progressed. In fact, the more Krieg played, the more fans he won over to his side.

One of the most emotional moments of the season came not at Arrowhead Stadium, but at a Kansas City pub where center Tim Grunhard hosted a weekly radio show. One night in early December, Grunhard told his standing-room-only audience that a special guest would join the show near the end of the scheduled hour. Most in the room immediately thought it was Joe Montana and anxiously watched the door for his arrival.

If there was disappointment when Krieg walked into the tavern, the crowd never showed it — quite the contrary. The room exploded in noise. The crowd stood and clapped, hollered and cheered. For nearly two minutes, they showered Krieg with the kind of ovation he had not received before in Kansas City.

And this was not about throwing a touchdown pass or scrambling away for a first down. This was simply a thank you from Chiefs fans for handling a difficult situation with more class and composure than most people could comprehend, let alone achieve in their day to day life.

"I've never had a reception like the one I had tonight," a visibly moved Krieg told the audience. "I want to thank every one in here for that reception. It was very wonderful."

Most impressed by Dave Krieg's performance in 1993 was Paul Hackett.

"As a backup quarterback, nobody in the NFL did it better than David Krieg," said Hackett. "He did everything: supporting the first guy, stepping in and performing when needed, contributing to the offense during the week and on game day.

"I just can't imagine where this team would have been without David Krieg."

CHAPTER ELEVEN

A MARRIAGE MADE IN . . . FOOTBALL

The day after the Houston disaster, the second guessing on Joe Montana's inactivity began in earnest. If the Chiefs were playing for home-field advantage in the AFC playoffs, how could they not start Montana? If it was not a serious injury, then why were the Chiefs babying him?

On his weekly radio show the day after the game, Carl Peterson defended the decision not to play Montana against the Oilers. In fact, Peterson said he had taken part in the decision.

"I think it's important that we get something straight," Peterson said that night. "Players don't make decisions when they play. That is the coach, and yours truly is involved in those decisions."

Listening at home, *Kansas City Star* columnist Gib Twyman decided Peterson's comments were a revelation. Several days later Twyman wrote a column, questioning the role of the general manager in the Montana decision. According to Twyman, decisions on playing time are traditionally the role of the head coach only, without front-office interference.

Peterson remembers the call he received from Twyman.

"I think the word I used over and over was incredulous; I just could not believe that we had been here for almost five seasons and people did not understand my role in this organization," said Peterson. "A major decision involving the status of an injured player, whether he is Joe Montana or anybody else . . . to think that I would not have some sort of input on his status, it was just unbelievable."

Here's an excerpt from the conversation between Peterson and Twyman:

Peterson: Why are you asking about this?

Twyman: I would disagree with the general manager making a game-day decision.

Peterson: Ha. Gib, every single personnel decision that has been made by the Kansas City Chiefs since I was named president-general manager has to have my stamp of approval. That's my responsibility. Didn't you realize that? Why do you think Lamar hired me? . . . Anything that has to do with player personnel, I have to have the final say on it.

Twyman: OK. How often do you get involved in the game-day decisions about who will play and who won't?

Peterson: When it regards injuries, all of the time. Marty and I discuss everything. We meet with the team doctors every single week. What do you think we've been doing here the last five years? That comes as a shock to you?

Twyman: The time-honored thing is that coaches make game-day decisions and general managers are the people who acquire personnel.

Peterson: Well, you are sadly mistaken in regards to what happens, certainly here and throughout the league. This is not just a game-day decision, not a last-minute decision. You are talking about a decision on quite obviously a very expensive, a very important player on this football team . . . I find it incredulous you find that as something that is wrong or out of the ordinary."

Twyman's column led to another salvo, this in the September 23 edition of a suburban weekly newspaper called *The Squire's Other Paper*. The editor, Tom Leathers, also expressed surprise at Peterson's involvement in the Montana decision. But he did not stop there. Leathers wrote:

"I'd been hearing the reports last season and into the start of this one: That coach Marty Schottenheimer and president Carl Peterson often aren't on the same wavelength."

The article went on to talk about past problems at Arrowhead Stadium between former coach Hank Stram and former president/general manager Jack Steadman. "They (Peterson and Schottenheimer) should get the word that it's not fair to Kansas City football or its fans if there is another tug of war for authority. Kansas City had it once, and it shouldn't have to put up with it again."

Leathers' publication is not widely distributed in the Kansas City area and the Chiefs do not receive a copy at Arrowhead Stadium. So it took more than a week before Peterson saw a copy of the article. His reply, however, was quick and to the point.

"It is obvious that you have no understanding of my administrative philosophy, nor how our operations are run at Arrowhead," Peterson wrote to Leathers. "This is particularly disappointing because of the many conversations you and I have had over the past four-and-one-half years. It seems the more we talk, the less you listen and understand."

So just what was Carl Peterson's involvement in the decision not to play Montana? Did he usurp what has traditionally been only the province of the head coach? Was Carl Peterson a football dictator and Marty Schottenheimer an unhappy servant?

Let Marty Schottenheimer tell the story.

"Carl came in and said, 'What do you think about Joe Montana?'" Schottenheimer said. "I said, 'I don't think we should play him.' Carl said, 'I agree with you,' and he turned around and walked out the door. It took 10 seconds. That was it. Period."

And what of the relationship between Peterson and Schottenheimer?

"It's never been better," said Schottenheimer. "We have our discussions, but I'll tell you something: Carl and I, we probably have had not more than two or three major disagreements on any major issues in the five years we've been together."

Said Peterson: "In the grand scheme of things, I agree with 95 percent of what he does. The five percent I disagree on, we discuss the circumstances. Sometimes he convinces me, sometimes I convince him. Sometimes we agree to disagree.

"There has never been a problem in our relationship, not from the day we first talked about this job."

It has been a football marriage that has worked; just look at the win-loss record (53-33-1) and other accomplishments (four straight appearances in the playoffs) over their five seasons together.

The success comes as a surprise to some around the National Football League. When Peterson hired Schottenheimer in January of 1989, one NFL executive, speaking on the condition of anonymity said:

"These two guys are control freaks. They won't last two years together before they are at each other's throats."

Peterson heard similar comments.

"There were some people, I think some writers from Cleveland who called me and said, 'You both have two big egos and it won't work,'" Peterson said. "I would bet Marty heard some comments about me."

"I did," Schottenheimer said with a grin. "I took the job anyway."

Five years after their football union, neither has any scratches around their necks. Arrowhead Stadium can still contain their egos. Unlike the explosive Dallas combination of Jerry Jones and Jimmy Johnson that ruptured after two Super Bowl championships, Peterson and Schottenheimer are not feuding.

"We both trust each other because we are after exactly the same thing," said Schottenheimer. "We are both interested in winning a world championship, and we both realize there are a lot of different ways to get there.

"The agenda is exactly the same. I've never seen him waiver ...we can disagree, but we are never disagreeable. We both have big egos, there is no doubt about that, yet I think we both manage them. It goes back to the decision with Joe Montana in the Houston game. Carl was involved for one reason: because he had a vested interest in a decision regarding a guy that we had made a very big commitment to.

"Did that bother me, that Carl came down to my office and asked? No. He's doing his job, what I would expect him to do."

Peterson and Schottenheimer have specific responsibilities in their contracts in relation to the players who wear the Chiefs uniform. Peterson has the final say-so on the NFL draft and the players signed or released from the roster. Schottenheimer has complete control over what happens on the field during the game. He decides who gets playing time and in what manner. Schottenheimer also has complete control of his coaching staff.

Does that mean each of them does not contribute in the other areas? Not at all. Quite the contrary; these two talk about every aspect of the football team.

"The only person, in my opinion, who is unwilling to take the input of another person is someone who does not have confidence in his own ability to make a decision," said Schottenheimer. "I try to gather as much information as I can. Carl tries to gather as much information as he can. Then we try to put the information together. We use all the resources available to us, from Lynn Stiles to Mark Hatley to Denny Thum to Tim Connolly to Mike Davidson, whoever it is.

"We don't always do what I want to do. We don't always do what Carl wants to do. But what is done is ultimately arrived at as being in the best interest of this football team. That is the singular question that is asked over and over again: Is this the best thing for the Kansas City Chiefs?"

There are many different ways to operate an NFL franchise. In some situations, the owner or the managing general partner has total control, as with Al Davis and the Los Angeles Raiders. In other cases, the general manager really has the final word on the football team, like George Young of the New York Giants and Charlie Casserly of the Washington Redskins. In some situations, the coach has more control than anyone else, as in the case of Don Shula with the Miami Dolphins. In other instances, coaches like New England's Bill Parcells wear both the hats of the GM and head coach. In still other cases there is a committee that makes the decisions, as usually happens in San Francisco with owner Ed DeBartolo, Jr., president Carmen Policy and head coach George Seifert. Finally, there are those franchises where nobody really knows who is in charge. Check the bottom of the league standings for those teams.

"Listen, the reason I was hired by Lamar Hunt in the first place was because he wanted a football person in charge of the organization," said Peterson. "I was asked to take this job so I would have input on what happens with the roster and the players that come to this team. That should not come as a surprise to anyone. Lamar made that clear from the start."

Peterson built the Philadelphia Stars into the class of the United States Football League, an upstart spring football league that began play in 1983 and survived for three years. Peterson was the Stars' first hire, stolen away from the Philadelphia Eagles where he was the player personnel director for head coach Dick Vermeil. When Peterson was hired, the Stars did not have offices, let alone football players. He started the franchise from scratch, arranging everything from office supplies to a head coach.

And players. Peterson went out and found enough talent that the Stars made the league's first championship game in 1983, losing to the Michigan Panthers. Philadelphia came back and won the USFL title in 1984 and again in 1985 when the franchise moved to Baltimore.

The new league found itself tied up with two problems: 1) the big egos of owners like Donald Trump, and 2) an anti-trust lawsuit filed against the NFL. Ultimately, the USFL won that suit, but was awarded just $3 in total damages. Without a big financial award, the league was unable to survive and soon became part of pro football history.

After the USFL folded, Peterson became the publisher of *PhillySport,* a monthly magazine devoted to the sports scene in Philadelphia. He fielded a number of calls from NFL teams over a two-year period. The New York Jets were interested and so were the San Diego Chargers and New England Patriots. Peterson was part of a group that considered purchasing the Dallas Cowboys.

In all of those cases, one thing kept Peterson in publishing and out of football.

"None of those opportunities provided me with the type of authority I needed," Peterson said. "I had been spoiled with the Eagles and then the Stars. Dick Vermeil had given me the power to run the organization and I had the same thing with the Stars; there was not a lot of interference from above or below. I knew that was the only way to get things done. I was not going to be able to work in a situation where there were road blocks between myself and the owner. To build a team, you must have authority."

Peterson learned the concept of building at an early age. His father, Eric, was born in Sweden and immigrated to the

United States through Ellis Island. Eventually, Eric Peterson settled in Long Beach, California, where he began a construction business.

"My father was in a volatile business and he had severe financial problems at one point," said Peterson. "He could have easily done what many of his colleagues did and declared bankruptcy. But he hung in there and worked and worked to pay off every single person. Then, he became successful again. I really respect that. I like to think that some of that rubbed off on me."

Eric Peterson liked to construct buildings. His son was more interested in building football programs. It started at California State-Sonoma, where Peterson helped revive the football program, spending two seasons as head coach (1970-71). He helped Vermeil build UCLA into a Rose Bowl winner (1972-76) and then followed him to Philadelphia (1977-82), where together they rebuilt the Eagles into a Super Bowl contender. The USFL had been the ultimate building project.

Early in November of 1988, Lamar Hunt had a franchise in desperate need of rebuilding. In the two seasons after firing head coach John Mackovic, the Chiefs finished 4-11 in 1987, and after 10 games of the 1988 season, they were 1-8-1. Several days after a 17-11 loss to Denver on November 6, Peterson received a phone call from Jack Steadman, who was then president of the Chiefs.

"He said, 'Mr. Lamar Hunt would like to talk to you about getting involved with the Kansas City Chiefs,'" Peterson remembered. "That's what started it."

There was a series of meetings between Hunt and Peterson — one in Dallas, another in Chicago. Hunt and Steadman flew Peterson to Kansas City under an assumed name and had him watch a game at Arrowhead Stadium in an empty luxury suite. Peterson drove from Philadelphia to the Meadowlands in New Jersey to see still another game on December 11.

Negotiations did not proceed quickly.

"About halfway through this process I told Lamar that the only way it would work for me was with full authority over the organization," Peterson said. "I think it took some real soul-searching and thinking on Lamar's part to even consider that."

The Chiefs had gone through several different front-office scenarios over their history. As one of the original American Football League franchises, Hunt had been in almost total control at the start, participating in the scouting, signing of players and daily decision making. Steadman was his general manager.

As the team established itself in Kansas City and enjoyed success, head coach Hank Stram became the dominant figure around the Chiefs. Hunt ultimately named Stram vice-president and head coach in 1972, and Stram signed a 10-year contract. With Stram's new title came new duties — negotiating contracts with players. Stram also had complete authority in deciding who played for the Chiefs.

To this day, Hunt says giving Stram what amounted to the authority of a general manager was one of the biggest mistakes he has made with the Chiefs. Stram had problems negotiating with some of his veteran players, and there were a lot of hard feelings. As the final word on personnel matters, Stram made a series of disastrous trades and draft choices, some that set the franchise back possibly 10 years or more.

Steadman was a bottom-line businessman with no football background. Trained as an accountant, Steadman helped write the team's incorporation papers in 1959 while working for Hunt Oil in Dallas. When the team moved to Arrowhead Stadium, Steadman's power began to increase. The lease at the new stadium gave the Chiefs operating responsibilities. In return, the team kept nearly all of the parking, concession and luxury suite revenues. It was a financial windfall for the Chiefs if the stadium was full of fans.

Stram thought Steadman knew just enough football to be dangerous, and they had many disagreements regarding the direction of the team. With seven years remaining on that 10-year contract, Stram was fired after the 1974 season. From that point until the discussions with Peterson, Jack Steadman was the man in charge at Arrowhead. In 1977, Steadman was named team president, and his power was absolute over every aspect of the operation. He also became the lightning rod for what few Chiefs fans remained after more than 15 seasons of bad football. The situation reached a boiling point in the 1988 season.

After much deliberation, Hunt gave Peterson full authority over not only the football team, but the entire organization. On Monday, December 19, 1988, Peterson was announced as the Chiefs' new president/general manager/chief operating officer. Steadman was bumped into the role of chairman of the board, and general manager Jim Schaaf was fired, ending a 25-year relationship with the organization.

When that lengthy title — president/general manager/chief operating officer — hit the Teletype that connects all 28 NFL teams, it created a few guffaws among league executives.

"It had everything but 'king,'" said one NFL executive. "It's the longest title in the NFL."

A *Kansas City Star* sports columnist wrote: ". . . the only things left out, I think, were Lion of the Desert, Duke of Earl, Sultan of Swat and Emperor of the Sun."

This analysis failed to comprehend that there was more than ego massage at work with the titles. Peterson wanted to erase any doubts in the minds of fans, players, coaches, the media and others around the NFL about who was now in charge of the Kansas City Chiefs.

"It was a new day at Arrowhead," said Peterson. "But they don't call Missouri the Show-Me state for nothing. A lot of people didn't believe it."

Steadman had been around too long and survived too many new faces. That he would walk away and no longer have any authority over the team was something many long-time fans and even those around the league could not swallow.

Early in his tenure, Peterson found his power challenged a few times by Steadman. In every instance, he prevailed. Steadman moved out of the plush Arrowhead office he had helped design and lost his prime parking spot outside the Chiefs offices. Both went to Peterson. Eventually Steadman left the building completely, moving to a downtown suite of offices created just for him. To this day, he is informed of decisions made by Peterson and he still attends league meetings and functions. But Steadman has little influence and no veto power in the organization.

When Peterson took over, he wasted little time in making changes. In the past, players and coaches had been caught in the revolving door. This time, front office administrators and the old way of doing things had to pay the price as well.

"I sensed that people were not intrinsically involved with the team," Peterson said. "People in the organization had divorced themselves from the football on the field. The feeling was, 'I've got my job, if the team doesn't do well, they will fire the coach and get another coach, but that doesn't affect me.' That was something we had to change."

Before Peterson took over, the Chiefs were a business that happened to have a football team. Ever the accountant, Steadman based his decisions on that discipline. Under Peterson, the Chiefs became a football business. Peterson earned a doctorate in administration from UCLA because he thought it would some day help him become an athletic director. When Peterson looks at the bottom line, he sees victories and defeats, not dollar signs.

"We are in the business of football," Peterson said. "That's what's important. It's not automobiles, real estate, mining, computers. It is a people business. We are dealing with egos that run the spectrum, that must be pulled together to work as a team. You have to have the right people in charge and committed to a common goal.

"That's the same for any business. The difference for us is scrutinization. Practically everything we do is immediately public knowledge. We are witnessed by 70,000 plus fans every week, millions more on television, and that's over 20 weeks a year. That means you must have an extraordinary commitment to your goal. There are going to be a lot of people trying to derail it. You must have the commitment to excellence that Al Davis has talked about so much with the Raiders."

Peterson views his role in the same manner as he would if his title was head coach.

"I told Lamar that I fully expected if I don't get the job done, he would fire me," said Peterson. "If we don't win, I should be fired. Period. The responsibility lies here. I also told him if I do well, then I should be rewarded, because I'm certainly going to reward the people working under me for success."

In many ways, Peterson is still a coach. It just so happens that some of his players do not wear helmets and shoulder pads, but suits and neckties.

"Without question, I consider myself a football coach," said Peterson. "Coaching is an extension of playing and once you have played this game, it is addictive. I was never that good a football player — average at best — but I never got my fill of it.

"In coaching, when you are a position coach, you take great pride in the work of your individual players. If they succeed, you feel very, very good about it. If they fail, you take it as a personal thing, that I did not do a good enough job of coaching.

Carl Peterson watches the closing moments of the AFC Championship Game at Rich Stadium in Buffalo. After success in Philadelphia with the NFL Eagles and the USFL Stars, Peterson was hired in December, 1988, to turn around the troubled Chiefs franchise.

Lamar Hunt (left) created the American Football League in 1960, and 34 years later remains the sole owner of the Kansas City Chiefs. From 1975 through 1988, a time when the Chiefs made the playoffs just once, Jack Steadman (right) was the most powerful person in the Chiefs organization.

Lamar Hunt greets Chiefs head coach Marty Schottenheimer on the field before the 1993 season opener against Tampa Bay. Unlike some previous Chiefs head coaches, Schottenheimer has developed a good rapport with Hunt.

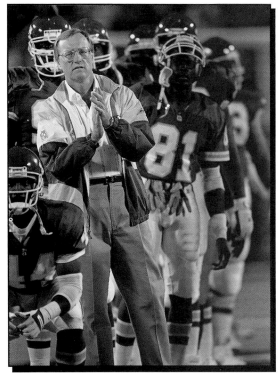

On the sidelines, Marty Schottenheimer can be one of the most demonstrative coaches in the NFL. Here, he's captured in one of his quieter moments. Schottenheimer said he had more fun in 1993 than in any previous season as a head coach.

Before he signed with the Chiefs in 1989, Tim Connolly would have done anything for a chance to work in the NFL. As the team's executive vice-president, Connolly has been instrumental in the franchise's turnaround.

The addition of offensive coordinator Paul Hackett with the Bill Walsh/San Francisco-style passing offense was one of the biggest changes in what turned out to be a 1993 season filled with change for the Chiefs.

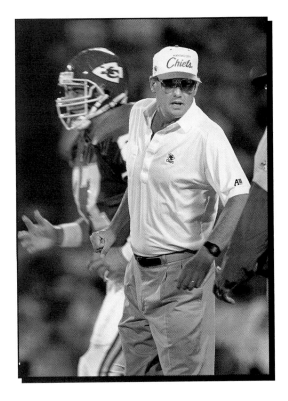

Schottenheimer confers with quarterback Joe Montana during the fourth quarter of the team's victory over Houston in the playoffs. Notice Montana's right elbow. Despite its ghastly appearance, Montana had no elbow trouble during the 1993 season.

After two seasons of inactivity, Joe Montana showed early in the 1993 season that there was nothing wrong with his arm. Here he is completing a pass in his first game in a Chiefs uniform, a preseason matchup against Buffalo at Arrowhead Stadium.

The key to the Bill Walsh/ San Francisco-style passing offense is the quarterback's ability to quickly read the defense and release the ball in less than three seconds, something that has always been one of Joe Montana's strengths.

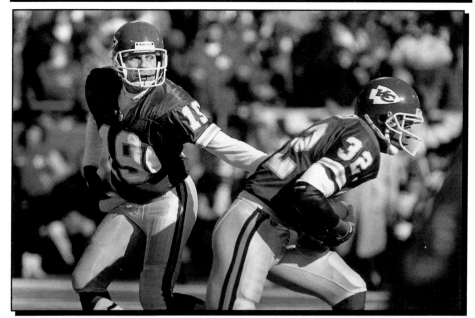

A snapshot for Canton, Ohio, and the Pro Football Hall of Fame: two sure-fire inductees – Joe Montana and Marcus Allen – exchange a handoff. Besides earning Pro Bowl berths for their on-field performances, Montana and Allen made big contributions in the Chiefs locker room, providing a needed dose of veteran leadership.

Marcus Allen goes airborne at the goal line for another touchdown. Only San Francisco's Jerry Rice scored more touchdowns than Allen's 15 during the 1993 season. Allen added three more in the playoffs.

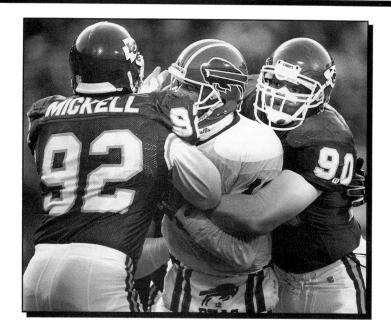

Defensive end Neil Smith (90) led the NFL in quarterback sacks during the 1993 season with 15. Here, he's picking up a pair of sacks against two different Buffalo quarterbacks, as he crunches Jim Kelly (above) with the help of Darren Mickell (92), and then snags Frank Reich (14) by himself (below).

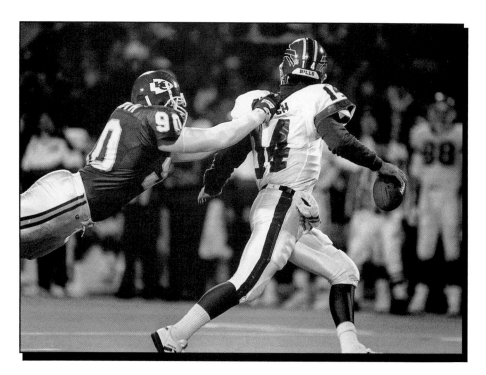

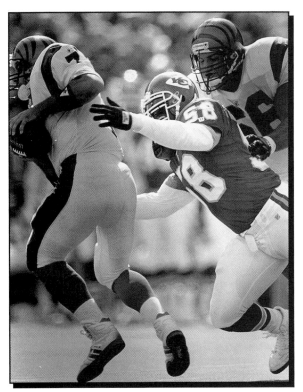

Although the season ended on a sour note in the title game loss in Buffalo, Derrick Thomas (58) had a good season in 1993, as he moved from outside linebacker to the defensive end position. Here he sacks Cincinnati quarterback David Klingler. In 1994, Thomas will move back to outside linebacker where he feels more comfortable.

For Albert Lewis (29), videotape study is the key to his skills as one of the NFL's top cornerbacks. On New Year's Eve, while many of his teammates were attending a birthday party for Derrick Thomas, Lewis was at home, watching tapes of the Chiefs' next opponent.

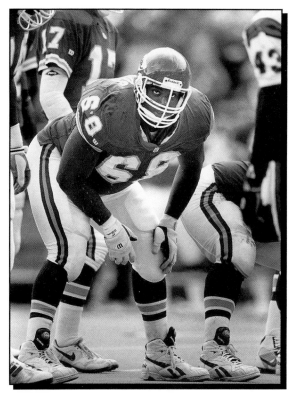

Will Shields (68) and Ricky Siglar (66) were probably the two biggest surprises of the Chiefs' 1993 season. As a rookie third-round draft choice, Shields ended up starting all but one game at right guard. Siglar had not played in a regular season game for two years, but started every game except one at right tackle.

"You learn in coaching that if you do not put together the right plan of action, no matter how good your players are, they are at a disadvantage. I feel the same way about what I do now. Before you face difficult decisions, you have a game plan or a business plan, something you have tried to think out thoroughly, objectively, without pressure. And once you've got your plan, then you go ahead with it. You can't have blinders on because things do change quickly and you have to be flexible. But overall, you must have a sense of where you are going, why are you doing this, and what your goal is.

"I learned that in coaching and I still do that every day."

That coaching background explains why Peterson and Schottenheimer have been able to make their football marriage work. When they sit down and talk, they speak the same language.

"I think the No. 1 key to our relationship is that we have the same goal in mind," said Peterson. "I think No. 2, and maybe more important, is that before I ever hired Marty, he had gained my respect as a very talented, bright football coach, going back to when we competed against each other as assistant coaches, he with New York, and myself in Philadelphia.

"We really do think alike. Whether it's because we are the same age and have had very similar experiences in pro coaching, I don't know, but there is little we truly disagree about. I can't tell you the number of times I have had a thought, and before I could express it, Marty expressed the same thought to me. I think that's happened with him a few times, too."

The similarities in their thinking can be seen when both are asked the same question at different times: if they could go into a laboratory and construct the perfect football player, what attribute would they start with?

Peterson: "The first piece is the heart — the heart that won't let this person ever quit, ever be satisfied with their performance. But most of all, under whatever conditions exist, this person refuses to give up. He may have inadequacies in some skills, but you can't beat him because of his heart. I can think of some examples I've seen: Sam Mills for one, and more recently, Rich Baldinger. Probably neither one should have played in the NFL based on size and skills. Yet, their heart not only allowed them to play, but in the case of Sam Mills, he became a Pro Bowl football player."

Schottenheimer: "The most important thing is a competitive spirit, the thing that as a coach you can't get out of them. If they don't have it, you aren't going to get it. That's why we see players with great athletic ability fail and see guys like Sam Mills succeed. We cut Sam Mills in Cleveland. He's not big enough, fast enough, he can't do this, he can't do that. But wait, what about that thing that goes on inside of him, that competitive spirit. You know, some of those other things you can work on, develop, nurture, but that competitive spirit, that willingness to sacrifice to do whatever it takes to win . . . that's the most important element in any football player."

Like Schottenheimer's incessant public statements that anything less than a Super Bowl championship is failure, Peterson believes there is only one reason to be part of athletics: victory.

"I always felt it was important to be the very best, and if you are not successful reaching that goal, then you have not done the job," said Peterson. "You can't be a winner 100 percent of the time, but if you don't strive for that, you begin to accept losing, and that's one thing that I have never accepted easily. I really believe that winning is a habit, just as losing can become a habit. People make choices and maybe they don't even realize they are choosing losing. It's like, 'Well losing is bad, but it's not the worst thing.'

"Let me assure you, losing is the worst thing."

Peterson and Schottenheimer both acknowledge their relationship is not without disagreements. The key is communication.

"Now remember, this is coming from a guy who has been through a divorce," said Peterson. "But the ability of both of us to say what is on our minds, without fear of hurting somebody's feelings and creating even bigger problems is what makes it work. Marty feels free to come in here, close the door and tell me exactly how he feels, that he's upset about this or he doesn't like this, or he disagrees about some decision that has been made. I can do the same thing with him.

"And yet, we talk it out, air it out, ask for other people's opinions. Then we open the door, walk out and we are on the same page."

If there are discussions and disagreements between these two, most often they are over personnel. Schottenheimer can remember several instances.

"I was interested a few years ago in examining the possibility of acquiring the first pick in the draft so we could take Steve Walsh," said Schottenheimer. "And Carl did not want to do that. I wanted to get Steve Walsh, but Carl did not. And he proved to be right.

"We had a debate a few years back over an offensive lineman, Larry Williams. I wanted to keep him because he was a veteran and Carl wanted to keep a younger player. We kept the younger player and Carl was right.

"I'm on record, I'm on NFL films as being the guy who said during the draft in 1990, let's take the linebacker from Michigan State, Percy Snow. That's who we selected. Did it work out? I'd have to say it did not.

"But there's one thing about me, if I make a mistake, it doesn't bother me. I just go on to the next decision. I just figure the odds are, if you use the right approach to these things, you are going to make more right decisions than wrong ones. I think we've used the right approach."

During the 1993 season, Peterson and Schottenheimer had discussions about the playing time of tight end Keith Cash.

"Carl pushed and pushed to get Keith Cash to play," said Schottenheimer. "And I wasn't ready to play Keith Cash. In the final analysis, we finally did play Keith Cash, and we were better for it.

"Now, does that mean Carl was right and I was wrong? I don't think it means that at all. I think it means that when you look at it from the perspective of a coach, you are charged with winning, so you put the people on the field that you have confidence in and trust can get the job done.

"If we had played Keith Cash earlier, would he have blossomed faster? He might have. But I don't necessarily believe that would have happened. I think the time was right for Keith to begin blossoming when he played. I think he was ready. I think he was confident. I had confidence in him."

Peterson has talked Schottenheimer out of making several decisions over the years.

"It was after the Pittsburgh game in 1989, where Steve DeBerg did not get a play off at the goal line because of the crowd noise, and we ended up taking a penalty," said Peterson. "Marty came in the next day and wanted to get rid of him. He wanted him on waivers at 4 o'clock that day.

"I thought we were throwing the baby out with the bath water, so to speak, and told him we couldn't do that. What if our other guys got hurt and could not perform? Who was going to be our quarterback?

"Eventually, Marty calmed down and he made a change in the starting quarterback. But we kept DeBerg. Sure enough, a couple weeks later we had some injuries and DeBerg was back in as the starter and we ended up winning four of our last five."

Schottenheimer has had to calm Peterson down as well. During some particularly nasty contract negotiations before the 1991 season between Peterson and cornerback Albert Lewis, it was Schottenheimer who kept both sides pointed in the direction of a settlement.

"The players will go to him and say, 'Carl's killing me with this negotiation, he's not fair, he's not doing this,' and so forth," said Peterson. "And certainly, we share that information. They know that the tenor of what they said will get back to me. Now, maybe it won't be in exactly the same language, because I think Marty sometimes leaves out the nasty stuff they've said about me. But their point will be presented to me by Marty.

"One of the things I respect most about Marty is how he handles contract holdouts. No coach, no general manager likes to have holdouts. It's disruptive, but it's part of the business of football. Marty says, 'Look, I would like to have the guy in camp, but in the grand scheme of things, he could come in, break his leg in the first practice and be gone for the whole year. I'm not going to waste my time worrying about things I cannot control.'"

When the changes were made on the coaching staff after the 1992 season and the new offense was installed, there were people who speculated the changes were mandated by Peterson.

Schottenheimer can only shake his head about that kind of thinking.

"Whoever said that does not know a thing about Marty Schottenheimer," he said. "I mean, if I wasn't willing to do it in Cleveland (in 1988) — if I left there because of interference from the organization on who would be on my coaching staff — then why would I allow it to happen here?

"There are some coaches in this league that have a sense of autonomy in what they do. I don't need that. I didn't need that in Cleveland and I don't need it in Kansas City. The only autonomy I need is who is on my coaching staff. To me, that is the one area the head coach must have complete authority. Anything less than that and the head coach is in trouble. You go back and check; head coaches who are handed assistants from the organization have never been successful. It has never worked.

"I had no problems in Cleveland until the moment Art Modell started to involve himself in who could and could not be on my coaching staff. That's where I drew the line in Cleveland. I would draw the same line here or anywhere in a similar situation."

That line can be drawn with players as well. When possible acquisitions have been discussed in personnel meetings, Schottenheimer has said, flat out, that he did not want them on his team.

"It would be a waste of time for us to draft a player who perhaps the scouts love, but the coach said could not play at all," said Peterson. "You have to be careful and remember that coaches coach and scouts scout, and they are two different things. But you want the coaches' input. I've always felt if you have a player available who the scouts love and the coaches love, then you've got a great chance that this guy is going to improve your team. The coach is going to work a little bit harder to produce and develop this player. The scout feels great about it; he's had an impact on this guy being in the organization.

"If you get to the point where there are dramatic differences of opinion, then you just stay away from the player and go on to the next guy."

Peterson and Schottenheimer rely heavily on the Chiefs personnel department, headed by Lynn Stiles, Terry Bradway and Mark Hatley. Both go out of their way to credit them with many of the successes the organization has experienced.

"Mark Hatley came to both of us and said that we should sign Barry Word," said Peterson. "I think we both had the same initial reaction: No. But we investigated, we did our research, we had Mark Hatley tell us why we should do it. After everybody did their homework, we all agreed that we should at least give this guy a look.

"That's how the personnel process works."

Peterson and Schottenheimer are not bosom buddies away from Arrowhead Stadium. Peterson tends more toward late dinners on the Country Club Plaza, while Schottenheimer can usually be found in Johnson County, grabbing a bite to eat on the way to the movies.

But when it comes to football, they very definitely operate on the same wavelength.

"When I hired him, I said, 'Listen, one of the biggest pluses is that you know I'm going to give you everything I can to win,'" said Peterson. "And I said, 'One of the biggest negatives is I'm probably going to second guess your ass all the way because I've coached in this league, and I've got ideas and I'm not always going to agree with you.'"

Schottenheimer has never had a problem with Peterson looking over his shoulder.

"It's not second guessing in the context that people generally define that expression," said Schottenheimer. "When you say somebody is second guessing you, there is a negative connotation, and his questions and comments have never been in that sense. He'll come in and say, 'I don't know about this, or is this exactly what we want to do?' He's not talking about X's and O's; usually it has to do with playing young guys.

"That's part of his job. He coordinates the finding of talent. I coordinate the playing of talent. We are both just doing what we are supposed to do. I don't know why anybody would have a problem with that.

"I don't."

CHAPTER TWELVE

NEIL'S DEAL:
A STORY OF SURVIVAL

There is no owner's manual for this thing called life, no map in the glove compartment to show us the fastest and easiest way to success, no auto club bulletin foretelling the potholes and detours that lie ahead.

We survive because we learn to adapt. We thrive once we understand destiny is but putty in our hands, frequently pushed and pulled by events, yet ultimately shaped by our own acquisition of knowledge.

Take the life's journey of Neil Smith, considered among the best defensive players in the NFL, the man Carl Peterson dubbed the Chiefs' franchise player before the start of the 1993 season.

As the Chiefs prepared to play the Los Angeles Raiders in the fourth game of the 1993 season, little had been heard from Smith. He missed all of training camp in River Falls and four preseason games. Smith signed his contract in time to play against Tampa Bay in the opener, although it was only on passing downs. The next week Smith started in Houston and sacked quarterback Warren Moon. In the third game of the season Smith was shut out — no sacks, no tackles, no assists — against Denver.

Then came a Smith explosion against the Raiders: four sacks for minus-35 yards and one forced fumble. He sacked Los Angeles quarterback Vince Evans in the first series of the game, then came back and dropped him late in the third quarter. Early in the fourth quarter, Smith got to Evans again, forcing a fumble that was recovered by teammate Tim Newton. On the very next series, Evans fell under Smith's rush for a fourth time; this sack went for a loss of seven yards.

The Chiefs beat the Raiders that day 24-9, pushing their record to 3-1. It also gave them a 2-0 record in the AFC West.

Smith's four-sack performance was one of the National Football League's best pass rushing efforts in 1993. It was a season where quarterback sacks were down across the board. A rule change that allowed quarterbacks flushed from the pocket to intentionally ground the ball without penalty, took one to two sacks out of every NFL game.

Neil Smith did not like the new rule, not one bit.

"All the pass rushers are trying to do is get to the quarterback," said Smith. "We aren't trying to hurt anybody. I'm not trying to knock the other quarterback out of the game. I just want to get him on the ground or knock the ball loose. If he gets hurt, it's his own fault. Somebody once said they should put skirts on the quarterback, and I think that's right."

Smith ended up leading the NFL with 15 sacks in 1993. That was the lowest leading total in a non-strike season since the sack became an official statistic in 1981. But for Smith, it was the best sack season of his career and earned him first-team All-Pro honors and his third straight selection to the Pro Bowl.

"It's hard to believe 15 was enough to lead the league," said Smith. "Teams were throwing the ball much faster against us then they had in the past. And then that damn new rule."

The NFL success experienced by Neil Smith is not a simple story to tell. It is not one of those nice, neat fairy tales of high school stardom, followed by college stardom, followed by professional achievement. This is the tale of a man who overcame a troubled childhood in the projects of New Orleans, a place where his best friend died in a drug deal gone bad. Labeled early in life as lazy, slow and, by some, retarded. Smith eventually was diagnosed with dyslexia, a learning disability that makes reading the printed page nearly impossible.

At the University of Nebraska, he arrived as a string-bean freshman, probably more adept at basketball than football, and was given one of the Cornhuskers' final scholarships. There was a disastrous rookie season in the NFL, when he was vilified by fans, the media, and even some of his teammates for his less than inspiring play, especially since he was the second player taken in the 1988 draft.

Yet, Neil Smith became a success, both in football and life. He survived. He adapted. He grabbed destiny, twisted it, turned it on its head, pulled it in his direction and made it work for him.

And Neil Smith wants more.

"There have been a lot of tough things in my life, the kind of stuff that can send you down the wrong path," Smith said. "Maybe I was lucky, but I'll tell you this: I worked for everything.

"Right now, it is very important for me to be considered the best. I want my peers to say my name and then say, 'He's the best guy in the league.' When people talk now about guys like Reggie White and Bruce Smith, I want them in five years to be talking about me."

As Neil Smith says this, he is sitting in Houston's Restaurant, in Kansas City's posh Country Club Plaza area. He is wearing leather pants that are so expensive he could buy lunch for everyone in the restaurant and still have money left over to take care of everybody's dinner . . . and lunch the next day. He is wearing a gold wrist watch, and there is a gold chain around his neck. On his belt is a mobile pager and sitting on the table is his cellular phone, which seems to ring every minute or so, as friends and family track down his location.

He is the picture of success.

"I want my peers to know that I overcame a lot, worked my tail off and did whatever it took to be the best defensive end in the National Football League," Smith said. "That's what I play for. That, and a championship ring."

"Hard" and "work" are words Marty Schottenheimer loves to hear in the same breath. As Smith strives to reach his goal of being the best, he has impressed his head coach.

"The biggest contributing factor to Neil's success has been his maturity," said Schottenheimer. "Under (assistant coach) Tom Pratt's guidance, he has developed an understanding of the importance of details and preparing yourself as a player. Because of the balance of his game as both a run defender and a pass rusher, he has the opportunity to become one of the very best in the league. More importantly, he wants to be the best."

This burning desire comes from growing up in New Orleans, where his mother Lutisha still lives and where Smith visits often.

"She worked two or three jobs and raised three kids, and if there is somebody I want to be like, it is her," Smith said. "There were times when she didn't eat because she fed us. She could have given up, allowed us to find our own way and taken care of herself. But she set an example. For me to have seen that, well, there is only one way to get it done after that, and that's the right way."

Growing up in the projects of New Orleans, Smith found himself sucked into the "wrong way." He stole bicycles, vandalized property and was on the road to more serious trouble.

"Eventually, we got out of the projects, and it kept me away from some of that," said Smith. "But one of my best friends still lived there. One time I went back to visit, and suddenly he was big into the drug game. He told me how great it was, all the money he had.

"Later, he got killed. I easily could have been with him. I could have been dead at 17. From that moment on, I started to be concerned about taking responsibility for my life."

Just a few years earlier, Smith's learning disability finally was diagnosed by counselors at his junior high school. For those with dyslexia, the printed page is a jumbled mess. The letters that make up the words are reversed and sometimes out of order. Ti nac ekam gnidear eht tseilpmis fo secnetnes a gnitartsurf echeirepxe. (It can make reading the simplest of sentences a frustrating experience.)

"I was told for years that I was lazy, and I believed it," Smith said. "I just didn't have it. I didn't learn. I didn't read books. My mother always thought it was because I was lazy. She never knew. My brother and sister never had those problems, and this was something new to her . . . I didn't do the school work because I couldn't."

Once diagnosed, Smith was sent to special classes so he could learn how to deal with the problem.

"Even right now, I'm not where I should be at the age of 27," Smith said. "There is so much that passed me by. I'm always trying to make up for lost time."

Smith still has trouble with the printed page. When the Chiefs defensive line takes a test before every game, assistant coach Tom Pratt asks Smith the questions, rather than hand him the written exam.

When he left New Orleans' McDonough High School for Nebraska, there was plenty of work Smith had to do in the weight lifting room if he was to survive and play major college football. As a freshman, he was 6-5, but weighed just 208 pounds. By his senior season, he had grown to 265 pounds. In spring practice, Smith was electronically timed in the 40-yard dash at 4.63 seconds. According to Nebraska coaches, that translated to 4.43 seconds on a hand-held stopwatch. The Cornhuskers staff had never seen a defensive lineman with so much speed.

Smith played in three New Year's Day bowl games for Nebraska, starting twice. He finished his career with 14.5 sacks while making his mark as one of the best run defenders in the country.

With the third selection in the 1988 NFL draft, the Chiefs decided they wanted Smith. Rumors abounded that other teams, including the Los Angeles Raiders, were also enamored with Smith. That sent the Chiefs hierarchy searching for a way to make sure they got their man.

Atlanta held the No. 1 choice that year and announced they were going to select Auburn linebacker Aundray Bruce. The Detroit Lions held the second choice, and the Chiefs were set to pick third.

To make sure they were able to draft Smith, then-Chiefs general manager Jim Schaaf worked out a trade with Detroit to move up one spot in the selection order. To do that, the Chiefs had to give up their second-round selection to the Lions. So, rather than selecting the third and 30th player in the draft, the Chiefs picked only the second, grabbing Smith. Coming off a 4-11 season with a team badly in need of a major talent infusion, it did not seem a smart move. The Lions ended up using that second-round choice to select Ohio State linebacker Chris Spielman. (At the time, the Chiefs desperately needed help at linebacker).

After making the aggressive move to select Smith, Schaaf became passive when it came time to negotiate a contract. Smith did not take part in any of the Chiefs' off-season programs and missed a week of training camp practices before finally agreeing to terms.

When he did show up, Smith's performance did nothing to quell the second guessing. Limited in two games because of an ankle injury and missing three others because of urological surgery, he finished the 1988 season with 53 tackles and 2.5 sacks in 11 games. The Chiefs were 4-11-1, and the media and fans zeroed in on Smith's lackluster play as one of the reasons for the poor season. Some of his veteran teammates questioned his work ethic.

"That rookie season was something else," Smith said. "The press tore me up, the fans tore me up, everyone looked at me like I lost the whole season. I thought I could beat guys in the NFL with my natural ability, just like I did in college. But I found out there are veteran players out there, and they know exactly what to do. The last thing they wanted was to let a rookie beat them.

"Coming from Nebraska, I had a totally different attitude than a lot of the veterans that were here," continued Smith who, in three years with the Cornhuskers varsity, had been on the field for only seven losses. "Winning was a part of everyday life there. You were crushed when you didn't win.

"But there were guys on that '88 team who didn't care. You could see it in the way they talked, the way they practiced, the way they talked to the coaches. I knew I didn't play well, but it wasn't because I didn't care. I lost a lot of respect for some guys on that team, but I never lost my desire for winning."

One veteran on that 1988 Chiefs team left a positive impression on Smith. Like his mother's example before, All-Pro free safety Deron Cherry showed Smith the road to turn around his career.

"That first season I was here, everybody would run out of the locker room after practice to go home or go run the streets," Smith remembered. "But this guy Deron, he was always running extra sprints or looking at video. He'd be in there, clicking the tape machine back and forth, back and forth, talking to himself as he did it, writing things down in this notebook that he kept. I'd look at him and say, 'This guy is crazy. What is he doing in there? He's wasting his time. We aren't winning any games. He doesn't need to do all of that. Nobody wants to win here.'

"The more and more I talked to him, I realized that he wanted to win and he wanted to be the best in the business. Everybody in this league is talented, but he wanted to be more than just another player. Deron became the best of the best because of all that work. I looked at myself in the mirror and I realized if I wanted to be the best, then I was going to have to start working like him.

"Deron sat me down and told me I had to start studying, so I started watching tape. I didn't know what the hell I was looking at when I started. But he gave me some pointers, and as I learned about my position and the league, I started picking things up."

Cherry also told Smith it was time to change his ways off the field. In that rookie season, Smith enjoyed the night life. For the first time in his life, he had money to spend. Plus, he was young and single; the candle very definitely was burnt at both ends.

"He told me to give up life on the streets," Smith said with a smile. "You know, when you are young, you think you can go all night and then come back the next day and practice like nothing happened.

"Maybe you can, but your butt will be dragging. Deron told me that all the stuff I was into on the streets would be there in 10 years if I still wanted it. He told me it was the same old thing out there, the same old people, and all that it did was get in the way of what I was trying to accomplish. That was tough to hear because I liked to go out to clubs and such. But he was right. I started cutting back dramatically on the time I spent running around, and I didn't miss a thing."

Another veteran provided an example of the kind of physical conditioning needed to reach the top of the NFL. When Mike Webster first arrived in Kansas City after 15 seasons with the Pittsburgh Steelers, his plan was to become an assistant coach. But Webster decided to continue his playing career, and in 1989, he was the team's starting center. Webster spent 1990 as a backup to Tim Grunhard and then retired. When he becomes eligible for the Pro Football Hall of Fame, he should be a first-ballot selection.

Webster became a legend in football for his training regime. While some players clocked their workouts in minutes, Webster's came in hours. He would lift weights before and after games, an unheard of combination. One of his former Steelers teammates tells the story of a young player who accepted Webster's invitation to train together one day during the off-season. This player was seven years younger than Webster, but was left in a heap after just 90 minutes. Webster went on to work out for another three hours.

Smith had trouble with stamina in his rookie season. The quickness and strength he showed at Nebraska was visible, but he had no endurance.

"Webby showed me how to train so I would be able to play at a high level on every play, first quarter and fourth quarter," said Smith. "He was an amazing dude. I don't think I've ever seen anybody work harder than Mike Webster."

And there was yet a third influence on Smith's career: former Chiefs defensive lineman Buck Buchanan. Before his death in July 1992 of lung cancer, Buchanan spent a lot of time talking with Smith. A member of the Pro Football Hall of Fame and one of the most inspirational members of the Chiefs glory teams, Buchanan tried to pass along some of his knowledge.

"He came here green as grass," Buchanan once said of Smith. "He reminded me a lot of myself, back in 1963 when I first came to Kansas City."

Said Smith: "Buck was a great man. When he talked, you had to listen. I had the chance to get to know him and his family, and they are special people. He helped, he helped me a lot."

After that disastrous 1988 season, the Chiefs made sweeping changes, with Peterson and Schottenheimer taking over as general manager and head coach.

"The one thing I remember about my discussions with Neil when we first came here, was that he was unsure of himself," said Schottenheimer. "He wasn't sure how good he could become, and a lot of that came from the pressure of being the second player drafted. That didn't matter to us because we didn't select him. So already, the expectations for him were not quite as heavy as they had been the year before."

Confident in his skills against the run, Smith knew he had to become a better pass rusher to survive in the NFL.

"I had to teach myself, so I looked at a lot of film," said Smith. "My hat's off to Reggie White, Bruce Smith, Charles Mann, Chris Doleman . . . there are parts of all of them in me. The guys I watched most were Reggie and Bruce.

"Bruce Smith is 280-some pounds and has the quickness of a cat. He can cut the corner and get around there quicker than anyone. Reggie is more of a power-type rusher, and he has that club move, where he just knocks the guy blocking him off-balance."

Smith has always been strong against the run, something he learned at Nebraska.

"This game is simply leverage, because the strongest guy doesn't always win, the quickest guy doesn't always win. It's the guy with the great leverage, who can counteract strength and quickness with the right positioning," said Smith.

"The other thing I have to do is look at a guy and try to figure out how I can get him off-balance. I need to get him going one way so I can go the other way. Most of the time, when it's an offensive lineman, I can't go through him; he's bigger than I am. I've got to figure out a way around him. It's as simple as that."

Smith also finds motivation in competing with teammate Derrick Thomas. Close friends off the field, they constantly try to out-sack each other on the field.

"Derrick is a guy who makes our job look so easy because of the talent he has," said Smith. "I will always be chasing him because he just has so much natural ability."

Deron Cherry also served as a role model for Smith off the field. During his playing career, Cherry was extremely active in the Kansas City community. His example led Smith to create "Neil's Deal" with the Ozanam Boys Home, a live-in treatment center for emotionally-disturbed youngsters whose behavior keeps them out of regular schools.

There are four rules the boys must follow if they join Neil's Deal:

1. Stay in school.
2. Stay away from drugs.
3. Always give your best.
4. Be a good friend.

Smith visits the home, talks with the boys and treats them to Arrowhead Stadium visits for games and practices.

"When I grew up, we lived right down the street from a boys home, and every time I got into trouble, my Mom would point down the street and say, 'I'm not going to take this mess anymore. I'll march you into that boys' home in a minute, if you don't get yourself together.'

"A couple times she walked me down the street to stand in front of the boys' home before she finally turned around. They had high fences there and they couldn't do what they wanted to do. It was like a jail, and I couldn't see myself locked up in a place like that.

"I relate to these kids. A lot of them have been labeled as troublemakers, slow learners and other things. I try to tell them it's only a label, that it doesn't describe the person inside, what is in your heart. What I want to give them is confidence. When those kids see me, they can see that there is a way out, that you don't have to be stuck with a label of being a failure or a delinquent.

"You don't get nothing free in life. You earn everything. I'm trying to teach that."

In 1993, Smith earned a piece of his goal.

"I feel like I can share the No. 1 spot at defensive end," he said."I'm not there yet, by myself, but I'm not far off, in my opinion.

"One year, I will be No. 1 all by myself. Right now, I'm halfway there. But to be considered the best, you've got to keep on going."

CHAPTER THIRTEEN

THE MONTANA EFFECT

Ask Paul Hackett to explain what it means to have Joe Montana on the Chiefs roster and then get out of the way as the offensive coordinator warms to his subject.

"It's amazing how much better the other players become when he is the guy taking the snaps," Hackett said. "The impact Joe has on a team is not simply his talent and performance; it's the impact he has on every other player on the team. Players of Joe Montana's caliber lift the performance of everyone around them. It happens in all realms of sport . . . that's why these guys become superstars. Play with a guy like Joe Montana, and you believe anything is possible. The confidence level goes way up. Players do things nobody thought they could possibly do because they are shot through with confidence.

"Once you've had a chance to be around Joe, you don't forget the experience."

Call it the Montana Effect.

The San Francisco 49ers know all about it. Is it merely coincidence that the 49ers have not won a Super Bowl since Montana was injured and lost his starting job? Certainly, Montana did not take San Francisco to a title every year. In 1990, his last full season as the starting quarterback for the 49ers, they lost the NFC championship game to the New York Giants. But in 1991, the first season Montana missed due to his elbow injury, San Francisco did not even make the NFL playoffs. And in 1992, when Montana played just 30 minutes of football, the 49ers lost the NFC title game to Dallas. San Francisco repeated that defeat to the Cowboys in the 1993 season. That's four consecutive seasons without a Super Bowl for the 49ers.

The Kansas City Chiefs learned very early in the 1993 season about the Montana Effect, possibly as soon as the season opener against Tampa Bay. There was also the Monday Night game on September 20 at Arrowhead Stadium against the Denver Broncos. Montana did not even throw a touchdown pass that night, but he was precision personified, as the Chiefs picked up a 15-7 victory.

The final confirmation of what his presence would mean to the Chiefs came on Sunday, October 17 at Jack Murphy Stadium in sunny San Diego.

Trailing the Chargers by four points, with no time-outs and just 3 minutes, 28 seconds remaining in the game, Montana led the Chiefs on a 9-play, 80-yard drive to the winning touchdown. Chiefs 17, Chargers 14. The victory pushed the Chiefs' record to 5-1, topping the AFC Western Division. It was also the best mark in the entire conference after six games of the regular season.

It was a vintage Montana performance — one that would have looked very familiar to the 49ers. But it was a revelation to the Chiefs, who knew about Montana's crunch-time cool only through the NFL grapevine.

"He walked into the huddle and it was so matter-of-fact," said center Tim Grunhard. "He didn't say anything but, 'Let's go; let's put it in the end zone.' There was no rah-rah speech, no 'Go out and kick butt' speech. The look on his face had not changed since the first play of the game.

"The way he approached it, we forgot completely the situation we were facing. It seemed like the first or second quarter, not the fourth quarter and our last chance to win the game. Any anxiety just disappeared. We were just going out and playing some football."

It was the 27th time Montana led his team to a come-from-behind victory in the fourth quarter. In that 91-second touchdown drive, Montana showed all the traits that have made him one of the greatest quarterbacks in football history. There was the coolness under fire, the refusal to wallow in failure and the ability to overcome physical pain. There was improvisation, accuracy in passing and deft handling of the football. He motivated 11 other players without raising his voice a single time. It was the Montana Effect.

"How could you not believe?" asked wide receiver Willie Davis after the game. "Can you think of anybody who you would rather be with, in that position, than Joe Montana?"

Davis paused, staring at the media standing in front of him, waiting for a response to his question.

"I can't think of anyone else," Davis finally said.

Hackett said: "I can explain things, draw them up, show them on tape, rehearse, teach, do all those things for months. And Joe can step on the field and, in a matter of moments, teach his teammates more about what we are trying to do than I ever could.

"I don't think he had to make believers out of anyone. That would be silly, considering his record. But it's one thing to hear about Joe Montana's coolness under fire and his ability to save a game in the face of all obstacles. It is quite another thing to experience it yourself, in the heat of battle."

A player like Montana not only lifts his teammates, but his mere presence can be devastating for the opposing team. With Montana, no fourth-quarter lead is safe. He proved that in 1980, his very first season as an NFL starting quarterback. San Francisco trailed New Orleans by 14 points in the fourth quarter. The 49ers ended up winning the game 38-35 in overtime.

The opposition is always looking over its shoulder with concern, hoping time escapes from the clock before Montana's magic has run its course. The Chiefs know all about that feeling of doom; it happened to them so many times against the Denver Broncos and quarterback John Elway. There are occasions when time does run out on Joe Montana. He does not win them all. It just seems like he does.

"I can't tell you how many times I've stood on the sidelines, late in the game, hoping we could pull something out, but knowing it would be almost impossible," said defensive end Neil Smith. "Sometimes we did pull out (a victory), but most of the time we just walked off the field a loser because nothing happened.

"Once you see this guy (Montana) in action, you know anything is possible. You don't ever want to give up on anything because he only needs a couple of seconds and a couple of yards. He's got the other team shaking in their shoes. They know it's coming; they just don't know how it's going to hit them. That makes you play harder; you never want to take a play off or relax. It pushes everybody."

There were many moments in the 1993 season that were key to the success of the Chiefs. The winning touchdown drive in San Diego must rank near the top of any list.

It began when Neil Smith blocked John Carney's 31-yard field goal attempt. With help from Dan Saleaumua, who went low on guard Joe Cocozzo, Smith penetrated the blocking and swatted the ball away with his left hand. It was the second blocked field goal of the game for Smith, and the Chiefs took over at their own 20-yard line. Instead of trailing by seven points, they were still four points behind. Even with the block, the offensive strategy did not change; a touchdown was mandatory.

"If you are listening back home, bring out the lucky charms, cross your fingers, knock on wood and pray to the football gods above," is how play-by-play announcer Kevin Harlan set the scene for listeners on the Chiefs Radio Network.

What happened next was football magic. It was pure Joe Montana.

"There was plenty of time," said Hackett. "Certainly 80 yards is significant when you have to get a touchdown. But the time was of no consequence when there is over three minutes to play. I think you've got to remain calm, you've got to remain relaxed. As a player, you've got to go out, do your job and let the offense work for you."

That is so much easier to do with Montana in the huddle.

"He's been through those situations in very big games — through them over and over again," said Hackett. "His poise tends to rub off on those around him. It allows them to operate more efficiently. They don't concern themselves with anything but their assignment."

Montana walked on the field for the first play, supremely confident about his team's chances.

"We had moved the ball on them before, so we felt there wasn't any way we could not go down and score again," said

Montana. "The guys were confident, and you could just feel it in the huddle."

Here's how the drive unfolded:

PLAY No. 1: A 22-yard completion from Montana to tight end Keith Cash, plus a 15-yard penalty against San Diego defensive lineman Shawn Lee for unnecessary roughness. The play and penalty moved the ball 37 yards from the Kansas City 20-yard line to the San Diego 43-yard line.

"The one thing you like to do is get the one big play at the beginning of the drive," said Marty Schottenheimer. "It is a momentum changer; it gets everybody rolling; it boosts everybody's confidence. To get that many yards (37) on a single play, on a drive like that, is pretty unusual."

Keith Cash was not the No. 1 receiver on the play. In the two-minute version of the short-passing game, the running backs tend to catch most of the passes. Defenses drop back into deep zone coverages, taking away the long passes to the wide receivers and tight ends, but conceding the short, underneath passes to the backs.

"The idea in a two-minute drill is that you must be patient, pick away, and eventually somebody on the defense will make a mistake," said Hackett. "On that first play, Kimble Anders was the guy we wanted to get the ball to. We wanted to get a completion, to get the drive rolling, and we weren't expecting a big yardage play."

The Chargers' coverage left an open gap in the middle of the field, and Cash found the spot. As Montana released the ball, Shawn Lee lowered his head and hit the quarterback in the chest. It was not a vicious blow, by any means. In that game alone, Montana had been hit much harder. But NFL rules these days are designed to do two things: 1) protect the quarterback and 2) keep players from lowering their heads and using the helmet as a battering ram.

After the penalty was walked off against San Diego, the Chiefs had a first down at the Chargers' 43-yard line with 3:22 to play.

PLAY No. 2: An incomplete pass to Anders, who was on the left side of the field. Montana threw the pass low and away. Anders had the ball momentarily, but it tumbled from his hands. Had Anders held on, the play would have gained just 3 yards.

It was now second down, with 3:16 left on the clock.

PLAY No. 3: Another incomplete pass to Anders, who was running across the middle of the field. Montana threw this ball low and behind his receiver, who was well covered by San Diego defensive backs Marquez Pope and Stanley Richard. The play would have gained no more than 3 yards.

The incompletion made it third-and-10, with 3:11 to play.

PLAY No. 4: An incomplete pass to Tim Barnett, who was crossing the field from right to left at the San Diego 29-yard line. The Chiefs were nearly penalized 5 yards for delay of game, but got the play off with just one tick remaining on the play clock. The Chargers brought a five-man rush, with linebacker Junior Seau blitzing up the middle.

The extra pressure forced Montana to step up into the pocket to throw the ball. Barnett was well-covered by Chargers cornerback Donald Frank, and the pass was so low, it banged off the turf. It was the third consecutive bad pass from Montana.

"I think the remarkable thing about Joe is his ability to put a bad throw or play behind him immediately," said Hackett. "He doesn't dwell on mistakes. In that drive, he did not throw the ball well on three straight plays. But it did not affect him on the fourth throw."

Said Montana:

"There is only one way to succeed in football and I guess one of the things that I've always been able to do is focus on what is happening that moment. I don't worry about the past or the future. I'm just concerned with the present."

"The present" was fourth-and-10, with 3:07 remaining on the clock.

PLAY No. 5: A 12-yard completion from Montana to Davis for a first down to the Chargers' 31-yard line.

This was another vintage Montana moment.

"It was solo-left, Z-cross with three wide receivers, and I was the Z receiver," explained Davis. "The play is designed for me to run a crossing route through the middle of the field. If it is zone coverage, I stop and wait. If it is man-to-man coverage, I just keep running.

"It was zone and I stopped in the middle of the field. Joe got flushed out of the pocket and as soon as he started running, I had to run with him. So it really turned into a man-to-man coverage route. I ran across the field and Joe found me."

Montana was under pressure up the middle of the pass protection from Chargers defensive lineman Chris Mims. But a late block by Tim Grunhard knocked Mims to the ground, allowing Montana to escape. That's when he drilled the pass between two San Diego defenders — Seau and Pope — and into Davis' stomach.

The play was not scripted. Davis learned way back in training camp how to react when Montana left the pocket and went on the run. It took instant recognition on the part of quarterback and receiver to make the play work. Montana and Davis had to react quickly, instinctively. That the play worked was evidence that, after six games, the offense was starting to pull together. Under pressure, everybody's thought patterns were on the same wavelength.

It was now first down at the Chargers' 31, and the clock was running; less than 2:50 remained to be played.

PLAY No. 6: A 12-yard completion from Montana to wide receiver Hassan Jones for a first down to the Chargers' 19-yard line.

This catch is the memorable moment of Jones' short eight-game career with the Chiefs. Jones was on the right side of the formation and ran a quick slant route, with cornerback Donald Frank on his back. Montana's pass was perfect — low and away — and only Jones could have caught the ball. The Chargers disputed the catch, saying the ball hit the ground first, but the game officials never hesitated in marking the spot where Jones was tackled.

Now the Chiefs were 19 yards away from the end zone, and the clock was still running, with less than 2:25 remaining.

PLAY No. 7: An incomplete pass to Cash on the left side of the field.

Montana was forced from the pocket by a strong pass rush and ran to his left. Stanley Richard, the Chargers free safety, moved forward towards Montana. Marquez Pope was covering Cash and did not react to Montana's scramble, staying with his man. That forced Montana to throw the ball away as Richard was bearing down on him. For the Chargers, it was a well-defended play.

For the Chiefs, it almost meant disaster. After releasing the pass, Montana landed and aggravated the hamstring injury he suffered two weeks earlier. With 2:12 showing on the stadium clock, Montana bent over at the waist and tried to deal with the pain shooting up the back of his leg. He took several steps forward and stopped. As the Chiefs held their breath, Montana limped back into the huddle.

On the sidelines, David Krieg looked for his helmet. By the time he found it, Montana had the Chiefs moving towards the line of scrimmage for the next play.

It was second down.

PLAY No. 8: An 18-yard run by Marcus Allen for a first down at the San Diego 1-yard line.

For those who love the strategy of football, the decision to use this particular play is a dream come true. Hackett made the call from the coaching booth, and it was relayed to Montana through hand signals by third quarterback Matt Blundin.

"I felt at some point we were going to have to do something other than drop straight back and throw the ball," said Hackett. "I would have called it earlier, but we had two straight completions and the clock did not stop, so Joe was calling the plays. When he threw the incompletion to Keith, I got my hands back on the wheel and felt it was time to try a run."

And not just any run. Called the "wraparound draw," the play has been around football for 40 years, but is seldom used by today's offenses.

A draw play is designed to look like a passing play, but instead is a running play. The quarterback acts as though he is going to throw the ball, and the initial movements of the offensive linemen indicate they are preparing to protect the passer. At the last instant, the quarterback hands the ball off to the running back.

The wraparound draw is a bit different, however. Instead of simply handing the ball to the running back from the front, the quarterback drops beyond where the back is standing. He then reaches around and slides the ball onto the running back's belly from behind.

Bill Walsh remembered watching the Chicago Cardinals teams coached by Pop Ivy use the play in the late 1950s. When Walsh was coaching for Paul Brown with the Cincinnati Bengals in the 1970s, he helped revive the play. From that point on, the wraparound draw was always part of Walsh's playbook.

When reading the actions of the quarterback on a potential draw play, linebackers and safeties are taught to wait until the quarterback moves past the running back. Once he does that, they drop into coverage. But the wraparound draw gives the appearance of being a passing play because the handoff comes from behind, instead of the front.

"You're trying to fool the man in the middle of the field — in this case Junior Seau," said Hackett. "Everybody else has dropped back into coverage. If you can take that guy in the middle out of the play, it should be successful."

Two split-second decisions turned the play into a big gainer for the Chiefs. Seau waited for his read, and when he saw Montana move past Allen, he took a step backwards. That was all the help center Tim Grunhard needed. Grunhard was waiting at the line of scrimmage, trying to make it look like he was blocking for a pass. He counted in his head the split seconds before he would spring the surprise on Seau. When the linebacker took his step backwards, Grunhard moved forward and secured a position of leverage on Seau.

Behind Grunhard, Marcus Allen was making a decision of his own. The wraparound was supposed to go to the right side. But as soon as he took a step forward with the ball, something told Allen he should run to the left.

"It was the first time we ran that play all year," said Allen. "For some reason, something told me to go left, and I did. Football is a game of instinct. Sometimes you make decisions when you're running with the ball that just happen. You can't get locked into doing everything the way it's drawn up on the blackboard. Sometimes you've got to be a football player."

As Allen ran to his left, San Diego defensive back Sean Vanhorse moved toward him. Allen shifted the ball from his right to left hand, and with a burst of speed belying his 33-year old legs, ran away from Vanhorse. Three Chargers finally tackled Allen as the officials stopped play for the two-minute warning.

The Chiefs had the ball, first-and-goal, at the Chargers' 1-yard line.

PLAY No. 9: A 1-yard touchdown run by Marcus Allen.

The Chiefs lined up with three tight ends, bringing in 300-pound tackle Derrick Graham to play one of those spots. Big fullback Ernie Thompson was in the backfield with Allen. In this situation, there was no doubt who was going to get the first shot at scoring the touchdown.

"He's the best I've ever seen around the goal line," Schottenheimer said of Marcus Allen.

Tight end Mike Dyal came in motion from right to left, then turned and moved back to the right just before the ball was snapped. Allen took the handoff from Montana. Thompson blocked Chargers linebacker Gary Plummer. Dyal walled off linebacker Lewis Bush, and Allen plunged into the end zone for the winning touchdown.

NBC-TV caught the reaction of Neil Smith on the sidelines as Allen scored. When the officials signaled touchdown, Smith bent backwards, raised his arms, smiled at the heavens and let out a scream that could be heard throughout the NFL.

"So many times we had been burned on those kind of deals," said Smith. "To get that touchdown, it was huge, just huge, a big moment in the season."

Said Allen: "We showed a lot of character. Different guys stepped up and made plays. Willie Davis' catch on fourth down ... there are numerous other players who came through. I think these sort of games are good for you. When you face these situations again, you just react; it's pretty instinctive. You've been there; you know what to do; you know how to deal with pressure situations. This is a great game for us ... we found a way to win."

After the game, Montana was asked if it felt like old times to him.

"Everything feels like old times to me," said Montana. "I can think of easier ways to do it, but this was fine. It is always important to be able to do that as a team. It gives confidence not only to our offense, but our defense. They know if they can stop them, we still have the ability to make it happen."

Montana was asked if anything he does still surprises him.

"It's all surprising," he said. "As an offensive team, you can't do this with one person. If our defense doesn't stop them and block that field goal, then all we did is go for a tie — and not an opportunity to win the football game."

Like the rest of his teammates, Allen heard so much about Montana's clutch performances over the years. The opportunity to see it up-close and personal was an important moment for him.

"It is definitely beneficial when you have a guy in the huddle who basically hasn't changed expression throughout the game," said Allen. "It's the most crucial time of the game and he's limping around out there, showing a tremendous amount of character and courage.

"When your leader doesn't show any signs of concern, why should you?"

CHAPTER FOURTEEN

"WE SUCK AND WE KNOW IT"

It was a perfect Indian summer night, the kind that makes November one of Kansas City's most pleasant months. The wind that continually blows through the Truman Sports Complex was but a whisper, barely able to wrinkle the American flag on the rim of Arrowhead Stadium.

Monday Night Football was back — this time for a game against the Green Bay Packers. As the Chiefs and Packers warmed up on the Arrowhead turf, a brilliant blue sky slowly disappeared behind a gray fog which rolled in over the eastern edge of the stadium. The Arrowhead lights were turned on, and this haze cast an eerie glow on the players preparing below.

This sudden fog was not caused by a temperature inversion, a nearby body of water, a change in the weather or even some freak of nature.

It was man-made — caused by the tailgaters in the Sports Complex parking lots, cooking everything from hot dogs and hamburgers to filet mignon and whole pigs as part of their pre-game parties.

Pro football veterans Carl Peterson, Marty Schottenheimer and Len Dawson, along with broadcasters like Bill Grigsby and Al Michaels, have seen hundreds of games in their lives. None had ever seen anything like the tailgate fog that enveloped Arrowhead that night.

"It looks like the whole parking lot must be on fire," said Grigsby, as the pungent fog began to obscure the very top of the stadium. "Those people are having some sort of party!"

Oh sure, they tailgate in Green Bay, Buffalo and Pittsburgh as well. There are times when San Francisco and Denver can throw a pretty good pre-game party. Every NFL stadium has some sort of tailgate activity.

But nobody does it like the fans of Kansas City. One of 1993's tailgate trends was fans who showed up at the stadium even though they did not have tickets to the game. When everybody went inside to grab their seat, these fans stayed outside and watched the game on portable televisions. Some rented trucks and brought big screen TVs. Others came with recliners and sofas to sit on, turning the parking lots into giant living rooms.

In a survey done before the 1993 season, Chiefs fans were asked: "Do you often arrive early to Chiefs games to tailgate?" An incredible 70 percent of those questioned said "Yes." When broken down into age groups, 84 percent of those polled between the ages of 25 and 34 said they have pre-game parties on a regular basis.

Tailgating has become part of the festive atmosphere surrounding any Chiefs home game. As big as the turnaround has been on the field for Lamar Hunt's franchise, what has happened off the field is just as remarkable.

Just one look into the Arrowhead stands will prove that fact. The Monday Night game against Green Bay was the 20th straight sellout at Arrowhead, and by the end of the season, that streak had grown to 25 consecutive games. During the 1993 season, the waiting list for season tickets grew to 5,000. From 1992 to 1993, there was a 96 percent renewal on season tickets. When tickets to potential home games in the playoffs went on sale, more than 90 percent of the season ticket holders bought the extra seats. Those seats that were left were sold to the general public in 100 minutes. Actual attendance for two preseason contests, eight regular season games and one postseason affair at Arrowhead in the '93 season was 827,367, an average of 75,215 per game.

Oh, how things had changed with the fans in the stands. Through the 1970s and 1980s, promises were made year after year to followers of the Chiefs. The promises came in the form of new head coaches. They came with the fanfare that followed the selection of yet another No. 1 draft choice, a player who was going to come in and make a difference. Every year was a "hump" season, one where the team finally would pull itself from the depths of the NFL and get over the hump to respectability.

The promises came in the form of marketing slogans that would highlight the team's season-ticket drives each year. There were ditties like:

"Coming On Strong"

"Excitement is Growing"

"Best Show in Town"

"We're Coming Back," followed the next year by "We're Coming Back, Come Along"

"The Fun Is With The Fans In The Stands."

But each year, the promises were broken. Coaches were fired and players were released. No. 1 draft choices flopped or found themselves highly paid excess baggage with a new coaching staff or scheme. The hump year never came; the Chiefs would climb only so high, and then something would send them falling back into the NFL abyss. The slogans rang hollow in the ears of fans who became more and more angry by the mounting defeats and management's reaction to them.

Out of sheer frustration in the mid-1980s, one member of the Chiefs staff came up with her own slogan, one that defined the fate of this franchise for nearly 20 years:

"We Suck and We Know It."

There is no question when the problems started. It was December 25, 1971. On that balmy Christmas Day, the Chiefs lost the longest game in NFL history to the Miami Dolphins, 27-24, in the first round of the playoffs. The teams played for six quarters that day before Miami kicker Gary Yepremian ended it with a 37-yard field goal. It was also the final football game played at old Municipal Stadium. The Chiefs opened 1972 in brand-new Arrowhead Stadium.

"You look backwards now, and there is little question that's where it all began," said Len Dawson. "After that game, nothing seemed to go right for this team."

The next 16 years produced so many stories of ineptitude and bungling by management, coaches and players that to repeat them all would create a manuscript whose size would rival *War and Peace*. But to give some sort of perspective of how bad things were, here are some of the highlights of the lowlights:

Season-Ticket Fiasco. More than 20 years after the move from Municipal to Arrowhead, it is hard to separate fact from fiction in this mess of relocated season ticket holders. If every person who has claimed they had 50-yard line seats at the old stadium is telling the truth, then Municipal was nothing more than one section, at mid-field, that reached thousands of feet into the air.

But many people with prime seats at the old stadium discovered in 1972 that they did not have similar prime seats at the new stadium. They found themselves at the 25 and 30-yard lines, with a bunch of unfamiliar faces sitting at the 50. Club president Jack Steadman was blamed for this mess, and 20 years later, there are long-time season ticket holders who still hold a grudge over the way they were treated in the move.

Trick or Treat: You're Fired. On Halloween Day 1977, the Chiefs fired Paul Wiggin as head coach after just 35 games over two and one-half seasons. When he was hired, owner Lamar Hunt and Steadman promised Wiggin patience and three years of drafts. After his second season, the Chiefs publicly reaffirmed their patience by adding three years to his contract.

Wiggin was fired seven games later, causing an uproar in the community and within Arrowhead Stadium, where the head coach was well-liked by staff and players. Later that night, Lamar Hunt visited Wiggin's home, in an apparent attempt to explain his decision further. He practically was chased out of the house by the coach's angry wife, Carolynn.

The 1982 Players Strike. For 57 days, the NFL players stayed away from the stadiums, leading to the cancellation of seven games during the season. No team was more militant about the strike than the Kansas City Chiefs. The season before, a salary survey showed the Chiefs to be the lowest-paid team in the league.

The day after the strike began, Steadman announced that the Chiefs had 45 new players standing by, ready to come in and take the place of the strikers. Behind the scenes, Lamar Hunt was pushing other owners for a resumption of play with replacement players.

That did not happen, and the strike dragged on. When they first walked out, the Chiefs players made a big show of holding their own practice sessions. But after about three weeks, they stopped showing up. Some stopped all physical conditioning work, figuring the season was over. When the strike ended after eight weeks, the NFL players had little to show for the walk-out except lost wages and a new collective bargaining agreement that really was not much different than the previous contract. The Chiefs reported back to Arrowhead out of shape and out of sorts.

The day the players returned to work, Steadman walked into the locker room and asked them to put aside their differences so the Chiefs organization could become a "family" again. It was the first time Steadman had ever spoken to the team as a group.

The Chiefs promptly lost four straight games after the strike. Steadman never spoke to the team again.

Stuck On A Plateau. When only 11,902 fans showed up for the final game of the 1982 season, Steadman panicked. The Chiefs finished the strike season 3-6. Despite the fact that progress had been made in each of head coach Marv Levy's first four seasons, he was fired. Steadman said the team had reached a "plateau," and that Levy was not capable of moving them farther.

Of course, Levy went on to become the head coach of the Buffalo Bills and led that team to four consecutive Super Bowl appearances. Each of those ended in disappointment, but Levy proved he was a far better coach than Steadman was a judge of coaches.

Ambush At Arrowhead. Levy was replaced by John Mackovic, who in 1986 led the franchise to its first postseason appearance in 15 seasons. Ten days after losing to the New York Jets in the first round of the playoffs, Mackovic was fired. He was the victim of a front-office and coaching staff coup, engineered by then-general manager Jim Schaaf.

In the events that led to the firing, Hunt made what many thought was an NFL first: he went to the home of a player, kicker Nick Lowery, and met with a dozen more players to discuss the coaching situation. Within hours of that meeting, Mackovic was fired.

The impression was created that the inmates were running the asylum. In this case, it was true.

The Great Paper Bag Caper. In 1988, the Chiefs had won only one game, yet still expected a large crowd for a Sunday home game before Halloween. A marketing "genius" in the organization decided the team should pass out large grocery sacks to the fans coming into the stadium. The idea was that these sacks would be taken home and used by the kids for collecting Halloween treats.

Just a few years earlier, fans in New Orleans started to wear paper bags over their heads during games at the Superdome as a protest over the poor play by the Saints.

Only the quick thinking of another club executive stopped what would have been an unforgettable NFL moment: an entire stadium protesting their terrible team, wearing paper bags on their heads, provided, no less, by the team itself. The bags were handed out as the fans left the stadium after yet another Chiefs defeat.

This was the mess Carl Peterson took over in December of 1988. His assignment was not only to turn the Chiefs around on the field, but also at the box office. Because of his background in coaching and scouting, Peterson was confident he could rebuild the team's talent base. Hiring Marty Schottenheimer as head coach helped immeasurably on the football side.

On the business side, Peterson knew he needed a lot of help as well. That's why he turned to Tim Connolly.

After graduating from George Washington University in the early 1970s, Connolly joined IBM and rose through the ranks of the computer giant, serving in various sales and management capacities. But the whole time he was climbing Big Blue's ladder, he was dreaming of a career in sports management. He eventually became an agent and represented baseball star Rod Carew in the late 1970s. He also represented the Philadelphia Eagles top draft choice in 1978, linebacker Reggie Wilkes of Georgia Tech.

That's when Connolly and Peterson really got to know each other, and they had several business dealings after the Wilkes contract. In 1989, Connolly was the president of the SORBUS Corporation, the largest independent computer maintenance organization in the world. When Peterson called with an offer to become the Chiefs executive vice president, Connolly jumped at the chance.

"I would have crawled on my belly on broken glass to get into the NFL," said Connolly. "I love the game of football. I loved playing it as a kid. I love being around it. I was 40 years old and all I wanted to do was be part of a football team."

When Connolly arrived at Arrowhead Stadium, he found a deeply troubled front-office operation.

"All the people in this building could tell me what was wrong," said Connolly as he sat in his Arrowhead Stadium office. "But they were tainted. There was a feeling from one department to another that, 'Hey we're doing it right; it's the coaching staff that's doing it wrong. The No. 1 picks haven't been worthwhile, the general manager doesn't know what he is doing, etc.'

"Hell, all that was obvious. Anybody could tell you things were messed up just by looking at the record. They were a 4-11-1 team. They had not been a contending team for nearly 20 years. All you needed to do was pick up a record book.

"We had to have more information than that to figure out how to fix all the things that were broken in the franchise. You cannot really understand what the problems are with your product until you talk with the customers and hear from their own mouths why the Chiefs were bad. We wanted to get a city's perception of the entire franchise."

Connolly commissioned a marketing study. It was to include focus group interviews with everyone from season-ticket holders to casual fans to people who simply enjoyed going to entertainment events and sometimes spent their money on tickets to Chiefs games.

"We had to have a broad group," said Connolly. "We could not have just season-ticket holders. Those poor people — they were so loyal; they were never going to go away, not if they were still there after everything that had happened.

"Our question was: how were we going to convert the casual fan? How can we convert the ones who said 'Yeah, I'd go to a game if I wanted to, but you haven't given me any reason.' We wanted to know how a Chiefs game compared as an experience to any other opportunity to spend your money."

Men, women, young, old... all demographic groups ended up being represented in the focus groups that met in April of 1989. Prepared by Buffy Filippell of TeamWork Consulting, Inc. and Matthew Levine of Levine Management Group, the report attempted to uncover the organization's problems and suggest possible solutions.

What they found startled everyone. Peterson and Connolly could not have predicted how deep the frustration and resentment for the team and its old management ran throughout the community. An entire generation had been turned off by the Chiefs' losing ways, and whether those questioned lived in Kansas or Missouri, there was very definitely a "Show Me" attitude toward the new arrivals at Arrowhead.

In the focus groups, fans were asked to describe their feelings about not only the Chiefs, but the Kansas City Royals baseball team and the then-active Kansas City Comets indoor soccer club. At the time, Kansas City was one of the few places where indoor soccer attracted crowds, thanks to the Comets' promotions and community involvement with youth soccer. The Royals were four years removed from their World Series victory over the St. Louis Cardinals and were still considered a pennant contender.

The fans' descriptions explained the problems facing Peterson and Connolly:

ROYALS: personable, fun-loving, energetic, enthusiastic, outgoing, winning attitude, class act, teamwork to win, steady.

COMETS: spirited, energetic, enticing, sparked, exciting, accommodating, total excitement.

CHIEFS: aloof, no will to win, untouchable, struggling, standoffish, arrogance, failed promises, chronic conflict, inconsistent, confused.

The consultants found a dysfunctional franchise, one that had disappointed its public so many times, the fans felt more like victims than supporters.

"They told us the organization was basically a cold one," said Connolly. "We were not user friendly. Doing business with the Chiefs and at this stadium was a trying thing. We didn't make it easy; in fact, we made it difficult.

"We heard horror stories, things like they would lock the bathrooms in the upper deck if there weren't many people up there. People were told to walk down to the next level to use the rest room. Do you know how bad that is, just to save a couple nickels, to make people walk up and down those spiral ramps?

"The Chiefs' image was one of no sense of humor, no give-and-take, almost completely defensive. You could understand why. They were under siege, from the fans and from the media, and it had become so bad, they just went down into the bunker and tried to protect themselves. They were crouched down, teeth gritted, saying, 'Screw all you people. This is the way we are going to do it; we are not going to defend it because no matter what we do, we can't do it right anyway.'

"The fans felt equally abused. It was like the team was their public park, and these people had let it go to such a state that the children couldn't go to the park anymore and play.

"The fans didn't like the Chiefs, and the Chiefs didn't like their fans."

The marketing report isolated three major problem areas, both inside and outside Arrowhead Stadium:

• MANAGEMENT/PLAYER GAP ". . . has been reinforced by a) the players' successful insurrection against head coach John Mackovic; b) the players apparent lack of commitment and integrity on the field, and c) ownership's long-term willingness to leave the team's performance destiny in the ultimate hands of a 'bottom-line' business executive with little football expertise."

• MANAGEMENT/COMMUNITY GAP "Is perceived as a pervasive disregard for the community, personified in Lamar Hunt's lack of presence in contrast to the highly visible and lionized owner of the Kansas City Royals, Ewing Kauffman. This exists despite Mr. Hunt's local holdings and ventures and the popularity of his amusement/theme parks.

"This gap also draws reinforcement from management's apparent failure to openly communicate any consistent and believable team-building philosophy to the fans . . . "

• PLAYER/COMMUNITY GAP ". . . is magnified by the contrast between the Chiefs' apparent community involvement and that of the Royals. Although the Chiefs can point to measures of increasing activity, the failure of their programs to gain memorable exposure among target audience supporters and prospects reflects poorly on the focus, breadth and effectiveness of these efforts, which appear to be of little value to the franchise.

"Players, with a few notable exceptions (Cherry, Lewis, Hackett and Lowery) are seen as being distant, unresponsive and perhaps embarrassed when interacting with fans."

But the greatest indictment of where the Chiefs ranked in the minds of the Kansas City sports fans came in the report's next paragraph:

". . . Fans view themselves as making emotional and financial investments in the team. Then, when high-salaried, militantly union-organized players openly and disdainfully withhold their services on a picket line or blatantly on the field, fans feel justified acting out their own withdrawal."

And they had withdrawn at an alarming rate. The best evidence came in two areas: season ticket sales and actual game attendance as a percentage based on the Arrowhead Stadium capacity of 77,622. In the 1972 season, the Chiefs had 72,885 season ticket holders and averaged 72,756 in actual attendance for seven home games. That included the largest crowd in Arrowhead history on November 5, when 82,094 jammed the place to see the Oakland Raiders. They played that season at 94 percent of Arrowhead's capacity.

Follow the numbers downward from there, each segment representing the term of the five head coaches before Schottenheimer:

SEASON	SEATS HELD BY SEASON TICKET HOLDERS	% OF SEATS USED BASED ON ACTUAL ATTENDANCE

END OF HANK STRAM ERA

1972	72,885	94%
1973	70,555	85%
1974	65,564	76%

PAUL WIGGIN/TOM BETTIS ERA

1975	47,274	78%
1976	45,251	70%
1977	40,628	66%

SEASON	SEATS HELD BY SEASON TICKET HOLDERS	% OF SEATS USED BASED ON ACTUAL ATTENDANCE
MARV LEVY ERA		
1978	30,861	55%
1979	29,428	73%
1980	32,105	66%
1981	31,016	82%
1982	32,225	40%
JOHN MACKOVIC ERA		
1983	28,523	61%
1984	29,151	64%
1985	28,007	58%
1986	26,074	62%
FRANK GANSZ ERA		
1987	30,454	52%
1988	26,594	65%

In a six-year span from 1972 through 1978, the Chiefs dropped 58 percent in the number of seats held by season ticket holders. It would be 12 more years before even half the stadium seats were held by season ticket holders again.

While the falling numbers indicated an obvious problem, the marketing study and focus groups pointed to the direction the new efforts needed to take. The first decision: there would be no more slogans used to sell tickets.

"There were all kind of great slogans we could have used, but after all the promises that had been made before, it would have been too much like the old days," said Connolly. "We wanted to make sure everybody in this community knew the old days were gone.

"We knew we would win. We were confident that Carl and Marty were going to build a successful team. What we had to do was address the event itself, the actual experience of going to a game. We had to find a way to get them committed.

"I had the chance over the years to be part of great game experiences, the kind you see at Alabama, Notre Dame, Clemson, the Pittsburgh Steelers in the 1970s. There was the tailgating, the wearing of the colors, the excitement around the stadium itself. Your purchase of a ticket was reinforced because you knew if you didn't have that ticket, you were out of luck.

"And we had to radically posture ourselves as being the opposite of what they were used to. We had to be warm and friendly and exhibit a sense of humor. We had to convey the attitude that maybe we aren't going to win every game, but we are damn sure going to play hard, and we are damn sure going to be polite and we are damn sure thankful for your business."

The comments from the focus groups led to many changes:

• The entire ticket operation was overhauled and computerized. Tickets to Chiefs games no longer had to be purchased at the stadium or through special outlets. The Chiefs signed with TicketMaster, giving them ticket outlets all over the six-state region where they drew fans.

• Complaints were overwhelming regarding the cleanliness of the stadium and the conduct of those few fans who bothered to buy tickets. The Chiefs instituted new policies, including attendants in the women's rest rooms. They also adopted a new code of conduct for the fans and increased the presence of security within the stadium on game day.

"Basically, we took a Disneyland approach," said Connolly. "We wanted to do whatever we could to make visiting the stadium an enjoyable experience. We said if they were going to tailgate, we were going to put charcoal bins out there. We put recycling points out there, and we had people hand out plastic bags in the parking lot so they can put their trash in bags and put it in the dumpsters.

"We put our security staff in green jackets instead of red, to make them easier to find on game day. And we don't call it security. We call it fan assistance. They are not securing them from the other beasts in the stands. They are there to help them."

• Rather than rely on the *Kansas City Star* to provide coverage of the message the organization wanted to send, the Chiefs bought space in the newspaper. It created a series of "advertorials" — paid advertising that is made to look like regular news stories. Through these ads, the ticket and stadium changes were stressed to potential ticket buyers.

• After 26 seasons with KCMO-AM (810), the Chiefs decided to change radio stations. The Chiefs sold their broadcasting rights to KCFX-FM (101), which until that time was a little-known and seldom-listened-to rock music station. KCFX offered more money than KCMO and WDAF-AM (610) for the rights, but the Chiefs' decision was based on demographics.

"KCFX had the audience we had to attract, the lost generation of fans from 25 to 45," said Connolly. "These were the people we were trying to reach with our message, so we had to go with a station they were listening to."

• Because of the credibility gap that developed between the team's previous management and the fans, the consultants advised that Peterson become the focal and vocal point of the franchise. They encouraged him to speak out publicly, to show that he was acting on the complaints that he heard. One way to do this was a weekly radio show, so Peterson became one of the few NFL general managers with his own call-in program, where fans could get answers directly from the man in charge.

Connolly made another change, one that would become the talk of the town. Almost from the time the franchise moved to Kansas City in 1963, part of the game-day experience around the Chiefs was "Warpaint," a horse that ran onto the field before the game, as well as each time the Chiefs scored a touchdown. Warpaint's rider was dressed as an Indian with a feathered headdress.

The decision was made in 1989 to put Warpaint out to pasture.

"The horse was almost a metaphor for the football team," said Connolly. "It was wonderful at Municipal Stadium where it could run on grass. But at Arrowhead, the horse had trouble running on turf because his hooves would slip on the AstroTurf. He had to sort of walk and trot. It became a thing where even the horse didn't seem like it hustled."

Connolly had to come up with another mascot.

"Back east, I had seen the Philly Phanatic," said Connolly. "There was nothing like that in the NFL, and that's what I wanted. Remember, we were cold, aloof and without a sense of humor in the eyes of the fans. We wanted something that was warm, huggable and made people laugh."

Thus was born K.C. Wolf, a giant ball of fur with a big head, an even bigger belly and a fluffy tail. K.C. Wolf was not met with universal acceptance. Some thought the costume looked like a giant rat.

"To everyone's chagrin, I got this big, portly, lovable wolf, who I was told did not look like the kind of mascot football teams had traditionally," said Connolly. "They had them in baseball and basketball, but in football you typically must have bulldogs, buffalos, gorillas — mascots that looked mean. This wolf was like Sesame Street. I was told it would never work.

"But the wolf was a hit from the very first day."

K.C. Wolf has become an industry in itself, spawning merchandise with wolf dolls, personal appearances and T-shirts. Skits involving the wolf are part of the festivities that have turned game day at Arrowhead into more than just a football game.

"It is a commitment to anything that can be done with entertainment," said Connolly. "We started with our first Monday night game (1990). We turned it into Mardi Gras. Fireworks went off. We did our own Monday Night opening, with our own video and our own music. People discovered there was more going on here."

In the 1989 season, the Chiefs had a single sellout, and that came only after Connolly convinced several businesses to buy the 6,000 remaining tickets.

"There was a lot of wait and see," said Connolly. "I don't know how many times we heard people say, 'We've seen this before.' As the team got better, we continued to listen and make improvements. There were not enough bathrooms, so we added to the size of the men's rooms, and we added women's rest rooms. We spent a lot of money. We put in handicapped facilities.

"The scoreboards . . . I was maniacal about communicating with people. Part of the money we got from the Sports Authority for the new lease (in 1991), we put into scoreboards, to a Sony JumboTron screen and a million-dollar control room to run it all. We wanted the fans to come here and get as much information as they would if they were sitting at home. We get replays on faster than the networks do because we have two hand-held cameras and our own control room in the stadium."

The improvements were noticed. So were the victories. Gradually, the attitude towards the team and attending games at Arrowhead changed dramatically.

Follow the numbers since 1989:

SEASON	SEATS HELD BY SEASON TICKET HOLDERS	% OF SEATS USED BASED ON ACTUAL ATTENDANCE
1989	31,863	79%
1990	39,725	90%
1991	52,867	96%
1992	65,628	94%
1993	69,219	98%

Everything did not always go smoothly. When so many changes are made, toes are bound to be stepped on, and the new regime at Arrowhead did that a few times. Some ideas were tried and quickly forgotten.

"One of our people saw on television this stadium where the fans were passing around this giant red ball," said Connolly. "This ball was just huge, and it would bounce around from section to section. Well, they talked me into trying out this giant red ball. Our fans didn't know what to do with it. This thing was so big, I think it almost crushed a couple people. We tried it once, and then the big red ball never returned."

Attending a Chiefs game has become one of the biggest social events of the fall and winter in Kansas City. It is not a stadium necessarily full of grizzled or sophisticated football fans. It is a building full of people enjoying the experience and rooting for the Chiefs.

"What helped clinch it for us was how the networks reacted when they came in here and saw what was going on," said Connolly. "The team was constantly improving, and the crowds were getting more and more excited. Before you know it, the league and networks come in here and say, 'Wow, look at this team! Look at this stadium!'

"And the fans puff out their chest and say, 'This is my team. This is my stadium. Monday Night football — nobody does it better than we do in Kansas City.' The pride factor came back."

Before the 1993 season, Connolly commissioned another round of focus groups to see how the organization was doing after four seasons. Here are two of the questions asked:

Overall, would you say that you are ..... with your overall experience of being a Chiefs season ticket holder?

VERY SATISFIED:	73.4 percent
SOMEWHAT SATISFIED:	21.7 percent
NEITHER SATISFIED OR DISSATISFIED:	2.0 percent
SOMEWHAT DISSATISFIED:	2.6 percent
VERY DISSATISFIED:	0.3 percent

Excluding the performance of the team or players, what do you believe to be the strengths of the Chiefs organization?

FRONT OFFICE	37.5 percent
COMMUNITY INVOLVEMENT	16.4 percent
FANS	13.5 percent
FACILITIES	12.5 percent
COACHING STAFF	9.2 percent
OTHER	10.9 percent

Remember the focus groups of 1989? It was almost a complete turnaround in four years.

"Now our problems are things like having too many people and too many cars in the parking lots," said Connolly. "The guys who did this study couldn't believe the numbers. They said in any survey, five percent of the people will tell you they are dissatisfied just in general principle. We had 2.9 percent.

"Our work isn't done. We keep trying to make it better."

And on this Monday night, 76,742 fans left happy, as the Chiefs beat the Packers 23-16.

The Chiefs trailed by six points at halftime, but scored early in the third quarter when Derrick Thomas sacked Packers quarterback Brett Favre, who fumbled. Dan Saleaumua picked up the ball and rumbled 16 yards for a touchdown. Later in the game, the Packers were going in for a potential touchdown when running back Darrell Thompson fumbled at the goal line after being hit by Saleaumua. Linebacker Tracy Rogers recovered in the end zone, assuring the Chiefs victory.

And they followed it up the next week, with an impressive 31-20 victory over the Raiders in Los Angeles. With Dave Krieg still starting at quarterback, the Chiefs overcame a 10-point halftime deficit. Krieg threw a touchdown pass of 66 yards to wide receiver Willie Davis and another for 4 yards to tight end Keith Cash. Playing in the L.A. Coliseum for the first time since he left the Raiders, Marcus Allen averaged 5 yards every time he touched the ball and scored a touchdown.

The Chiefs were 7-2, alone atop the AFC West.

CHAPTER FIFTEEN

TACKLING THE KANSAS CITY STAR

The spring of 1993 found the *Kansas City Star* newspaper beginning an investigation of the criminal charges filed against some members of the Chiefs over the previous three years.

In 1991, three players — Bill Jones, Percy Snow and Albert Lewis — were arrested on charges involving domestic battery, assault and leaving the scene of an accident. In 1992, three players — Kevin Porter, Tim Barnett and Bennie Thompson — were arrested on charges that included domestic battery and driving under the influence of alcohol.

And in early 1993, three players — Barnett, Thompson and Dale Carter — were charged by metropolitan police departments with crimes involving terroristic threats, transporting an open container of alcohol and driving under the influence of alcohol.

Despite the fact that most of the team over that three-year span were law-abiding citizens, the track record of those few who were arrested cast a big shadow. There was concern about the situation within Arrowhead Stadium's locker room and front office. At least two players were released, in part, because of their attitudes and continuing legal problems. Others were fined and disciplined by the team. The Chiefs pushed still others toward counseling programs.

Reporters for the *Star* first contacted the Chiefs about the subject in May. There were several conversations with the team's public relations department, and an interview was arranged with Carl Peterson over the summer. But as the 1993 season began, no story appeared in the newspaper, and the subject seemed to have been forgotten as the Star chased other stories.

But in the early morning hours of September 30, a Chiefs player became involved in a very public mess. It was enough to re-pique the interest of the newspaper.

Cornerback Dale Carter was with two male friends at a well-known night spot — the Harris House — in the Westport section of the city. One of the men got into a disagreement with some of the other patrons in the establishment. A fight started, and Carter's friend was cut on the face by a shattered bar glass.

Carter and his friends left the Harris House, planning to take the injured man to a hospital for treatment. As they drove away, gun shots rang out from a vehicle across the street. Someone in Carter's party returned the gun fire as their vehicle sped away from the scene.

Police later found Carter and his friends several blocks away with a flat tire and bullet holes in the body of their truck. They also discovered a pistol inside the vehicle, but were unable to pinpoint who had returned the gun fire. All three men were taken into custody, but later were released with no charges filed against them. It would be almost three months later before Carter was hit with a misdemeanor charge of attempting to carry a concealed weapon.

Whether Carter was an innocent bystander or a major actor in the incident did not really matter to most people. There had been a gun battle in Westport involving a Kansas City Chiefs player — one with a previous arrest that year for driving while intoxicated.

A phone call informing Peterson of the Carter incident woke him from a sound sleep. It was not the first time the Chiefs general manager had a perfectly good snooze ruined by such a phone call. For months Peterson and head coach Marty Schottenheimer talked with the players about being more careful with their behavior. In fact, Dale Carter received a number of those lectures.

The Chiefs' first-round draft choice in 1992, Carter was selected as the National Football League's Defensive Rookie of the Year in '92. He was a sensational punt returner, taking one kick back for a touchdown in the opening game of the 1992 season against the San Diego Chargers. Later in that season, he had an 86-yard punt return for a touchdown. His play at cornerback was stunning, and his 36-yard interception return against the Denver Broncos at Arrowhead Stadium made every reel of league highlights for that season. He finished 1992 with seven interceptions, the second highest total for a rookie in team history.

More than a few people around the Chiefs and NFL thought Carter was one of the most gifted athletes in the sport. But his abundance of physical skills was matched by his lack of social graces. Carter's poor judgment and quick temper showed on and off the football field, causing the Chiefs major headaches.

Born and raised in humble surroundings in Covington, Georgia, Carter seemed ill-equipped emotionally for life as a professional athlete. When he went to the University of Tennessee in 1990, he carried all his worldly possessions in a single sack. Two years later, Carter signed a four-year contract with the Chiefs worth millions. He went from being dirt poor to filthy rich almost overnight and had problems handling his new wealth. During his rookie season, the Chiefs received several calls from restaurant and bar owners complaining of Carter's behavior in their establishments. Peterson and Schottenheimer sat him down and explained that he could not continue to act in a manner that drew attention to himself.

Carter would be quiet for awhile, and then the Chiefs would hear of another incident. It seemed the only people Carter listened to were his mother and older brother, Jake Reed, a wide receiver with the Minnesota Vikings. At one time, Peterson considered moving Carter's mother to Kansas City from Atlanta, and even contemplated making a trade for Reed.

After hearing of Carter's latest problem, Peterson hurriedly dressed and drove to the Chiefs' offices at Arrowhead Stadium. He stopped first in Marty Schottenheimer's office and told the head coach that he wanted to speak with the team after practice.

Peterson was livid — Schottenheimer said later that he had never seen his general manager so upset — and spent the rest of the day trying to stifle his anger. At the end of the team's practice session, everyone but the players was asked to leave the field. For the next 15 minutes, Peterson delivered a verbal blast at the squad. His words were not delicate, his tone hardly subtle.

"My point was quite simple," Peterson remembered. "Ninety percent of the team was keeping itself out of trouble, acting like professionals. They were preparing to play each week and were taking care of themselves.

"The other 10 percent was screwing it up for everybody else with their behavior."

Several players said they realized how upset Peterson was when they discovered he was wearing two different shoes as he spoke to them.

"One was a brown loafer with a tassel and the other was a brown loafer with no tassel," said one player. "Once I noticed, I had to keep my head down so he would not see me laughing. I guess he was so mad, he didn't even look when he put on his shoes in the morning."

It was not long after the incident involving Carter that about a dozen players received letters from the *Kansas City Star*. The newspaper acknowledged that it was looking at criminal problems involving the players. But it also revealed that it was investigating civil legal actions filed against players in the five-county Kansas City metropolitan area.

Some players took their letters to Peterson.

"I had never heard of anything like that: writing about civil lawsuits and lumping them together with criminal cases," said Peterson. "Certainly, we had those players who had been ar-rested and charged with crimes. That was all public information and had been written about in the newspaper. As an organiza-tion, we don't like to see negative news about any of our employ-ees, but there's nothing we can do about it."

Being arrested or convicted of a criminal act and being hit with a civil lawsuit are two very different matters. In today's litigious society, the filing of a lawsuit seemingly happens with every tick of the clock. Especially vulnerable to legal actions are those in the public spotlight, such as entertainers and athletes.

The letters sent by the *Star* to the players mentioned civil lawsuits ranging from the failure to repay loans to paternity suits. Of the 23 cases mentioned, nine involved business ven-tures by players like Bill Maas, Chris Martin, Kevin Ross, Derrick Thomas and Harvey Williams.

"The addition of civil cases to this story they were working on really bothered me," said Peterson. "Anybody in the public eye today is a target for lawsuits. Frankly, some of the cases the newspaper uncovered were disputes over goods and services that had been settled. Disputes like these happen all the time. I'm sure the *Star* has their share. If they didn't, why would they need a staff attorney? It's the price of being in the public eye."

The Chiefs team captains met to discuss the letters and considered a boycott of the *Star*'s reporters. Some players like wide receiver Willie Davis stopped talking to the newspaper as soon as he received the letter.

"They were digging around in my past, dredging up stuff that happened to me back in college," said Davis. "Why would anybody do that? Once I got that letter, I wasn't going to help them with anything. I could not understand what they were trying to do with this story."

Peterson could not understand, either. However, he had a sense that his unwillingness to discuss the criminal cases in detail with the newspaper's reporters was what kept the story alive.

"When one of our players got into trouble, the *Star* wanted me to come out and make some sort of statement about the arrest," said Peterson. "They wanted me to discuss disciplinary actions we were taking against the player. They basically wanted to act as judge and jury on these players, with me as their prime witness, before the players ever had their day in court. I wasn't about to do that to a player, or anyone else who works for this organization who finds himself in trouble with the law.

"First of all, we are all innocent until proven guilty, and I'm certainly not going to comment on a player who hasn't had his day in court. Second, how we deal with our players is the business of the team and no one else. The *Kansas City Star* does not comment publicly on what happens in the employer-employee relationship within its own building."

Peterson requested a meeting with the *Star* hierarchy and the reporters working on the story. He had planned to take with him only Chiefs attorney Jim Seigfreid and public relations director Bob Moore. But attorneys representing the players asked to be included, and eventually, there were more than a dozen people sitting around the conference table on Tuesday, October 12 in the *Star*'s downtown Kansas City offices. The newspaper demanded the meeting be "on the record," meaning anything said could be repeated outside the room and even used by the *Star* in a possible story. That was fine with Peterson.

"We weren't there to hide anything or provide them with anything," said Peterson. "It was our opinion that the story was already written. We were simply trying to find out their motivation, why they felt it necessary to dig around in the lives of our players. Why had they included the civil cases? Why had they decided it was of importance to the readers of the *Kansas City Star*?"

The newspaper's editor Art Brisbane tried to answer Peterson's question during the meeting.

"Our motivation is simply to report the news and try to serve the public interest," Brisbane told the group. "If there have been several separate, relatively small stories that have appeared in the paper that represent part of the picture, and there is a larger picture when you look at things taken together, then we would consider that to be news and we would consider that to be in the public interest. And that's it."

That left many in the room still wondering about the point of the investigation. It led to several heated exchanges. One was started by one of the lawyers representing a player named in the story.

Player Attorney:	"I guess my question is, what is the public interest here? I fail to understand that at this point, particularly when the information is already public."
Brisbane:	"Are you telling me the public is aware that 15 players have criminal charges against them, have had some kind of criminal problem? I don't think they are aware."
Chiefs attorney Jim Seigfreid:	"That's not accurate."
Tom Jackman, Star reporter:	"Art, those aren't all criminal charges."
Brisbane:	"Whatever is the figure, whether it is nine or 10 . . ."
Seigfreid:	"That's a pretty important figure for the editor to know."
Player Attorney:	"What I'm asking is what do you think the public interest is and why would you go out . . ."
Brisbane:	"Carl, I would like to address the question to you. What exactly do you hope to get out of this meeting, because if it's about a group of attorneys raising questions about whether we have the right to make this inquiry, we are kinda on the

wrong track here . . . you are in the football business and we are in the newspaper business, and we feel there is a potential public interest in this story."

The meeting revealed the basic premise behind the *Star's* investigation: the Chiefs' legal problems made them a menace to Kansas City society, and the team's management was unwilling to admit there was a problem, let alone do anything about it. Players were allowed to continue playing after being arrested, with no visible repercussions from the club. The Chiefs were renegades, and the team had lost control of them.

To validate its premise, the Star had to compare the Chiefs to another team in the NFL. Clubs like the Cincinnati Bengals, Buffalo Bills or New Orleans Saints would have been excellent choices, since they operate in cities of approximately the same size as Kansas City.

If not another pro football team, then the newspaper needed to make a comparison with a business of similar size. The Chiefs have approximately 200 employees and annual revenues in the range of $75 million.

That's what Peterson asked for during one portion of the discussion with the *Star:*

Peterson:	"You want me to comment on the Kansas City Chiefs regarding this. I can't do that. I'm not going to do that. First of all, it is a private matter. But secondly, I don't understand the motive of this story. Where is the journalistic value that (a Chiefs player) couldn't or failed to pay for his credit card, if indeed that is true? Can you answer that question?"
Brisbane:	"Let me try to respond. I would start by saying the criminal charges are of a different character . . ."
Peterson:	"And there were 11 (criminal charges) of those out of 34 (incidents detailed by the paper), of which six are pending."
Brisbane:	"Like I say, the criminal charges are clearly of a more serious character than the civil. The civil is a different category."

Peterson: "But you have put them together for the reason of
. . ."

Brisbane: "What we have set out to do, is to first of all
identify what are the outstanding legal issues and
see whether there is a pattern there, and whether
it is significant."

Peterson: "Define significant."

Brisbane: "Significant is whether there is a substantial pattern there."

Peterson: "In comparison to what?"

Brisbane: "We compared it to the Royals."

Peterson: "Is that a fair comparison?"

Brisbane: "That's a good question. I think we are in the
process of trying to determine . . . "

Peterson: "I asked you before, why don't you do it with one
or all of the 27 other franchises in the National
Football League?"

Brisbane: "We may yet do that Carl . . . if in order to test the
validity of this we have to compare it to another
NFL team, we would be willing to do that."

But the *Star* wasn't willing to do that, and it stayed with its
comparison of the Chiefs and Royals. The newspaper said its
check of court records in the five-county Kansas City metropolitan area found no criminal proceedings against any baseball
players and no civil lawsuits beyond divorces.

However, matching the Chiefs and Royals was an apples-
to-oranges comparison. The Chiefs' roster has double the number of players, since football employs 55 to 60 players in a season
and baseball has 30 to 35. Far more Chiefs players than Royals
players make their permanent home in the Kansas City area; the
newspaper reported 70 percent of the Chiefs called Kansas City
home, compared to 20 percent of the Royals. Although the
baseball season is six months long, compared to four months for
football, Royals players actually spend less time in Kansas City
because half of their 162-game schedule is on the road. When the
Chiefs travel away from home they are gone for one night. The
Royals sometimes can be gone for 10 days or more.

Peterson left the *Star* building after the meeting feeling like
the whole process had been futile. He hoped the newspaper

would reconsider lumping the civil lawsuits with criminal charges, but . . .

"The story was already written," said Peterson. "I was convinced of that. It was going to appear. They had spent too much time with it. Maybe we made them go back and read the story more carefully. Maybe they went back and added some things. But that meeting essentially did not change a thing.

"But I'll tell you what: we weren't going to sit back and be defensive about this. We went on the offensive."

It would be nearly two months before the Chiefs heard again from the *Kansas City Star* about the story. On Thursday, December 9, four *Star* reporters walked into Arrowhead Stadium. Like all NFL teams, the Chiefs' locker room is open to the media after practice each day. The players had been warned about the arrival of this journalistic swat team, so it did not come as a shock when the newspapermen fanned out across the room.

The *Star* reporters were greeted by indignation, anger and indifference. Most players simply ignored questions that were asked, as they had been advised to do by their attorneys. One player involved in a child support case asked that the name of the child be kept out of the story. Some swore at the reporters. Marcus Allen, whose name was not even part of the investigation, went nose-to-nose with one of the reporters, asking why the story was so important that it required digging into the personal lives of players. The reporters left with empty notebooks and complaints about how they were treated by some of the players.

There was still the matter of a football game to be played in Denver, and the Chiefs left Mile High Stadium just as empty-handed as the *Star* reporters left the locker room. For the third consecutive year, they had jumped out to a lead on the Broncos. And for the third consecutive year, John Elway rallied his team for another victory, this time 27-21.

The game's pivotal play came with just over 12 minutes remaining in the fourth quarter. Some would argue that it was the most crucial blunder of the season. Certainly, it must be considered among the reasons why the Chiefs did not have home-field advantage in the playoffs.

The situation: fourth down, eight yards to go for a first down at the Denver 42-yard line. The Chiefs held a four-point lead as Bryan Barker prepared to punt the ball. On the left flank of the punt protection was Bennie Thompson, the Chiefs' special teams captain.   Thompson's assignment was to block one of Denver's rushers and then head down-field to get in on the tackle.

Up to that point in 1993, Thompson was not having the kind of season that earned him Pro Bowl honors with the New Orleans Saints in 1991. Opponents were more aware of Thompson and had special blocking assignments set up to stop his punt and kick coverage. Going into the Denver game, he had just nine solo special teams tackles in 12 games.

As he stood in the punt formation, Thompson made a decision: he was not going to worry about blocking the man in front of him. He decided to run down the field as quickly as possible, and try to participate in the tackle. Thompson did the same thing earlier in the season against the Los Angeles Raiders and made the tackle. But he drew the ire of the coaching staff for not handling his protection duties first. There is nothing more devastating in football than the blocked punt; it can change the momentum of a game faster than any other play.

The Chiefs would learn just how devastating such a play could be. Thompson sidestepped the Broncos' Reggie Rivers and headed down-field in coverage. Rivers sprinted past Thompson and blocked Barker's punt. After the ball rolled around, it finally was recovered at the Chiefs' 11-yard line. Denver scored three plays later, with Elway finding Shannon Sharpe for the third touchdown pass of the day. The Broncos added a late field goal for a 27-21 victory, and the Chiefs now were 0-11 in Mile High Stadium dating back to 1982.

The loss stung the Chiefs deeply because they knew the 1993 Broncos were not a very strong football team. Denver relied almost completely on Elway in the second half of its season. The Broncos defense was suspect and fell apart down the stretch. Elway and his teammates were eliminated in the first round of the playoffs, losing to the Los Angeles Raiders.

The next Sunday, December 19, the Chiefs hosted the San Diego Chargers. That morning, the *Star* finally ran the story on the legal problems of Chiefs players. It appeared on the front-page of its Sunday edition under the headline, "Some Chiefs have troubles away from the game." The story took up nearly two full pages of the news section.

The *Star* listed eight players who had been arrested since 1991. They also listed 10 players with 23 civil lawsuits filed against them. In total, there were 15 different players named in the story. Five of those players no longer were with the team.

After waiting so long to see the story, reaction in the locker room was muted when the article finally appeared. Some players continued their policy of not talking with reporters from the newspaper. Others who had stopped talking now made themselves available.

"To me, the article turned out pretty funny," said Willie Davis, who still refused to speak with *Star* reporters. Davis was mentioned in the story because of a civil suit filed against him by an Arkansas women seeking child support payments. Through his attorney, Davis said he was unaware of the suit and had been making support payments. "I mean, they went to all this trouble, all this investigating; you would have thought they had turned up some major scandals or something.

"They dug some stuff up about me from back home. But I haven't been arrested; I haven't been convicted of anything. But they wanted dirt, so they went out and found it."

Among the people of Kansas City, reaction was mixed. Some thought the *Star* story did nothing but rehash old news. Others were upset that the story came out as the team was making a drive to the playoffs. Some people agreed with the newspaper's premise that the Chiefs were out of control and that Peterson and Schottenheimer were not firm enough in handling the troublemakers.

The reaction was muted, however, by the Chiefs' 28-24 victory that Sunday afternoon over San Diego, leaving the team 10-4 and on the doorstep of their first division title in 22 years. The game featured another of those come-from-behind efforts from Montana, as the Chiefs found themselves down 17-0 early in the second quarter. But Montana threw touchdown passes of 9 and 28 yards to Willie Davis and 4 yards to J.J. Birden. Combined with a 1-yard scoring run by Marcus Allen, the Chiefs picked up another victory.

Whatever controversy the *Star* story caused, it would have passed very quickly if not for subsequent events. Before Schottenheimer's regular Tuesday afternoon press conference, Peterson took to the microphone and blasted the newspaper in a prepared statement.

"One can only speculate as to the purpose and timing of the *Kansas City Star*'s recent series of reports detailing legal troubles for Kansas City Chiefs players," Peterson said. "Lumping civil cases involving credit card bills and business dealings with criminal cases, however, goes well beyond what any clear-thinking person would consider fair play.

"As I indicated to the *Star*'s reporters, we do not accept or condone criminal activities from any Chiefs employees. Nevertheless, we are under no obligation to comment on such activities, since any comment may compromise the swift and proper solution of any charges. As an employer, we have a larger responsibility to protect an individual's rights no matter what station he may hold in the public eye. Moreover, many of the allegations seem frivolous and of no public interest. Does anyone really care if a player fails to pay on a credit card account or has a piece of furniture repossessed? What is the journalistic value of this information? What crime has the player committed? Is this the *Star* making moral distinctions and condemning those who fail to meet the *Star*'s designated moral standards?"

Two days later, Peterson told the *Star*'s football writers — who were not part of the investigation of legal problems — that he no longer would speak to them. It was just another episode in what was a three-year battle between Peterson and the newspaper, one that began in the days just before Christmas of 1990.

An investigative reporter from the *Star* began making phone calls and asking questions about Peterson's relationship with Vince Costello. At the time, Peterson's weekly radio show was held at a restaurant operated by Costello in south Kansas City.

Costello is a former NFL player, who spent 12 seasons with the Cleveland Browns and New York Giants. He also was part of the Chiefs coaching staff in the mid-1970s under Paul Wiggin, a former teammate with the Browns. After Costello was fired by the Chiefs, he drifted into the restaurant business, and his Costello's Greenhouse was a well-known fixture near the Ward Parkway Mall.

It also turned out that Costello gambled on pro football games. In fact, in the summer of 1990, he testified about his gambling under a grant of immunity during a trial against a Kansas City bookmaker with connections to organized crime. Costello admitted to wagering between $300 and $1,000 per game on as many as six to 13 games each weekend of the NFL season.

In the world of sports, the most serious allegation that can be made against anyone is a link to gambling. There are players in the Baseball Hall of Fame who have been arrested on drug charges. Yet, Pete Rose — the game's all-time hit leader — cannot find a spot in Cooperstown because of gambling charges made against him and the resulting lifetime suspension. Remember the furor in the summer of 1993 surrounding basketball star Michael Jordan and his gambling habits on golf courses? Athletes in football and basketball — Paul Hornung, Alex Karras, Connie Hawkins — have seen their careers interrupted because of allegations involving gambling. The sports world has welcomed back all sorts of ne'er do wells over the years, but the taint of gambling makes one an outcast.

On December 23, 1990, the *Star* ran a story on the front-page of its Sunday edition headlined: "Chiefs Show is hosted by ex-gambler." It detailed Costello's gambling and the fact that his restaurant was the site of Carl Peterson's weekly radio show. The premise of the story was that Peterson was breaking NFL mandates that team officials should stay away from known gamblers.

There were several problems with this story line. Costello was not a "known" gambler to the Chiefs, the NFL, Peterson or the radio station. Costello's testimony in the trial against the bookmaker had taken place in March of 1990. It was not until late December, just as the Chiefs were about to make the playoffs for the first time in the Peterson/Schottenheimer Era, that the Star reporter began asking about the connection. There already had been 15 Carl Peterson Shows held at the restaurant, going all the way back to the first week of September. When asked about this, the *Star* reporter replied: "We just noticed it."

Peterson did not pick the broadcast site for his radio show. That was decided by the station, KCFX-FM, with no consultation with Peterson. Had the station known of Costello's past, it would not have taken the show there in the first place. That fact was not mentioned until the sixth paragraph, after the story had already jumped from page one to an inside page.

Peterson and Costello were not friends. During the shows, Costello would stop and say hello to Peterson. Several times after shows, Peterson had dinner in the restaurant and brief conversations with Costello when he stopped by the table. But they never talked on the phone, never visited each other's homes and Costello never had been to Peterson's office in Arrowhead.

These facts were provided to the *Star* reporter by several people (including the author) before the story was written . The newspaper made one call to Peterson, which was passed on to the team's public relations office. When he was told Peterson was not immediately available for comment, the *Star* reporter told Chiefs public relations director Bob Moore the story was not urgent, and probably would not run in the near future.

Incredibly, despite the seriousness of the connection being made by the newspaper, it went ahead with the story. In the seventh paragraph it said: "Peterson did not respond to requests for an interview."

The day before the story ran, three *Kansas City Star* reporters had access to Peterson in San Diego. None of them were asked by their editors to find Peterson for some sort of comment.

The *Star* took the easy way out, an unbecoming act for a newspaper that has won a number of Pulitzer Prizes over the years and once carried the reporting of Ernest Hemingway. Press box pundits said the whole story could be filed under the heading: "Never let the facts get in the way of a good headline."

But it was no joking matter to Peterson. He had been painted with a brush that had no paint, but he still was stained. As the team's charter flight back to Kansas City cruised across the Rockies, Peterson stood in the back of the plane and railed against the newspaper. The error was compounded when the Associated Press in Kansas City picked up the piece and sent it around the country, still without any comments from Peterson. The next day, Peterson had to explain to his mother in Long Beach, California why somebody was linking him with a confessed gambler.

Peterson demanded a meeting with the officials of the *Star* over the story. After nearly two hours of conversation, much of it lively, he still had a bitter taste in his mouth.

"I learned a very valuable lesson," said Peterson. "I learned that the individual really doesn't have freedom of the press, just the newspaper does. I learned I had little or no recourse against the linking of my name publicly with someone linked to gambling. I learned I had to sit there and swallow the whole damn thing. There was nothing I could do.

"How could they run a story like that and not talk to me? They say I did not respond to requests for an interview, but nobody asked me for an interview. They had reporters with the team in San Diego. I would have been happy to tell them their story was nothing, that I barely knew Vince Costello, that I didn't know he was a gambler, and that I did not pick the place where we held the radio show.

"But they did not want to hear that. That would have spoiled their story. I guess a headline like "Peterson doesn't know ex-gambler" wasn't good enough."

From that point on, Peterson held a great distrust for the *Star* and most of its reporters. Three years later, the newspaper's story on the legal problems of Chiefs players only re-confirmed his feelings and led to his decision to stop talking with *Star* reporters.

Did this feud affect the amount of coverage given the team by the *Star*? Probably not. Did it affect the quality of the paper's coverage? Absolutely. Chiefs fans learn more about their team from radio and television than they do from the *Kansas City Star,* and that's unusual among the cities that make up the NFL.

The relationship between the media and professional athletic teams has changed tremendously in the last 15 or 20 years. But then, so has the entire world of journalism. Since the Watergate coverage of Woodward and Bernstein helped bring down the Presidency of Richard Nixon, the media has taken a much tougher approach in its coverage of everything. As the dollar amounts have increased in the world of fun and games, so has the scrutiny by the press.

As Peterson says, that is "the price of being in the public eye." What rankles those in the world of sports is the "holier than thou" attitude carried by many in the media. There are some journalists who consider themselves to be the "watchmen" of our society, which begs the question, "Who watches the watchmen?"

"Let's be honest; they are in the media *business,*" said Peterson. "It's a business. As much as they hate to admit that, they are there for one reason: to sell newspapers or to make sure people watch or listen to their station.

"They don't want to operate under the same scrutiny they put us under. Ask the media to detail their internal problems and they will tell you it's nobody's business. They have just as many problems as any business does. They are not pure. They have people who break the law. They have people with personality problems, with family problems, with health problems. They have their own scandals.

"I've been told, 'Don't get in a fight with people who buy ink by the barrel.' It's probably hurt me personally, but I won't sit back if I believe something is wrong.

"Listen, there is no mystery in this; they are in the entertainment business, just like we are."

CHAPTER SIXTEEN

WILLIE'S CLOCK
IS TICKING

Outwardly at least, the other Chiefs players did not express anger or resentment regarding the attention Joe Montana received from fans and media during the 1993 season.

For the most part, Montana's teammates tolerated the crush. Marty Schottenheimer explained during the team's May mini-camp that the spotlight might get red hot with Montana around, but there was nothing anyone could do to stop the fascination with the quarterback.

"The media decides what they are interested in," Schottenheimer told the players. "We can't tell them what to cover or decide for them what should get their attention. It's out of our control, so don't get wrapped up in it. Cooperate as much as you can, but don't let it bother you."

Early in the season, reporters and television cameras shadowed every move Montana made on and off the field. The Kansas City media soon discovered what their brethren in San Francisco already knew — Montana was available and fairly cooperative in interviews, but he was not going to fill notebooks and tapes with timely dialogue. In the world of journalism, Montana is considered a great story, but a bad quote. With newspaper inches and television-radio seconds to fill, reporters sought comments from his new teammates.

Most of the Chiefs cooperated; wide receiver Willie Davis did, for a time. Day after day, the questions came from reporters in different forms and different faces, but always with the same subject: Montana. In training camp, Davis tried to answer all the Joe Montana questions, but his patience quickly wore thin. He called a halt to all interviews dealing with the subject of Joe Montana. When reporters approached his locker, Davis would throw up his hands and stop them before the first word left their mouths.

"No questions about Joe," Davis said.

These were not angry words, although at times he sounded as if he was upset. In a city like New York, Denver or Philadelphia — where any contrary word creates headlines in the tabloid newspapers — Davis would have found himself in the spotlight for his silence. He would have been painted as a malcontent over Montana.

But in Kansas City, nobody wrote or said much about Davis' reticence in speaking about his quarterback.

"I was just tired of it," Davis said. "Everybody was coming up and asking the same questions, 'What's it like to catch a pass from Joe Montana? What's Joe Montana really like? What about this thing that you Kansas City receivers are not Jerry Rice and John Taylor? Tell us something about Joe.'

"It was the same people coming up, asking the same questions. One guy asked the same question about three different times during one week in training camp. I began telling them if they wanted to know, they should go ask this other person, or just go back and get my answers from a week ago.

"Anybody that had a new question about Joe, I answered. But ask me if I have been over to his house for dinner? Or how does it feel to catch a pass from Joe Montana? Come on, those are silly questions."

Davis insists he was not jealous of the attention bestowed on Montana.

"There wasn't any envy towards Joe," he said. "It wasn't like I wanted all those people asking questions about me instead of him. It would be fine with me if no reporters were ever around. Joe can have all the attention. I don't want it; I don't want any of it. I don't know how Joe puts up with it."

The words tumble out as Davis sits in a pizza restaurant not far from Arrowhead Stadium. It is a Tuesday — the players' day off — and Davis has been out running errands. It is late in the

1993 season, long after those crazy early days of Montana Mania. The playoffs loom ahead. Questions about Joe no longer raise his ire. Willie Davis has accepted that the media's interest in him is largely tied to the fact he is on the other end of Montana's throws.

"The start of the season — that was just crazy," said Davis, a big smile creasing his face. "Things kind of died down after awhile, and there weren't so many silly questions. I haven't been asked if I can be Jerry Rice or John Taylor in weeks."

Guys like Davis, J.J. Birden and Tim Barnett heard questions like that from the time the trade was announced. Sure, Kansas City now had Montana, but it did not have his favorite receivers Rice and Taylor. With a reputation as a running team, the Chiefs receivers were little-known and under-appreciated around the league.

"There's no way we are going to be like Rice and Taylor," said Davis. "We are different people. But I don't think that means we can't play and we can't produce in this offense. Man, it gets to the point where after you hear so much about what you aren't, who wants to talk about what you are?"

Rice is 6 feet, 2 inches tall and weighs 200 pounds. Taylor is 6-1, 185 pounds. Davis is 6-0, 165 pounds. Birden is 5-9, 165 pounds. Those physical differences make for different results in the San Francisco-style offense. Davis/Birden are faster than Rice/Taylor, but because Davis/Birden are not as big, they have trouble breaking tackles. Rice/Taylor can turn a 5-yard pass into a 30-yard gain. Davis/Birden can turn a 30-yard pass into a 60-yard gain. The offensive scheme with Montana at quarterback is built more to highlight the abilities of Rice and Taylor than Davis and Birden.

"I don't think I really lived up to the expectations of everybody around here," Davis said. "Not that I was trying to do that. I just wanted to satisfy myself and help the team win games.

"People said all year that our receiving corps wasn't that good, or wasn't the type that Joe Montana needed around him to succeed and go all the way to the Super Bowl. So, since I didn't put up Jerry Rice numbers, I know that I haven't fulfilled the expectations of people who wanted that. There's nothing I can do about it. People have talked about how this team doesn't have big physical receivers who can break tackles and gain extra yardage in this offense. And I guess that's true. There's no way

I'm ever going to be a big physical receiver. It's just not going to happen because I don't think I'm going to be growing anymore.

"I've met my own expectations. After two years on developmental, I didn't expect to come in and be starting and catching balls. I'm happy with it."

Montana frequently came to the defense of his new receivers.

"These guys are talented receivers who have not gotten a whole lot of attention because of the offensive style this team had before," said Montana. "I don't have to apologize for them. There were a lot of seasons (in San Francisco) where we did not have a receiving corps as talented as this one. I'm very comfortable with them."

It has taken Willie Davis some time just to grow comfortable with the idea of talking about himself, let alone speaking of Joe Montana. It is another part of what has been a remarkable transformation for the quiet native of Altheimer, Arkansas. In two years, he went from National Football League nobody to one of the league's game-breaking receivers. He led the NFL in average yards per catch — 21 yards — during the 1992 season. Davis followed in 1993 with an average of 17.5 yards per catch, the best among receivers with more than 50 receptions.

Off the field, this transformation into a big-league receiver also brought Davis out of his shell. A member of the Chiefs coaching staff once described Davis as having the "doe in the headlights" look about him. Sometimes painfully shy, Davis did not engage in a lot of locker room banter early in his career. Eye contact was not one of his strong suits. His position coach, Al Saunders, remembered that it was several weeks of working with him as a rookie before Davis let down his guard.

"You have to remember how I came here and what happened to me when I got here," said Davis. "A lot of people forget about that. I wasn't supposed to make it. I had everything going against me."

One of 11 children, Davis played football, basketball and ran track at tiny Altheimer High School, where his graduating class totaled 56. His dream was to play college basketball, and he drew limited recruiting interest from schools like Georgetown, Arkansas and Tulsa. None offered him a scholarship.

Davis ended up just down the road from Altheimer at the University of Central Arkansas in Conway. At the time, Scottie

Pippen was making a name for himself there on the basketball court. Davis dreamed of joining him, but ended up playing wide receiver in Central's wishbone offense, where his No. 1 assignment every week was to block. As a three-year starter, Davis caught 63 passes, averaging more than 20 yards a catch with 10 touchdowns, including a 99-yard touchdown catch in his junior season.

The Chiefs accumulated limited information on Davis before the 1990 NFL draft. He did not play in any postseason all-star games and had not been invited to the Scouting Combine workout session. That meant most of the NFL teams did not consider him among the top 400 prospects in the country. The odds of a player so far down on the talent ladder getting a shot at the NFL are slim. The odds of that same player surviving and thriving in pro football are infinitesimal. There are one or two cases a year where an undrafted rookie free agent survives long enough to make a name for himself in the league.

When the Chiefs looked at a highlight tape prepared by the folks at Central Arkansas, Davis was a tiny figure in the grainy picture who kept running the same pass patterns over and over.

"He ran a streak route up the field and ran past a few guys," said assistant coach Al Saunders, who evaluated the film. "Then he ran a post route. That was it. He was very raw in everything — his ability to catch the football, his understanding of the game, his work ethic; everything."

After the 1990 draft was completed and Davis was not selected, the Chiefs and New York Giants showed interest in signing him as a free agent. After going through several mini-camp practices in New York, Davis felt the Giants were not serious about giving him a chance to make the team. So he left New York and signed with the Chiefs.

Not long after he showed up at Arrowhead Stadium, Davis questioned how serious the Chiefs were about giving him a chance for a roster spot.

"A person in this organization told me at the time that the only reason they got me was to fill the roster in training camp," Davis said. "My head just dropped when he told me that. I said to myself, 'I have no way of making this team.'"

Davis will not divulge the name of the person who told him he was nothing but fodder for training camp practices. He will say only that the man still works for the Chiefs and that Davis sees him almost every day.

"I remind him all the time about what he told me," Davis said. "Earlier this year, when a story was written and I mentioned about what he said, he sought me out. 'Hey, why did you bring that up?' he said. I told him, 'Because it's true.'"

Before the start of the 1992 NFL season, the only Willie Davis most sports fans knew was the Hall of Fame defensive lineman for the Green Bay Packers in the 1960s. Nearly 30 years later, Willie Clark Davis spent two seasons on the Chiefs developmental squad and was activated for just one game during the 1991 season. Davis played a season in the spring-time World League of American Football, where he caught 20 passes for 242 yards as a member of the Orlando Thunder. But that WLAF experience did nothing to elevate Davis into the football consciousness of Kansas City, let alone the NFL.

Davis finally received his shot with the Chiefs when he made the final roster coming out of the 1992 training camp. It would take several more weeks of anonymity before he exploded. Davis put together three consecutive 100-yard receiving games, something no other receiver in the league was able to duplicate in 1992. That's right, not even Jerry Rice and John Taylor put together three straight 100s that year.

As his playing time increased, so did his confidence off the field. Several times early in the 1992 season, Davis refused to do media interviews. It was nothing personal and there was no statement meant in his silence; he just did not feel comfortable talking with people he did not know and even then, many of his teammates did not really know Willie. By the end of the season, Davis had not exactly become a chatterbox, but he no longer sought refuge from the cameras and microphones.

"We didn't have a lot of people watching us in college," Davis said. "And there weren't a lot of people watching in the World League. When you are on the developmental squad, there aren't a lot of people trying to talk with you. It wasn't something I had ever done much. It took me time before I felt good about talking like this."

Despite his personal breakthrough in the 1992 season, Davis knew changes were coming in the Chiefs offense.

"It was very disturbing at the end of that season when our defense was playing so well and we couldn't help out with our offense," said Davis. "Nobody knew what was going to happen, but you figured something had to give. We couldn't stay with what we had done."

When the change to the San Francisco-style offense was announced, Davis reacted with caution. "I was pretty successful in the old offense," he said. "I spent three years learning the old offense, so now there was something new to learn. I didn't know what it meant for me. Plus, remember, I wasn't Jerry Rice or John Taylor. Maybe those guys were going to come with Joe, too."

For Davis, the transition to the new offense was fairly easy. He led all Chiefs receivers in 1993, with 51 catches for 909 yards and seven touchdowns. Only Marcus Allen finished the season with more touchdowns for the Chiefs than Davis. Combined, the rest of the wide receivers grabbed only three touchdown catches. Davis caught at least one pass in every game and had 14 receptions of 20 yards or more.

And he has become a big-strike touchdown-maker, with 10 scoring catches in two seasons that average nearly 35 yards per score. In 1993, most of his seven touchdown catches were memorable:

1) A 19-yarder against Tampa Bay in Game No. 1 was Joe Montana's first touchdown pass as a member of the Chiefs.

2) Montana found him for 15 yards and a touchdown in Game No. 4 against the Raiders, which proved to be the winning points in a Chiefs victory.

3) In Game No. 9, Davis and Dave Krieg combined on a 66-yard bomb that was the key play in the Chiefs' come-from-behind victory over the Raiders in Los Angeles. Davis had five catches for 115 yards in the game.

4) A 29-yarder from Montana in Game No. 13 against Denver gave the Chiefs a third-quarter lead. They ended up losing in the fourth quarter, victims of yet another John Elway comeback.

5) and 6) Both came in Game No. 14 against San Diego. Davis caught a 9-yard touchdown pass from Montana and then a 28-yarder from Krieg. The second score proved to be the winning points, as the Chiefs beat the Chargers.

7) Montana found him for a 14-yard touchdown in a Game No. 16 victory over Seattle.

"I think I could have done a little more," Davis said. "I dropped a few passes here and there that I should have had. Like

I said, I don't think I met the expectations of some people, but I was happy."

Davis is philosophical about what the future might hold for him and teammate J.J. Birden.

"I'm sure they will go out and try to find a big, physical receiver for the (1994) season," said Davis. "I guess that might mean the opportunities for me would decrease. Man, that's just part of the game. That's the business."

About midway through the 1993 season, Davis signed a new three-year contract with the Chiefs. The deal came not long after the team's salaries were printed in the *Kansas City Star*, listing him as one of the lowest-paid players on the squad at a reported $115,000. "I don't think I was even making what they said I was," Davis said with a laugh. If it was true, Davis would have been the Chiefs' lowest-paid starter.

His new deal brings him considerably more money, although not the stratospheric numbers that are becoming commonplace in pro football.

"I think I surprised a lot of people in the front office," said Davis. "I don't think they expected me to do what I did. I signed around the middle of this year. I just wanted to get something done and concentrate on football. I didn't want to get into an argument with them and have them upset and then me upset, and then it would have dragged out for a long time."

When the salary list became public, Davis took plenty of ribbing from his teammates about his paycheck. A couple of years ago, that kind of verbal abuse would have left him in a deep funk. A more confident Davis just shrugged it off.

"I wouldn't say it was embarrassing," said Davis. "You have to understand what that locker room is like. If you don't have thick skin down there, then you are going to be in trouble. Those guys pick up on anything, and they'll hit you with it. It got a little tough, and I got down, but you've just got to learn to laugh with them.

"I'm just thankful for what I'm getting. Most people don't see that much money in their lifetime. What I'm making now, the folks back in my hometown can't even believe."

Davis remains one of the least quoted players in the Chiefs' locker room, which is just fine with him. But it is a shame, because the public does not know that Willie Davis is one of the most level-headed players in the NFL, wise beyond his 26 years, especially when it comes to the world of pro football.

"I'm not campaigning for anything," said Davis. "I don't need the publicity. I've only ever wanted to do one thing, and that's play football."

Not only is he playing; he is succeeding beyond anyone's wildest dreams for him four years ago. Willie Davis does not picture himself as a role model, but his NFL story is one from which anyone can learn.

"He came here with tremendous speed, but he probably weighed 158 pounds soaking wet," said assistant coach Al Saunders. "The thing is, 58 pounds of that had to be his heart. He's very determined, very intelligent, a very hard-working individual. It has not been easy for him, but he has overcome all of it. He is very definitely an NFL player."

That "58-pound heart" was the driving force that allowed him to survive his start as an undrafted free agent. That, and one of life's greatest motivators, the fear of failure.

"I think what kept me going was that I didn't want to fail," Davis said. "I was not used to failing. From little league to college, I was the man. I got here and everything changed because everybody has talent in the NFL. They have vets they rely on, and young guys have to prove themselves over and over before anybody gives them a shot. I didn't want to leave until I got that shot.

"I just didn't want to fail myself, or fail for my family and friends."

It's possible to take Willie Davis out of Altheimer, Arkansas, but taking Altheimer out of Willie Davis cannot be done. As the sixth of 11 children — with a sister and brother still in high school — Davis remains tied to his family home.

"On a good day, if nobody died, there are 1,200 people," Davis said. "Everybody knows one another. Growing up, there were no problems. If somebody got out of hand, then someone down the street would set them straight. You didn't have to wait until you got home to find out you did something wrong. If you did get in trouble, sometimes your brothers and sisters would try to get you out of it. Sometimes they would tell on you anyway, and get you in even more trouble."

Altheimer is never far from Davis' thoughts; that's where he plans to return when his playing career ends. And that finish could be sooner than a lot of people might imagine, considering his success over the last two seasons.

"I've got a five-year plan, and I've got three years left on my plan," said Davis. "Hopefully, I can reach the end of my five-year plan, take my money back to Arkansas and relax. I can't see playing this game that much longer."

Those are unusual words coming from a young man with two good NFL seasons on the books and the potential for more. But overcoming his rough start in the NFL has Willie Davis pragmatic about life as a professional football player.

"When I stop having fun playing football, it's over," said Davis. "I'm going to stop. I don't care how much money is involved. I think after five years of this, it is over. I can't think it will be that much fun.

"The body wears out and that takes the fun out of the game. I hate getting up on Monday mornings, feeling like I feel; it's terrible. During the game, you have so much energy that when you get hurt it bothers you for awhile, and then the pain goes away.

"But on Monday mornings, you realize your whole body hurts because of people hitting on you. Anything can happen to you at any time. You see guys all the time who can barely walk, and they are still in their 20s. It's all from football. You can't look at it like you are going to play forever; if you do, you are fooling yourself. I look at somebody like Brian Bosworth, who is not even in football anymore. He was smart, and he is set for life financially. But physically, he's going to have problems."

Davis spent the 1993 season marveling at his newest teammates, Joe Montana and Marcus Allen, and watched with amazement another 30-something veteran, Albert Lewis.

"That Marcus and Joe are still playing and doing it at a high level is amazing," said Davis. "But Albert Lewis is the guy that is beyond belief. He's got to be in the best shape of anybody in the locker room. That makes me mad. That's where I get jealous. How could this dude still be doing this? I think Albert Lewis is the best cornerback in the league. As far as man-to-man cover guys, I don't see anybody better, and I watch them all. I see him working in the off-season, and there is no way I could work like that, no way. I would be exhausted before I ever got to training camp.

"Then there's Marcus. He went through so much with the Raiders, I think anybody else would have said, 'The heck with this, I've accomplished a lot of great things, I'm going to quit, I'm going to retire.' I'm sure he's probably set financially, but he's still out here playing, trying to win another championship.

"And Joe, I mean what's he playing for? He's won the Super Bowl, he's set the records, he's going to the Hall of Fame. I asked Joe in training camp why he wanted to keep playing. He's playing because he's still having fun. That's what he told me. He wants to go see if he can win another Super Bowl with another team because no one thinks he can do it. I think Marcus is the same way. He's still having fun. You can see it in the locker room. Both of them are laughing, joking around.

"The thing is, those guys are unusual. Most of us aren't ever going to have the chance. I'm not expecting it, and I know my body sure isn't. I could go out any Sunday and blow my knee out, and the whole thing could be over. I'm on borrowed time.

"The clock is ticking and I can hear it. "

CHAPTER SEVENTEEN

MONTANA MANIA

Over the last 15 years or so, there has been a serious devaluation of the language surrounding sports. Words once used to describe the extraordinary, now explain the commonplace. What once was considered poor is now mediocre. What once was merely average, today is called good. And good is now great. The words "great performance" are thrown around so frequently these days, truly outstanding efforts sometimes are lost in the humdrum of hype.

The dominance of television and its insatiable appetite for programming is the key reason behind this change. Everything must be bigger and better to tickle the short attention spans of today's sophisticated TV viewers. This forces the "talking heads" who fill our screens to new levels of hyperbole — just to make an impression. Thus, "great" becomes a word used in every conversation. "Outstanding" comes along every day or so. "Unbelievable" is now very believable; it happens so often.

Twenty-five years ago, it took a team like the Boston Celtics, with 11 National Basketball Association championships in 13 years, to be called great. It was the same with the New York Yankees, who won six World Series titles in seven years. A "dynasty" was considered the seven consecutive NCAA basketball championships won by UCLA.

A team wins a title today, and it is immediately crowned a "great" champion — one of the best teams of all time — even if

12 months later it is nowhere near the victory stand. And should this team win two championships in a row, it would be declared a dynasty. Already, the Dallas Cowboys are being called the team of the 1990s with two Super Bowl victories, even though half the decade remains to be played.

Like "great," the value of the word "superstar" has been depleted. Originally created by sports and entertainment writers to designate the very best of the very best, a superstar was a performer who left even his peers stunned by his gifts and efforts. In the sports world, it was used to describe on-field production that reached such a high and sustained level, it elevated not only the player, but the team around him to remarkable accomplishments.

So memorable is the superstar that his name and face are known beyond his sphere of influence. Sporting superstars used to be people recognized even by those unfamiliar with the fun and games. They appeared not just on the cover of *Sports Illustrated*, but on the covers of *Time*, *Rolling Stone* and *Esquire*.

Superstars were people like Babe Ruth, Jack Dempsey, Red Grange, Muhammad Ali, Joe DiMaggio, Wilt Chamberlain, Gordie Howe, Arnold Palmer, Ted Williams, Jack Nicklaus, Magic Johnson, Larry Bird, Michael Jordan, Mickey Mantle, Willie Mays, Jim Brown and Wayne Gretzky.

That may seem like a lot of superstars, but it is nearly 75 years from the era of Ruth to the time of Gretzky. Superstars are the ones mentioned when informed fans discuss questions like, "Who was the greatest hitter of all-time?" or "Who was the most complete basketball player in NBA history?" or "Who was the greatest quarterback to play the game?"

This is not what "superstar" means today. A baseball player is considered a superstar when he hits higher than .300. Should a running back gain more than 1,000 yards in 16 games, he is suddenly a superstar. In basketball, if a player averages more than 25 points per game, he is acclaimed one of the game's greats. Consistency of performance is no longer part of the criteria for defining superstardom. One achievement elevates an athlete into the stratosphere of greatness. Today, producing results on the field sometimes is not necessary; appear in television commercials with catchy slogans like "Bo Knows," and there are those who will call you a superstar.

The truth is, excellence in the world of sports does not fall from trees every day. Superstars cannot be found in every sport, in every city, in every generation. At any given point in history, there are but a handful of superstars running around the world of sports.

Take Joe Montana, for instance. By every definition — new and old — he is the embodiment of a superstar. On the field, he has produced immense success both individually and as part of championship teams. His image transcends the game. He appears in television commercials for Hanes clothing without holding a football in his hands or even having his name flashed on the screen. It is not necessary; viewers know his face.

On Thursday, August 12, 1993, as the Chiefs were preparing to play the Buffalo Bills in a preseason game, I was quoted in *USA TODAY* as saying:

"Kansas City has had Len Dawson, Tom Watson and George Brett, but they've never had a superstar. This guy (Joe Montana) is a superstar."

It did not take long for angry phone calls from the provincialists. "You were misquoted, right?" said one caller. "What kind of fool are you?" asked another. "How could you say something so stupid?" commented one irate fan, threatening bodily harm with the next breath. Accusations were made that I besmirched the careers of Dawson, Watson and Brett. I was accused of suffering from Montana Mania.

Well, I was not misquoted, and I am not a fool. I will allow the reader to decide the question of my stupidity, and nothing I can ever say will tarnish the achievements of Dawson, Watson and Brett. They are true stars in their sports.

But are they *superstars*? Are their names mentioned among the top two or three quarterbacks, hitters and golfers of all time? Are their faces instantly recognizable in every corner of the country, by fans and non-sports fans alike? The answer to all three questions is no. That does not belittle their accomplishments. It is simply fact.

In May of 1993, the Sports Marketing Group of Dallas, Texas released the results of a survey it did on the popularity of athletes. Michael Jordan was deemed the most popular athlete in the country, named by 47 percent of those who were questioned. No. 2 was Joe Montana, named by 44 percent.

While some Kansas City sports fans were bothered by the characterization of Montana as the city's first sporting superstar, many others were busy proving the point throughout the 1993 football season. Kansas City prides itself on having a Midwestern sensibility that supposedly allows its sporting stars to live normal lives. But Kansas City dropped its reserve and began to drool over Montana from the moment his name was first mentioned in the same sentence with the Chiefs.

Montana sightings came quickly and often. *The Kansas City Star* reported regularly on the location of his home, the school where his children were enrolled, the household help he employed and places where he had dinner. When Montana made one of his few scheduled public appearances at a Venture department store in Independence, Missouri, 4,000 people jammed the aisles, and management was forced to close the doors. As mentioned earlier, when Montana appeared on teammate Tim Grunhard's radio program, it took six off-duty Kansas City policemen to get him safely into and out of the building.

Montana Mania was not only a Kansas City malady; it showed itself in the very first days of Chiefs training camp in River Falls, Wisconsin.

Past visits by the Chiefs to this hamlet always saw a few kids hanging around the dining hall and dorms, looking for autographs. Never was it a security concern. But with Montana around, it became a problem. Extra security was necessary just to move him from one building to another. Autograph hounds buzzed the campus at all hours. Early one Sunday, as the morning dew still glistened on the grass, two men stood outside the Chiefs' River Falls dormitory. They looked to be in their 30s, and each had an armload of pictures and notebooks. They were not the least bit interested in anybody else that morning — not Marcus Allen, Derrick Thomas or Neil Smith, who all walked past the men.

"We just drove up from Chicago," one of the men said. "We are going to wait for Joe."

When Montana and Dave Krieg journeyed to a River Falls pub on their first night in camp, they found the locals friendly and not too pushy as the quarterbacks enjoyed a beer. But as soon as the quarterbacks walked out, one woman grabbed the beer can Montana was drinking from and put it in her purse. A souvenir? A keepsake?

"I don't know," said the woman. "I just know that he touched it."

One night, Montana walked out of the players dorm to his car. As he was getting ready to put the key in the ignition, one of his teammates yelled at him to wait—lying underneath Montana's car was a young boy. Montana opened his door in time to see him scurry away. Why was the kid under the car?

"I don't know," Montana said the next day. "But at least I didn't hear any ticking."

When the Chiefs visited LaCrosse, Wisconsin to scrimmage the New Orleans Saints, several small children nearly were crushed as a wave of adults began pushing at a fence separating Montana from those seeking his autograph. When Marty Schottenheimer decided not to play Montana in that scrimmage, one woman publicly berated the Chiefs head coach afterwards.

"You disappointed a lot of people," she screamed.

"Take it up with the Commissioner," shot back a startled Schottenheimer.

But Montana Mania was not limited to Kansas City and Wisconsin; it also included . . . Montana.

Ismay, Montana is the smallest incorporated city in the state. Named after the daughters of a railroad official, Ismay sits in the southeast corner of the vast state, on the way to nowhere and near nothing. Its population hovers around 30 people. Few beyond Ismay know the town is even there.

Until the city changed its name to Joe, Montana 59336.

It began with a phone call from Kansas City radio station KYYS-FM (102). Officials at the station were trying to find some way to ride Montana Mania to higher ratings and exposure. Some folks at the station came up with the idea of convincing a town in Montana to change its name to Joe. Ismay was the second town they called. After a town meeting around city clerk Wayne Rieger's kitchen table, the folks of Ismay voted to change their name to Joe. The change was made official during a July 4th parade.

The story of Joe, Montana received national attention and spawned at least one imitator, as Troy, Texas changed its name to Troy Aikman, Texas.

With the help of the radio station and the real Joe Montana's shoe company (L.A. Gear), 22 citizens of Joe, Montana visited

Kansas City for the Chiefs game against the Cincinnati Bengals in October. The trip included a meeting with their slightly embarrassed namesake.

In fact, Montana remains uncomfortable with most of the adulation that comes his way. It has brought him a lot of money over the years in endorsements and opportunities, but those riches do not seem to have gone to his head regarding the attention he receives.

"I don't play the game for those things (endorsements and notoriety)," Montana said. "But I know that I am in a position where people are interested, where kids look up to me, and I take that seriously. I can't satisfy everyone. I'd love to take care of all the kids, but that's not possible, either."

Montana tries. When approached politely and without a large number of people lurking in the background, Montana will sign autographs. He has learned the art of signing as he walks; if he were to stand still and autograph items, it would cause mass commotion. He will not sign when he's with his family. Several years ago, he was with his kids at Disneyland and stopped to sign an autograph. Within seconds, his oldest daughter disappeared into a crowd of people, causing Montana moments of panic before she was found.

Montana has a contract with the Upper Deck Company for his signature. When the Upper Deck Authenticated catalog comes out several times each year, it has a two-page spread on Montana memorabilia. An NFL football autographed by Montana sells for $229. An autographed Chiefs or 49ers jersey sells for $289. An autographed Chiefs or 49ers helmet fetches $389. Combine the football, jersey and helmet into one 41"x48"x6. 5" framed display for an everyday low price of $1,199.

Along with Hanes, L.A. Gear and Upper Deck, Montana has an endorsement contract with Sega. During the football season, Tuesdays are usually the players' day off. But one Tuesday, Montana spent most of the day at Arrowhead Stadium, filming a commercial for Sega. His few public appearances — like the visit to the Venture store — came as part of one of his endorsement contracts.

Overwhelmed by requests from charities, Montana limits his active involvement to those such as the Make A Wish Foundation, a group that helps children facing terminal illness.

And when he does help out, usually it is done with a request of anonymity. When the Chiefs were at training camp in River Falls, the lower Midwest suffered through a month of severe flooding. Entire communities along the Missouri River near Kansas City were wiped out. Damage totals reached into the billions of dollars. One day, general manager Carl Peterson asked the players to make a donation to a flood relief fund. By the time they were done, the players collected $30,000, which was promptly matched by the Chiefs organization for a total of $60,000. Montana's part of the donation was $10,000.

The day after the Chiefs' regular-season finale at Arrowhead Stadium, Joe and Jennifer Montana visited Children's Mercy Hospital in Kansas City. There was no fanfare, no publicity release, no television or newspaper reporters to record the moment. No one outside the hospital would have known about the visit, if it had not been for a letter to the editor that appeared several weeks later in the *Kansas City Star*. Marilyn Miller of Lee's Summit wrote:

"My child was one of the children Mr. and Mrs. Montana visited and I know he will never forget it. For days afterward, many otherwise distraught parents had something besides their children's illnesses to talk about."

The amount of mail Montana receives is overwhelming, and it takes a team of people in Kansas City, San Francisco and Cleveland to handle the crush. Letters addressed to him and sent to Arrowhead Stadium are separated from the rest of the Chiefs mail, and every two days or so, they are boxed up and sent to San Francisco. There, a woman hired by Montana does her best to answer each and every letter.

Each box of Montana mail sent from Arrowhead holds approximately 400 letters. At least three boxes a week leave the stadium for California. In a month, that is almost 5,000 letters. And that does not include letters meant for Montana, but are addressed simply to "The Kansas City Chiefs." That's another two or three hundred a week. Packages sent to Arrowhead are not even opened; they immediately are returned to the sender. In all, the Chiefs' mail tripled with the arrival of Joe Montana.

The letters are not just from Kansas City and San Francisco; they are from all over the country. Most are from children seeking advice, an autograph or just some connection with the man they see on television. A random reach into a mail bag produced a wide-range of requests, including the following:

From Glen Cove, New York: ". . . I saw you last night on Monday night football. You played a good game. How did it feel when you had that standing ovation? . . . I play junior high school football. I think I am the starting quarterback . . . when you were a kid did you practice a lot? How old were you when you new (sic) you wanted to play professionally? Do you have any advice for me that I could use to make me a better football player?"

From Provo, Utah: "My 11 year old son Shane . . . has several hundred Joe Montana football cards. The happiest day of his life and yours too was when you came back to play after your long recovery . . . you have been an inspiration to all of us."

From Lee's Summit, Missouri: "I am writing this letter because I am your best fan and I am in the fifth grade and I am ten years old and I am writing a letter to you for homework."

From Hacienda Heights, California: "I am your fan, I am eight years old, I want to be like you."

From Madison Heights, Virginia: "How old are you? Are you married? Do you have any kids? I know I ask a lot of questions, but I am your biggest fan. I am 12 years old. I like the way you play."

The incredible demands on Montana created extra work and headaches for the entire organization. In a little more than six months — from July 19, 1993 through January 31, 1994 — the Chiefs public relations department handled:

• 22,906 phone calls. In 1992, the PR department handled around 23,000 calls over 12 months.

• 3,974 donation requests.

• 4,558 phone calls on player appearances.

• 1,491 interviews in person or by phone.

Everyone wanted a piece of Montana, most especially the media. It started in training camp, and by the time the 1993 season hit the midway point, just about every network in the country had requested an interview with Montana: ABC, NBC, CBS, CNN, ESPN, ESPN2, CNBC, MTV, A&E, TNT, WTBS, HBO. Throw in the international requests from networks in England, Japan and Germany, and it seems that only the Weather Channel was not interested in an interview. One Japanese network arrived at training camp and requested an hour of Montana's time for a one-on-one interview. They got 10 minutes, along with all the other television stations in River Falls that afternoon.

Montana's time with the media was managed by the Chiefs public relations department. They tried to handle as many of the requests as possible, without overwhelming Montana, taking away from his time for preparation. During training camp, Montana spoke to the media at least once a day. During the season, Montana spoke at least once a week, sometimes more.

Several times, Montana turned down interview requests from networks simply because he was tired of talking and was sensitive to the possibility of overexposure. Twice, he refused requests from ABC-TV to tape interviews before Monday Night football broadcasts. That sent ABC producers into apoplexy, and they called Carl Peterson, Lamar Hunt, Montana's agent — anyone they thought could change Montana's mind. Eventually, the quarterback gave brief interviews to the network.

Chiefs training camp had never seen so much media, coming from . . . everywhere. TV stations and newspapers in the San Francisco Bay area were early visitors. Writers from Los Angeles, San Diego, Dallas, Chicago, Boston, Phoenix, Atlanta, New York, Washington and Philadelphia all made stops. Throughout the season, the Chiefs had so many requests for credentials to home games that some of the smaller Kansas City media outlets could not get into the jammed press box.

Sometimes the requests from fans, media, even people in the NFL turned toward the bizarre and ridiculous:

• In September, the Chiefs public relations department fielded a call from a widow, whose husband recently had passed away. She said her late husband was a big Montana fan, and she wanted Montana to autograph the urn that held her husband's ashes.

• At least four different times during the season, NFL game officials — yes, the guys in the striped shirts who officiate the game — asked Chiefs personnel if they could take articles to Montana to be autographed. Opposing players did the same, sending footballs and jerseys through other stadium personnel.

• Requests for personal appearances included everything from a school breakfast in Wichita to a church's chili supper in central Missouri.

• When the Chiefs opened their preseason schedule in Milwaukee with a game against the Green Bay Packers, Montana did not play. Before the game, a fan walked out of the stands at County Stadium and into the Chiefs' warm-up drills, where he asked Montana to sign a Chiefs helmet.

• When Montana was injured, the Chiefs' phones rang early and often with calls from fans and bettors checking on his status. There were also many calls with home-made remedies for his maladies.

"I can't tell you how many messages and letters I received from fans that knew exactly how to cure Joe's hamstring and wrist," said Carl Peterson. "I didn't realize there were so many home remedies for a pulled hamstring."

If there was jealousy among his teammates from all this attention, it remained hidden. In fact, as the season wore on, more and more Chiefs marveled at the way Montana handled the whole situation.

"There are so many people that ask so much of him," said tight end Jonathan Hayes. "And he still responds in a great manner. He never acts offended. He tries to do as much as he can. The guy is a class act all the way around."

CHAPTER EIGHTEEN

CARRYING THE TORCH TO A DIVISION TITLE

On Sunday, December 5, the Kansas City Chiefs soundly defeated the Seattle Seahawks in the Kingdome, 31-16. As the players walked off the field, they stopped to watch the closing moments of the Denver-San Diego game on the stadium's giant television screen. A late field goal gave the Chargers the victory.

At the end of that day's National Football League action, the Chiefs held a two-game lead in the AFC Western Division with just four games left on the schedule. As the 1993 season headed down the home stretch, the Chiefs were positioned perfectly for a drive to the division title, something that had eluded the franchise since 1971.

In the Chiefs' victory over Seattle, Marcus Allen scored three touchdowns, giving him a total of 13 for the season. Allen dazzled the Seahawks with his final touchdown, a twisting 30-yard run to the end zone that proved beyond any doubt he still possessed the necessary moves, speed and ability to star in the NFL.

If there was one player who should have been excited in the postgame locker room, it was Marcus Allen.

But as he stood before the media, buttoning his shirt and preparing to talk about the victory and his performance, Allen was not smiling or laughing. The interview session began, and Allen answered the questions in a voice just above a monotone. His replies were matter-of-fact and did not show any sense of vindication, contentment or celebration. Watching Allen, it was impossible to tell if his team won or lost the game.

As he walked back to the locker room to grab his bag and head for the team bus, Allen was asked: "Marcus, why not a little emotion? This was a big day for you and this team. Aren't you happy?"

Marcus Allen cocked his head and yelled over his shoulder: "We've got four more games to play."

A few days later, that story was told to Marty Schottenheimer. The Chiefs head coach could not suppress his grin.

"That's why Marcus Allen is here," Schottenheimer said.

Level headed, focused, dedicated to the team — those are the qualities Marcus Allen displayed throughout the 1993 season. That's why his teammates voted him the team's Most Valuable Player award in an election that gave new definition to the term "landslide." He scored 15 touchdowns during the regular season and three more in the playoffs. Allen led the team in rushing with 764 yards.

But those numbers tell only a small part of the Marcus Allen story. Schottenheimer explains the rest.

"At the end of the (1993) season, I met with every player individually," Schottenheimer said, "and it was remarkable how many of them mentioned Marcus Allen in their comments about the season. It was 15 or 20 different players who talked about the effect Marcus had on the locker room and the team."

Like Marcus Allen, Carl Peterson is a man who chooses his words very carefully. Hyperbole is not his nature. A person could grow old waiting for the Chiefs general manager to make an outlandish statement. His thoughts are always well-measured before they are revealed. But when Peterson talks about the leadership efforts of Marcus Allen and Joe Montana during the Chiefs' 1993 season, the words tumble out quickly, like a mountain brook in the warm sunshine of spring.

"The best part of what those guys brought to us came in the locker room, in the classroom and off the field," Peterson said. "I would have paid them their entire 1993 salaries just for that, even if they had never set foot on the field.

"That's a big statement, I know," Peterson admitted. "But I really mean that. What they brought to our team on the field was obvious. The extras are what made the biggest difference."

There were concerns before the season started about mixing two big names like Marcus Allen and Joe Montana into the Chiefs' locker room. How would it affect team chemistry? Would these guys be accepted immediately? Would there be resentment over the attention given to them? How would Allen and Montana handle the situation? Would they be aloof or approachable?

The concerns were unnecessary. Allen and Montana blended seamlessly into the Chiefs' locker room. Neither was aloof. Neither spent a lot of time thumping their chests. They did not chase the torch of leadership; Allen and Montana simply went about their business. In due course, the torch was handed to them by their new teammates.

"They brought to us what we lacked the year before," said Peterson. "These guys stepped in from two different organizations and made a big contribution in molding our team. You wonder how much of a leader a player can be in his first year, without getting up on their stools in the locker room and beating their chests, shouting 'I'm Marcus Allen. I'm Joe Montana.'

"They did it their own ways. They are two very different guys. But you talk about respect. It's like those old E.F. Hutton commercials; when Joe and Marcus talked, people listened."

Leadership is frequently a misunderstood concept when it comes to the world of athletics. The average fan sees an outgoing player — one who is vocal with the media — and figures he must be a team leader. Everyone expects the best players on a team to be locker room leaders as well. Hollywood has created an impression that successful sports teams thrive on emotional speeches every week from players who roam the locker room with fire in their eyes and brimstone in their words.

The leadership process is not nearly as melodramatic as the movies would like us to believe. The loudest voice in the locker room frequently does not always have the most listeners. The best athletes are sometimes ill-equipped for the mantle of leadership.

Real leadership on a football team does not come in pregame speeches and loud exhortations during halftime. Real leadership comes in the not-so-sexy, ho-hum handling of everyday life.

Like Marcus Allen.

"A lot of people don't realize what a student of the game Marcus Allen is," said Peterson. "Marcus Allen knows the blocking assignments for every one of our running plays. He knows what the offensive linemen are supposed to do. He studies the opponents. The hours in the classroom are things the fans can't see.

"But his teammates do. They see. If that doesn't have an influence on you as a player, then you are a hopeless case. If Marcus Allen is spending extra time looking at film, then why aren't you?"

Teammates did notice. Kimble Anders is a man of few words. Ask him about Marcus Allen, and Anders cannot talk fast enough.

"I just watch him and try to learn," said Anders. "It's the way he approaches everything: practice, preparation, before the game, during the week, during the game. I always thought Marcus made everything look easy. Now I know why—because he works so hard."

Sometimes Allen does more than just lead by example. There are times when he feels compelled to speak his piece, as he did during a training camp meeting when he told the Chiefs that "scared men can't win." And sometimes his words come in private conversations with teammates. Cornerback Dale Carter was walking through the locker room after practice one day when he yelled to another player, "Hey nigger, you ready to go?" Carter said this right in front of Allen's locker. It may not be politically or morally correct, but nigger is a word sometimes used between black teammates in locker room banter. No offense is meant and none is taken. The only problem is the continuation of one of the most hateful words in the English language.

"Why do you use that word?" Allen asked Carter.

"What word?" Carter said, a quizzical look on his face.

"Nigger," Allen replied. "Why do you use that word?"

Carter was suddenly silent and looked very uncomfortable. Allen got up, put his arm around Carter's shoulder and walked him to the quiet of the trainer's room, out of earshot. What followed was not a lecture; there was no finger-wagging under Carter's nose or a raised voice. It was simply the case of Marcus Allen trying to impress upon Dale Carter how dreadful his choice of words had been.

"I don't do a lot of talking," said Allen. "I try to lead by example. I think the game is a great game and it's a lot of fun. But this is a great platform to really challenge yourself and see what you are or what you want to become.

"I think you become what you expect to become, and I expect great things."

Allen may not do a lot of talking, but compared with Joe Montana, he is positively loquacious. Speeches from Montana are few and far between. His leadership talents come not from words, but deeds, recalling the words of Napoleon Bonaparte:

"A leader is a dealer in hope."

Hope is what Joe Montana is all about.

"With Joe, you see the effect of his presence on the field in San Diego, against Pittsburgh in the playoffs, and down in Houston in the playoffs," said Schottenheimer. "This team developed an attitude that was different than it had in the past; there was a belief that it could overcome anything. I think you can chalk that up to a maturing process through the team. But I think most of the credit has to go to Joe Montana. His teammates believed in him."

Montana's physical skills have eroded somewhat, but that has not depleted his other abilities. His important qualities—the coolness under fire, the refusal to be ruffled by a bad start, his ability to concentrate on the task at hand—were vital ingredients in the chemistry of the 1993 Chiefs.

"When he talks, you had better listen closely because nine times out of 10, when he tells you something, later on he's going to do it in a game," said wide receiver Willie Davis. "So, we were always asking questions to make sure we understood exactly what he was saying. And no matter what was happening on the field or how things had gone, he always left you feeling like everything was about to fall into place."

Montana went out of his way to make sure the chemistry was right with Dave Krieg. Right after the trade was made, Montana and Krieg played a round of golf together and talked about the situation. Montana wanted to ward off another feud like the one that developed with Steve Young in San Francisco.

"I respect the things that he has done and accomplished and overcome," Montana said of Krieg. "I had a long talk with him and I said, 'Hey, if things don't work out, the last thing I want is an adversarial relationship.' I tell you, if he plays before me, or if I get hurt and he plays and he is playing great, then I'm all behind him. It's a completely different situation than the one I left in San Francisco, and that's what I wanted him to know. That conversation really helped us understand each other a little more."

That rapport between Montana and Krieg became one of the key elements of the season because it allowed the offense to develop at a faster pace. Let offensive coordinator Paul Hackett explain:

"The way Joe has always operated is that he takes the lead from whoever is coaching him, and then he puts his stamp on the offense. So I would lead the discussion, and that would draw Joe into talking about situations and plays.

"But with David Krieg around, we had a guy that was always questioning. David is always willing to say, 'Hey that doesn't seem quite right' or 'That doesn't make sense.' Here was a guy who was thirsty as hell for information about this offense. And that was beautiful because it stimulated Joe's thinking. That got Joe and David to a place where they were communicating together on this offense.

"On game day, the conversations those two had were great. That really put some teeth into what we were trying to do."

Montana and Allen share the distinction of being Super Bowl most valuable players. One day they will share space in the Pro Football Hall of Fame. But in the Chiefs' locker room, they are as different as night and day. Willie Davis explains:

"With Joe, you can't turn your back on him because he's liable to smack you in the back of the head. Joe will wad up a ball of tape and fling that thing at you, and then duck out of sight so fast, you can't figure out where it came from. He'll walk through the locker room and reach in and grab somebody's clothes and just throw them around a little bit. He'll sit there eating a banana and he'll throw the peel over his shoulder and into his locker. Sometimes it will sit in there all day. It would sit there for weeks if the equipment guys didn't come along and pick up after him. You have no idea that this guy is a Hall of Fame quarterback, maybe the greatest who has ever played the game.

"Joe came in, and he relaxed everybody right from the start. The media and the fans were the ones that hyped him up. He came in and showed everybody, 'This is how I am. I'm Joe Montana, but I'm not arrogant. I'm not just here to play on Sunday, and I don't not want to talk with you because I'm some superstar.' Everybody just took to him.

"Now Marcus, it was a little different. One time Marcus is playing and joking around, and the next time he's sort of aloof and real serious. Once you get to know him, you find out that's just the way Marcus is.

"He's a lot more meticulous than Joe. Marcus won't let you eat any food in front of his locker. He'll chase you away. He'll tell you, 'Get away from here with that food. Get those crumbs out of here.' With Marcus everything is always in its place."

With Allen and Montana came a more mature Chiefs attitude. After having problems with team chemistry in 1992, the mix at Arrowhead was much more productive in 1993.

"There were too many outside influences that were affecting this ball club last year (1992)," said tight end Jonathan Hayes. "There were some players that were unhappy. But then they made some changes. The addition of Joe and Marcus really made a difference. For the guys that have been here for awhile, it adds stability. For the younger players who need stability, there are guys like myself, John Alt, Albert Lewis, Kevin Ross, guys who have been here through the bad times. We can say, 'Hey guys, we have been here when it hasn't been fun, and we don't want to go back to that.'

"I think all that combined made for good chemistry."

There has been a shortage of leadership in the Chiefs' locker room, dating back to the retirement of the great players from the Chiefs' glory teams of the late 1960s.

Any conversation with members of the Chiefs' Super Bowl teams from 1966 and 1969 will include mention of the strong veteran leadership on those squads. Ask one of those Chiefs players for the names of their leaders, and they likely will rattle off a dozen names without taking a breath: Len Dawson, Ed Podolak, E.J. Holub, Jerry Mays, Johnny Robinson, Willie Lanier, Bobby Bell, Buck Buchanan, Jim Lynch, Fred Arbanas, Ed Budde, Emmitt Thomas.

"There were a lot of stand-up guys on those teams," said Holub, considered by many to be the No. 1 stand-up guy in Chiefs history. "What I mean by that is, they were guys who laid it on the line every Sunday. There were guys that did what was necessary to win the football game. They sacrificed for their teammates. We were a family. That sounds corny to people who do not understand what athletics is about, but we were a family.

We fought among ourselves, but you had better not pick on one of our guys, because then you had the whole team breathing down your neck."

In 1971, E.J. Holub passed the torch of leadership to a young offensive lineman named Jack Rudnay, who went on to play 13 distinguished seasons with the Chiefs. Rudnay was the 1994 inductee into the Chiefs Hall of Fame.

The problem for the Chiefs came when there was no one to receive the torch from Dawson, Podolak, Buchanan, et. al. The poor drafting by Hank Stram left the cupboard bare. Those great leaders retired, and with them went the legacy of what it takes to win a championship.

During the dry years around Arrowhead Stadium, Chiefs players found all sorts of excuses for losing games. They blamed the front office, the head coach, the coaching staff, the media, the fans — even, at times, their own teammates. Show me a team with a lot of excuses, and I will show you a team with a lot of losses.

Each and every NFL season does not follow a perfect script. Things go wrong, players are injured, bounces go the other way, outside influences intrude. The teams that learn how to deal with those distractions are the teams that make the playoffs and win championships.

In 1993, the Chiefs learned how to be one of those teams. There were plenty of problems during the season — the type that could have been used as excuses:

• Struggles with the new offense.

• The injuries suffered by Joe Montana.

• Possible resentment of all the attention given Montana and Marcus Allen.

• The *Kansas City Star* story detailing the legal problems of some Chiefs players.

Late in December, the NFL established a deadline for signing players to contract extensions. With the salary cap starting in 1994, teams could extend contracts before December 23, and part of any signing bonus would not be counted against the cap. Several teams signed some big-money players before the deadline.

Other teams made no attempt to sign any players, and that caused some locker room dissension. The Pittsburgh Steelers, for instance, did a lot of public complaining when management did not sign several top players who were scheduled to become free agents.

The Chiefs had more than 15 players who were scheduled to become free agents in 1994. They made offers to several players, but could not get anyone signed before the deadline. Yet, there was not a peep in the locker room. Highly vocal players like Albert Lewis and Kevin Ross were headed for free agency and wanted contract extensions. But they did not say anything during the season about the situation.

"I think everybody checked their egos at the door," Jonathan Hayes said of the 1993 Chiefs. "Everybody just went about their business. That's maturity. That's understanding what is important. Anytime in life, you are going to have distractions. It comes down to how you let those distractions affect your life.

"I think (in 1993) for a change, we did not make the distractions a major part of what was going on around here. An attitude developed that, 'There is nothing you can do about it now, so we'll worry about it later.' I think that helped this team a lot."

Said Willie Davis:

"Number one, everybody looked at it like this: 'If we get everything going, nobody in the league can beat us. If Joe stays healthy, and everybody on offense and defense stays healthy, there isn't anybody that can beat us.'

"I think the guys with the contracts just said, 'Hey, either they are going to get something done, or they are not. If not, then we'll go somewhere else and play next year.' But that's next year. You are getting paid for this year and if you have a good year, then it improves your chances of getting a better deal next year. To go around moping about them not signing you to an extension or a new contract doesn't do you any good. It doesn't get you a new contract and, if it affects your play, it hurts you next year, too.

"In the past, I don't think they thought they could go all the way with the teams they had. So they were looking for something to blame everything on — distractions. This team (1993) was fighting to get somewhere."

Ask members of the 1993 Chiefs the names of team leaders beyond Allen and Montana, and the name mentioned most often is Hayes.

"With Jonathan, it isn't so much what he does, but what he doesn't do," Willie Davis said. "You never see Jon go out and get into trouble. He's the kind of guy that you would move all the rookies into his house and say, 'This is how you live, this is how you take care of yourself, this is how you live in the community, this is how you play the game.'

"Jonathan goes out and practices hard every day, day after day. He doesn't like practice any more than the rest of us do, but he's always out there. I can't tell you the last time he missed a practice."

It was the kind of example that sent the Chiefs off to Minneapolis on Christmas evening with a chance to win a division title for the first time in 22 years. Kansas City was 10-4. Denver and Los Angeles were both 9-5. The Chiefs held a tie-breaker advantage on both the Broncos (they had a better division record) and the Raiders (they beat them twice during the season). With just two games to play, a Chiefs victory in a Sunday night game against the Vikings would give them first place in the AFC West.

Sub-zero temperatures were made even colder by a howling wind which whipped around the Metrodome. As the players sat in their hotel rooms, the Raiders were losing to the Green Bay Packers in an early game. The Broncos were hosting the Tampa Bay Buccaneers in what should have been an easy Denver victory.

But the Broncos stumbled, losing to the Bucs. Combine that outcome with the Raiders loss, and suddenly, forty-five minutes before kickoff against the Vikings, the Chiefs had clinched the AFC Western Division title.

And then the Chiefs went out and ruined the moment, as Minnesota handed them an embarrassing 30-10 defeat. Every aspect of the team fell apart in this game. The offense turned the ball over three times, including a pair of interceptions thrown by Montana. Defensively, the Chiefs could not stop Vikings' running back Scottie Graham, who gained 166 yards on 33 carries. Minnesota wide receiver Chris Carter caught a pair of touchdown catches, beating Dale Carter on both plays.

As division champs, the Chiefs played their worst game of the year.

"I don't know what happened," center Tim Grunhard said afterwards. "Most of us knew we had clinched the division; some guys were talking about it in the locker room. But I don't think you can blame that as the reason we played so poorly."

Montana said: "Fortunately, we didn't have to win. But you hate to play a game like that any time. This was probably the worst game since I've been here."

Schottenheimer called it "humiliating." He was especially distressed because there was really no chance to celebrate the AFC West title.

"This team, this organization deserved a celebration," Schottenheimer said. "After 22 years of chasing this thing, and everything that has happened to this team and the fans of this team, everyone deserved a chance to yell, scream and jump up and down. But we blew it."

There were real concerns in the Chiefs camp after the loss to Minnesota, especially with the defense against the run. Through the first six games, opponents averaged just 64.5 rushing yards per game. Over the last 10 games of the regular season, the Chiefs defense gave up an average of 123 rushing yards per game.

The problems began in Game No. 6, when free safety David Whitmore suffered a season-ending knee injury. At that point, Whitmore was the leading tackler on the Chiefs defense. In the next game, Charles Mincy stepped into Whitmore's starting spot, and the Miami Dolphins ran for 139 yards as the Chiefs were slapped with a 30-10 defeat.

The next week, Schottenheimer decided to make major changes in his defense. Mincy and strong safety Doug Terry were benched. Cornerback Kevin Ross was moved from cornerback to free safety. Dale Carter stepped into Ross' spot at cornerback and Martin Bayless became the starter at strong safety. It was the second straight year that major changes were made to the defense at mid-season.

Derrick Thomas was having problems as well. Although his overall play improved at defensive end, Thomas was not getting the quarterback sacks as frequently as he had over his career. He ended up with more quarterback pressures in 1993 (47) than the season before (27), but with nearly six fewer sacks.

When the Chiefs returned home from Minneapolis in the wee hours of Monday morning, there was no one at Kansas City International Airport to greet them. No screaming fans, no bands playing music, no television cameras recording the moment.

The Kansas City Chiefs were 1993 AFC Western Division champions. But as they drove home through the frigid night, no one felt like celebrating.

CHAPTER NINETEEN

AT THE MOVIES WITH ALBERT LEWIS

It is early in the evening on Friday, December 31, and around the Kansas City area, celebrations of the new year are already underway. In the Westport section of the city, linebacker Derrick Thomas is throwing himself a birthday party. When the clock strikes midnight, he will turn 27, and Thomas invited all of his teammates to celebrate with him at a private bash.

But in a quiet Overland Park neighborhood, there are no celebrations for the first moments of 1994 in Albert Lewis' house. And there will be no trips made to any parties, either.

On New Year's Eve, Albert Lewis is sitting in his living room, preparing for the Seattle Seahawks, the Chiefs' next opponent.

"Maybe when I was younger, I might have gone out," Lewis said, a slight smile creasing his face. "Don't get me wrong; it's not like I never go out now. Maybe on Monday or Tuesday. But man, I'm too old to be going out on a Friday night before a game.

"Those young guys think they will play forever. I know there aren't that many more seasons left for me."

In the real world, Albert Lewis was 33 years old during the 1993 National Football League season—not even halfway through his life, according to the projections of normal life expectancy. But in the world of professional football, Albert Lewis is consid-

ered ancient, especially because of the position he plays —
cornerback. There are not many men who can play the corner
with skill after the age of 30. Those who do, survive on remarkable skills and qualities.

Albert Lewis is a gifted athlete. Even as one of the Chiefs'
oldest players, Lewis might be in the best physical condition of
anyone on the roster. Watch him run, and the image is of a horse
— a thoroughbred. There does not appear to be an ounce of fat
on his body. His muscles are lean, long and explosive. Pound-
for-pound, he's probably one of the strongest players in the
league. In a race against a stopwatch, he is fast. Put him on the
field covering a wide receiver, and his speed becomes world
class.

But his skills are not just physical. Lewis has the other
assets necessary — dedication, intelligence and fortitude — to
still be playing the cornerback position.

"He is playing excellent, excellent football," Marty
Schottenheimer said near the end of the 1993 season. "There has
been no drop-off in the play of Albert Lewis from the first day we
came here as a coaching staff in 1989. If anything, he's playing
better.

"In my mind, Albert Lewis is the complete player. He has
great range and great skills for man-to-man coverage. Seldom,
if ever, does he have a mental error. I can't remember the last one
he had."

Lewis' mental errors are few and far between because on
New Year's Eve, he is not thinking about a party. He is sitting at
home, preparing for his next opponent, viewing the same tape of
Seahawks games that he watched the day before, and the day
before that, trying to detect a flaw, a pattern, a foible in his
opponent.

"Studying gives you an opportunity to dissect," Lewis said.
"No matter what aspect of the game you are studying — whether
it is another team's offense or the techniques of a receiver — it
gives you the opportunity to break it down. I think that's the way
you build a defensive plan."

Lewis' home is part of an upper-middle class neighborhood not far from Johnson County Community College. There
is no indication from the street that a professional football player
lives inside; this is not some huge mansion that screeches, "I am
a celebrity."

The interior is decorated in white and black. The baby grand piano is white. The leather wraparound sofa in the television room is black. The walls are white. The decorations are white and black.

The color scheme does not come as a surprise. The world of a cornerback is always black or white. On the corner, there is no grey; it is feast or famine on every single play. When a cornerback makes a mistake, the whole stadium knows about it because his man is usually running towards the end zone. Along the crush of the line of scrimmage, a mistake won't be noticed by the untrained eye. With cornerbacks — where everything happens out in the open — one does not have to be Vince Lombardi to recognize a badly-beaten defender.

That is why cornerback is the hardest position to play in professional football. A cornerback must have physical skills (speed, quickness, strength) and mental prowess (intelligence, intuition and memory), but he also must have an attitude about him. A cornerback must be able to forget the personal victories and defeats that make up every game. There is no celebrating a job well done at cornerback, and no time to get down in the dumps over a mistake. There is only time for the next play.

And that's the other thing about being a cornerback: he can do everything right, use proper techniques, anticipate the play and have great coverage on the receiver . . . and still be beaten for a touchdown.

"A cornerback is on an island, and he's all by himself," Lewis said. "There aren't too many jobs where you can do everything exactly the way it is supposed to be done and still fail. On the corner, it happens all the time."

Few have recently played cornerback as well as Lewis did in the prime of his career. In Schottenheimer's mind, Lewis is one of the best ever at the position.

"With all due respect to a Hall of Famer Mel Blount, in my view Albert Lewis is a better corner than Mel Blount," Schottenheimer said. "He does all the things that Mel did, plus plays man-to-man coverage and covers them everywhere they go. And I'm a big Mel Blount fan.

"He (Lewis) is clearly one of the three best defensive players I've ever been around."

Lewis learned plenty about the pitfalls of playing cornerback in the NFL as a rookie in 1983. The Chiefs had some veteran defensive backs at the time who helped him through the shock; guys like Gary Green, Deron Cherry and Lloyd Burruss. At the time, all three were considered Pro Bowl talents.

"There isn't a whole lot that happens in college football that prepares you to play this position in the NFL," Lewis said of cornerback. "No matter what skills you bring to the game, you have to start from scratch."

And that means becoming a student of the game. When Lewis entered the NFL, games were still recorded on film. One of his first purchases as a rookie was his own projector. He learned that from the veterans.

"I never studied film individually in college, only what we studied as a team," Lewis said. "The first day in the NFL, it became obvious that film study was going to be necessary. When you're a rookie and in training camp, you see guys in the secondary studying more film — as the other guys rush out for a before-bed beer. You get the idea that film work is necessary.

"Then you start the season, and as a rookie, you see guys carrying home films. You find out every guy in the secondary on the team has his own projector. And the next day, they take more film home, and the next day even more. It happens every day and every week, and you learn very quickly that it is a vital part of the job."

In that first season with the Chiefs, Lewis joined a veteran group that had been together for several seasons. He had to study just to keep up with them.

"They did a tremendous amount of film study, but seldom as a group," said Lewis. "They studied as individuals. Whenever we did study as a group, it became so detailed that when we went back to doing it alone, we were all thinking on the same terms. It was pretty remarkable, actually. These guys would look at the film and all have the same thoughts. Sometimes they didn't even have to communicate them; they just understood how each other was going to react.

"Once you've reached that level — where everyone understands how a certain situation is going to be played — then I think it's more important to study alone so you can get your part of that down."

On Lewis' big-screen television on this New Year's Eve 1993, the Peach Bowl is being played at the Georgia Dome. The compact-disc player is also turned on, as songs by Toni Braxton and James Taylor fill the room. Lewis pops in a videotape of the last three games played by the Seattle Seahawks. The Peach Bowl disappears, and on the screen it's Seattle against Phoenix. Lewis starts dissecting the action.

"When you first start looking at tape, you're really studying yourself more than the other team," said Lewis. "You're trying to develop good habits. You are trying to see how you react to different situations, rather than individual receivers. Once you've got your game put together, then you can start studying opponents and figuring ways to handle them."

Against Seattle, Lewis spends most of his time covering the Seahawks' talented young receiver, Brian Blades. But as the tape begins, he does not watch Blades so much as he watches the Phoenix defense. He notices how the Cardinals handle different Seattle formations and translates that into what the Chiefs plan to do against the Seahawks.

"OK, a three-deep cover," says Lewis, speaking the language of defensive pass coverages. In this case, he's talking about a coverage with three safeties providing deep help. "Now, in our three backer, if both receivers run short patterns, I have the outside guy. If we are in three sky and they both run short patterns, I have the inside guy. If they crisscross, you just have to wait and see what happens. That's when it gets to be hairy, because you are making decisions on the move."

Lewis watches tape so he does not have to make decisions "on the move." He wants to make his decision on how to handle a situation on Friday, so that come game-time on Sunday, he can simply react.

One play rolls into another play on the tape, and occasionally Lewis will rewind, pause for a second or two, and then move on. He's watched this tape three times already this week. This night will make the fourth viewing. He'll watch it one more time on Saturday, maybe even on Sunday before the game.

"Now, in this type of coverage in our defense, my responsibility . . . you see No. 89 (Blades) there . . . when he comes back to the slot, I have to try to get a jam on him, knock him off stride and then get back out and cover No. 84," Lewis explains. "What I'm trying to do is disrupt him as much as I can, so they won't throw the quick pass. Then, I've got to make sure I get over to the other guy, so they can't dump it to him."

The untrained eye misses these little things, the stuff that Lewis soaks up quickly.

"OK, this is a zone, and the corner's responsibility is the deep third," said Lewis. "But he's guessing the receiver is going to run a stop route. And look, the corner squats right there, waiting for the receiver to stop, but the receiver goes right by him.

"Seattle runs a lot of stop routes, but if this corner had studied his film, he would know they always run their stops on the numbers (yard-line markers on the field). When the receiver lines up wide of the numbers, like he did, he's going to run a go or a deep comeback, not a stop route."

That's the kind of information the tape provides only to the seasoned viewer like Lewis. The tape is not from the television broadcast that fans can see every Sunday. It is a special coaching view of the game, so that all 22 players on the field are visible on the screen.

"Once you know what you're doing — and that takes five or six years — you see more and more things you never saw in the beginning," said Lewis. "When you start, you are looking at yourself and the player across from you. But that doesn't give you the whole perspective of the offense. You have to know what it does, how it does things and what it does in certain situations. Things like: what does the offense do when the quarterback is flushed from the pocket? What does the quarterback do under pressure? It takes some time before you look and see the whole field."

The tape now has rolled into a game between Seattle and Los Angeles, and Lewis has spotted something on the very first play, as a Raiders defensive back tackles a receiver from behind.

"Ok, they went away from their tendency and that's why the cornerback got caught," Lewis says."The only time Seattle throws to the left side of the field is when the defense is in a zone and the cornerback is playing off the line. Seattle is a strong-side passing team, but on this play, they threw to the weak side."

Earlier in the week of preparation, Lewis had spent an evening studying the tendencies of individual Seattle receivers, searching for clues that might make his job easier. Most of that time was spent looking at Blades.

"I study everything," said Lewis. "From where he lines up, to how he comes off the line, how he runs, what his body position was when he did this, and what his body position was when he did that.

"What does he have trouble with? How fast is he? If he is faster than me, then how fast can I let him get to me before I have to turn and run? I found the answers to all those questions.

"Sometimes you freeze the tape when they run a particular play, especially when you're playing against a real fast guy, because you can't let him get behind you. You look at the field, you see where the ball is thrown, when the ball is thrown and you try to develop the ability to play in your mind the angles, how long would it take for this ball to get from this point to that point. You look for the perfect position.

"That's not really something that coaches coach. They say, 'Take this away, give this up,' but I think all the great players — especially cornerbacks — try to find a spot on the field where they can put their body in a position so they can take away just about everything."

The doorbell rings, and Lewis gets up to welcome — not a friend looking for a New Year's Eve party — but his chiropractor, complete with portable table. For the last several days, Lewis has been bothered by soreness in his neck, and regular visits to the chiropractor are just part of his weekly routine.

"I've heard people say you can get addicted to chiropractors," Lewis says as his back is being adjusted. "I can believe it because it feels so good when they're finished."

At the NFL level, players seek any edge they can find. If it means having a chiropractor over to the house on New Year's Eve, then by all means, invite him and his portable table. Some players have their own masseurs who make house calls. Lewis has one. Others use acupuncture. Lewis hates needles. Some have their own psychologists.

"I haven't ever used a psychologist," Lewis said with a laugh. "I don't know why anybody would go to a psychologist for football — maybe other things, but not football. Coaches think they are psychologists themselves, so we've got plenty of those around.

"I guess the martial arts is the only psychological thing I've done. It has helped with mental toughness, concentration and confidence, especially during times of fatigue. When you get tired and start thinking about being tired, you are in trouble. But the martial arts have taught me you can get into a zone of total concentration when you're dog-tired, and overcome it. "

Injuries were a big part of the Albert Lewis story over the 1991-92-93 seasons, costing him 18 games in all. First, came a knee injury that ultimately required surgery, robbing him of eight games in the 1991 season. The next year, he suffered a broken right forearm and missed the final seven games.

And then in River Falls before the 1993 season, Lewis broke the same right forearm when it became tangled in the jersey of a running back he was trying to tackle. It wiped out his entire preseason, and Lewis missed the first three games of the regular season.

"In the big picture, it all probably helped me because I was on ice for about two seasons," Lewis said. "There wasn't so much wear and tear on my body."

The wear and tear on his psyche has been limited, too. Throughout 1993, Lewis displayed a demeanor of contentment, something that had been missing in recent seasons. Several years ago, he had a very public and loud contract squabble with Carl Peterson and asked to be traded. When he suffered his knee injury in 1991, Lewis had a public disagreement with the Chiefs over treatment by the team doctors. He was also one of several NFL players who attached their names to lawsuits against the league, seeking free agency.

In 1993, all that seemed distant history.

"I am content," Lewis said. "There have been situations and things that have been part of my life in the last few years, and they all seemed to resolve themselves. They all worked out.

"All a person can do is what he thinks is right at the time. We don't always do things the right way; we don't always say the right things, but the most important thing that you have to remember as a player is, how do you play the game? Everything else outside of football, whether it is contracts, politics or whatever it is, all that has to go out the window.

"My contentment comes from the fact that this organization has gone out and acquired good players and veteran players who have been there before. That helped me resolve some of the discontentment that I have had in the past."

After 20 minutes, the chiropractor's work is finished and Lewis turns his attention back to the television screen.

"The No. 1 thing I've got to do in this zone is jam Blades," Lewis says, as the Raiders and Seahawks battle it out on the tape. "The corner didn't hit him hard enough to move him off his line. I've got to get as much contact as I can, and then I've got to locate the next receiver."

After watching the tape for nearly an hour, some of the Seahawks' tendencies become obvious, and even an untrained observer is guessing correctly on whether the coming play is pass or run.

But Lewis never guesses.

"When I'm studying the film, 90 percent of the time I can guess correctly what the play will be," said Lewis. "But all players can do that. At cornerback, you never want to guess. It takes away from your spontaneity to react to whatever they do, because just when you think you've got it all figured out, they'll spring something on you. If you are guessing on the play, then you can get burned very badly.

"Sometimes it can be detrimental to know too much or think you know too much. It becomes the paralysis of analysis. Game day is not the time to do a lot of thinking. You have to react. You can't hesitate. On some of the big plays where I have just missed in my career, like the postseason game in Miami (a touchdown pass from Dan Marino to Mark Clayton where Lewis went for the interception and missed) . . . those have been plays where I hesitated mentally.

"That will get you every time."

Lewis has the highest regard for receivers who study as much film as he does.

"What increased my film study was playing against guys like Steve Largent and Charlie Joiner," says Lewis. "They played the game as a chess match. They didn't have the great speed, but they could set you up — with a little weave here, a little weave there, a cross-step there. Every time they came off the line, they were trying to make you think one thing, when they were preparing to do another thing.

"I was talking before about angles . . . those guys were trying to put themselves in the right angles, the right positions to make plays. I can tell you a perfect example. In my second year in the league, we played Seattle and I studied films of Largent on how he ran a particular route. It was a dig route; he would take off down the field, straighten you up and then break inside. What I tried to do was be very patient and wait. Every time Largent broke in, I was there. The quarterback never threw the ball, and he didn't catch that particular pass that day.

"Well, we played them out in Seattle a few weeks later. They ran the same play, the same way, with that same little move and I broke in, just like before. But this time the quarterback pumped him the ball, and then Largent broke back to the corner of the end zone — touchdown. I knew then that Steve Largent was watching just as much film of me as I was of him."

The Seahawks tape ends and the telecast of the Alamo Bowl pops up on the television screen. As a student of defense, Lewis can watch just about any game of football and pick out the defense.

"The colleges are easy because you know in a heartbeat what they are playing, who did something wrong, who didn't drop deep enough or get wide enough," Lewis says. "It gets frustrating because you sit there and you know what happened, and the commentator at the game will say something totally different. You are sitting there saying, 'No, that's not the way it happened, Stupid.'"

That's why Lewis seldom watches NFL games on television with the sound on. And he almost never watches network telecasts of Chiefs games. He made one exception during the 1993 season, watching the NBC broadcast of the Chiefs' December loss at Denver.

"Shannon Sharpe caught three touchdowns against us that day, and on the first one, we were in a man-to-man defense," said Lewis. "The commentator (Bob Trumpy) said Sharpe beat Doug Terry man-to-man. Well, I know he didn't beat Doug Terry because Sharpe was my man.

"What happened was this: we had this special call between me and Martin Bayless. It was based on the back and receiver on that side of the field and what they did on the play. The situation came up and I made the call. Martin heard the call, but because Martin didn't think we should have run the call, he didn't execute the call. Doug ended up taking Martin's place in the coverage and boom, he ends up with Sharpe.

"A couple days later, I'm sitting there watching the TV tape and I know that No. 1, it was my fault for making the call because

I never should have called it. No. 2, it was Martin's fault for not executing the call. Finally, No. 3, you get to Doug Terry, who got caught by our mistakes."

The first meeting in 1993 between the Chiefs and Seahawks was not one of Lewis' best performances. Blades caught seven passes for 134 yards that afternoon. Lewis and several of his teammates had trouble breathing in the Kingdome that afternoon. "I couldn't catch my breath all day," said Lewis. "Maybe it was from running after Blades."

Lewis waited until the day before the second game with Seattle before he looked at tape of the first meeting.

"It becomes more of a chess game when you play your division teams twice a year," he says. "You want to depend on the film from the previous game. If they have plays that were successful, you really have to pay attention and find a way to stop them. On the other hand, sometimes a team will come out and do just the opposite because they know you've been studying them. Sometimes they'll come out and change everything.

"When we played Seattle before, Marty (Schottenheimer) and I were watching film on the plane. I showed him this particular play. Now, in years past, they've been running bench routes with a motion receiver. Well, after looking at this film, I convinced myself they are going to change; they are not going to run a bench route with a motion receiver.

"In the game, the first opportunity, they motion a receiver and he ran a bench route just like they always do. But I had talked myself into something else, so I leaned this way, he went that way and they completed the pass.

"You know I think great players, the more they play become less of a big-play maker and become more consistent. They want to make sure of what they are seeing. Whereas, the feast or famine players, they are always reacting, bam, right there, right now. Sometimes they will make a great play and sometimes they will get beaten.

"Dale Carter is a prime example. He just reacts. There is no thinking there. Now that's not bad, if he can funnel it and control it. But if he can't, he'll have a lot of problems."

Lewis did not have any problems that Sunday in the rematch with Seattle. Blades caught five passes for 69 yards and was kept out of the end zone as the Chiefs finished the regular season with a fairly easy 34-24 victory.

"They caught us once (a 33-yard completion from Rick Mirer to Blades)," said Lewis. "I hate to see that happen. But we won, and we get to fight another day."

In this case "another day" meant the NFL playoffs.

CHAPTER TWENTY

MONTANA TIME

Something was very wrong inside Arrowhead Stadium.

Seventy-four thousand-plus fans were standing in the aisles, eyes fixed on the field below and they were barely making a sound. Only the shuffling of feet and chattering of teeth in the January chill could be heard. What is always an emotional cauldron during Chiefs games — with noise from the fans sometimes reaching the decibel level of a jet airplane's engine — was suddenly as quiet as a cathedral.

Joe Montana knew he was not in a place of worship, although sometimes it seemed as if the Chiefs fans were going through a religious experience on game day. And, there was that one guy who always came to the stadium with a sign that read "Joe Is Good", except that one "o" was crossed out so it read "Joe is God". But this was football and in Arrowhead that meant noise. As he walked towards the Chiefs' bench, unbuckling his chin strap and pulling off his helmet, Montana could not help but notice the silence.

"It was so quiet," Montana remembered. "I went over there and I did not have any trouble hearing what people were saying. I put on the headset and talked to Paul (Hackett), and he didn't have to yell.

"It was like the whole crowd was holding its breath."

There was 1 minute, 48 seconds remaining in the fourth quarter of a first-round National Football League playoffs game between the Chiefs and Pittsburgh Steelers. The Chiefs trailed by seven points and held possession of the football when Montana called Kansas City's final timeout. It was fourth down-and-goal at the Steelers' 7-yard line.

Actually, it was fourth down-and-the 1993 season for the Chiefs. After three weeks of training camp, four preseason and 16 regular season games, the football year had come down to a single moment. Either the Chiefs would score a touchdown and tie the Steelers, or their season would be finished, far short of the intended goal of an NFL championship.

Fear, doubt and worry populated the Arrowhead stands. Throughout the 1993 season, the Chiefs showed the ability to come from behind and win games. Certainly, there were few better in last-minute, pressure situations than Montana. But what happened on this frigid Saturday afternoon strained the limits of fan loyalty.

Start with the fact Pittsburgh was the final team to make the NFL playoffs in 1993, sneaking in with a final-game victory over Cleveland. The Steelers needed help from the Houston Oilers, who beat the New York Jets in a Sunday night game at the Astrodome that secured the last postseason berth for Bill Cowher's team. After a strong 11-5 record in 1992, Pittsburgh struggled to reach 9-7 in '93. The key to their offense was running back Barry Foster, and he missed the second half of the regular season with an ankle injury and was not available for the playoffs. Quarterback Neil O'Donnell battled a sore elbow all season that limited his passing range. On special teams, the Steelers were atrocious, giving up big play after big play and never contributing anything in return.

Yet, in the first week of the postseason, the Steelers held a 10-point halftime lead on the Chiefs, 17-7. As the home team walked off the field, a smattering of unhappiness was audible from the Arrowhead crowd. This was not the playoffs script everyone expected; most especially, they did not expect this with Joe Montana on the field.

Was the postseason not the time when Montana was supposed to shine? Had not many fans and members of the media theorized after the Chiefs made the trade with San Francisco, that Montana was nothing more than "postseason insurance"? Kansas City reached the playoffs with Steve DeBerg and Dave Krieg at quarterback for three seasons. Joe Montana could take them further, all the way to the Super Bowl.

It was MONTANA TIME.

"December and January have been months where Joe has performed at a higher level," said Chiefs offensive coordinator Paul Hackett. "He's always been at his best when the games mean the most and that's always late in the season and in the playoffs. That's something you have to have to win a championship."

It was MONTANA TIME.

"Hasn't everybody said from the beginning that if the Chiefs could just get to the playoffs and have Montana healthy, they'll make a run at the Super Bowl?" said Chiefs head coach Marty Schottenheimer.

Coach, do you agree?

"I've always felt that," said Schottenheimer. "The only chance you have of winning on the road in the playoffs is if you have a top quarterback. You've got to have somebody other teams fear.

"A guy like Joe Montana is feared."

Opponents fear Montana in the clutch. Why? Take one look at his performances in prime time; his record as a starting quarterback in January was 12-5, a .706 winning percentage. There are four Super Bowl victories with San Francisco. At one point the 49ers won seven consecutive playoff games over three seasons.

"That's what you play for, to keep playing," Montana said in the days before meeting Pittsburgh. "Sure, there are a lot of rewards for winning in the playoffs, but the thing I've always liked is that you get to keep playing. You see teams eliminated and they go home and they don't have anything to do.

"You want to keep playing until they tell you to go home."

With a championship?

"That's the best," Montana said with a smile.

As the Chiefs began their first postseason game of the Montana Era, they had a problem: Joe Montana. As a quarterback with a career completion percentage of more than 63 percent, Montana seldom had problems getting the ball to his receivers. Against Pittsburgh, however, Montana was throwing the ball like an unproven rookie who had never suffered the postseason pressures before.

Montana missed on his first *seven* throws against the Steelers. At no other point during the 1993 season did Montana throw seven straight incompletions. When it counted most, Montana was having trouble connecting with any of his receivers.

PASS No. 1: Montana was hit just as he threw by Steelers linebacker Kevin Greene and the ball fluttered incomplete, over the head of running back Marcus Allen and in front of tight end Jonathan Hayes (0 for 1).

PASS No. 2: One of Montana's strengths is his ability to "look off" defenders: he focuses on a certain point on the field or on an individual receiver and then at the last instant, turns his head and finds a receiver somewhere else on the field. Defensive backs are trained to watch the quarterback's eyes. By looking away from his intended receiver, a passer can fool the defense.

But on his second pass, Montana zeroed in on wide receiver J.J. Birden from the time Birden left the line of scrimmage. It made it very easy for cornerback Deion Figures to reach in and knock down the pass (0 for 2).

PASS No. 3: The key to the San Francisco/Bill Walsh/Joe Montana offense is dumping the ball off to the backs when the downfield receivers are covered. On the first play of the Chiefs' second possession, Allen was wide open on the left. But Montana badly overthrew the ball and Allen had no chance at making the catch (0 for 3).

PASS No. 4: Montana looked for Birden again and found him open on the right side, but his pass was underthrown (0 for 4).

PASS No. 5: On a third-down play, Montana dropped back to pass and found solid protection. He looked right and then left, throwing the ball towards Birden near the sidelines. But he threw the ball five yards short of where Birden had made his cut, and the pass sailed into the Steelers bench. Montana came off the field muttering to himself, brushing past Allen who tried to encourage him (0 for 5).

"I was hot, mad at myself," Montana said.

PASS No. 6: There was a change when Montana took the field for the Chiefs' third possession of the game. After practicing all week and then throwing his first five passes while wearing gloves, Montana was bare handed.

Montana never wore a glove on his passing hand before the Pittsburgh game. Few quarterbacks had ever been able to wear a glove and still throw the ball effectively. Jim McMahon seemed to be the only quarterback who had any success with a gloved passing hand. But McMahon always wears gloves, even when he plays indoors.

The week leading up to the Steelers-Chiefs game had been frigid in Kansas City. Actual temperatures were running in the single digits, with a wind chill factor around minus-20 degrees. Throughout the week, the Chiefs practiced indoors.

Even though he was inside, Montana started wearing gloves. These were not the gloves associated with winter weather, complete with rabbit-fur lining. These were ultra-light gloves, the type worn by wide receivers in football, hitters in baseball and golfers. Montana did not want the gloves to keep his hands warm.

"What happens in cold weather is your hands dry out," said Montana. "They get cold, dry and slick. Then the ball gets slick and you have trouble handling it. The gloves have little rubber strips on the fingers that make gripping the ball easier."

Montana may have been able to grip the ball better, but it did not help his throwing. After missing the first five throws, he left the gloves on the sidelines with equipment manager Mike Davidson. Yet, he was still not able to complete a pass, as his sixth throw of the game — this one to Birden — was high (0 for 6).

Pass No. 7: On the next play, Montana threw his best pass of the first quarter, but Willie Davis was not able to hold the ball (0 for 7).

Pass No. 8: Finally, success! It came on a third-down pass to Davis that gained 25 yards and a first down.

But after he released the ball, Montana was hit by Pittsburgh defensive lineman Donald Evans in the right side of his back. Evans lowered his head and drove his helmet into Montana's ribs. Although some opponents felt the officials protected Montana during the 1993 season, no penalty was called on Evans for his hit. Montana wobbled a bit as he got to his feet and then walked off the field.

Dave Krieg stepped in for Montana, and on his first play he handed off to Marcus Allen, who was stopped for a 2-yard loss. Away from the tackle, wide receiver Tim Barnett and Pittsburgh cornerback D.J. Johnson were battling. The Chiefs wide receivers are some of the most feared blockers in the NFL because they are constantly running downfield and throwing their bodies in front of defenders. On some teams, receivers block only occasionally; on the Chiefs, a receiver cannot get on the field if he does not block.

Barnett came down the field and dove at Johnson's legs. This type of block drives defensive backs crazy because they fear injury. Upset that Barnett had gone after his legs, Johnson kicked at the wide receiver's face. Only Barnett's face mask kept him from getting a mouthful of Johnson's shoe.

Johnson had a problem, however. He kicked Barnett with four officials watching. All four threw their flags, assessing Johnson with a 15-yard unnecessary roughness penalty. Then, referee Gary Lane stunned everyone when he ejected Johnson from the game. That set off Steelers coach Bill Cowher, who had to be restrained by some of his assistant coaches and players from going on the field and after the officials. It was a high price to pay for the Steelers.

"It was not a smart move," said Johnson. "I should not have kicked him. I don't feel like I should have been thrown out of the game, but I should not have lost my head."

While this mess was being straightened out, Montana was on the sidelines trying to get back on the field.

"After everything that had happened, I did not want to spend any time watching," said Montana. "I got it in the ribs and it took my breath away. They hurt, but that's something you can play with."

Montana just *had* to get back on the field. The quarterback who everyone thinks never gets nervous had to chase butterflies from his stomach before this game. Playing in the postseason meant everything to him:

—There were his own expectations; that was the reason he left San Francisco in the first place. Everyone thought his career was over. Under the microscope of the playoffs, Montana was intent on making sure everyone understood there was still something left in his battered body.

—There were the expectations of the Chiefs, who had come to see Montana as the last link in their Super Bowl puzzle. Although Montana fought that perception and took every opportunity to play it down with the media, he knew that was how he was viewed by the organization, fans and even his teammates.

—And in this first playoff game with the Chiefs, Montana was facing the Pittsburgh Steelers. Growing up in western Pennsylvania, he was a fan of the great Steelers teams of the 1970s. During his career he always seemed to have mixed emotions playing against Pittsburgh and it showed in his performances, as the 49ers won just two of the four games he started against his hometown team.

"I was so nervous," Montana said in the days after the Pittsburgh game. "I kind of got myself all balled up with the idea of the playoffs, the Steelers . . . I wanted to do so well. I wanted to come out and get us moving right off the bat, just take us right down the field, with that crowd roaring.

"I tried to be too perfect. I ended up putting us in a hole."

Montana did not dig the Chiefs' hole by himself. Pittsburgh reached the scoreboard first when O'Donnell found tight end Adrian Cooper wide open for a 10-yard touchdown pass. No Chiefs defender covered Cooper on the play, signalling yet another coverage breakdown, something that plagued the team all season. Another problem for the Chiefs secondary in 1993 was poor tackling. The big play that set up Cooper's touchdown was a 32-yard screen pass from O'Donnell to running back Merrill Hoge. Both safeties — Eric McMillan and Martin Bayless — had chances to tackle Hoge, but could not bring him down.

After the incident with D.J. Johnson, the Chiefs tied the score. Krieg's only pass in his four plays in relief of Montana was a pretty 23-yard scoring toss to Birden that burned Rod Woodson, the Pittsburgh cornerback. Woodson is notorious for his aggressive play and the Chiefs took advantage of that, as Krieg pump faked to Birden, who had made a move to the inside of the defensive coverage. Krieg's fake caused Woodson to stop backpedaling and move forward. When he did, Birden cut his pass route back to the outside, making a terrific catch as he had to go horizontal to the field and still keep his body in the end zone.

"It was a play we put in just for Woodson because we saw on the film that he was biting on those double moves," said Birden. "It was a slant and go. And just like we expected, he bit on the slant and then I turned it up. The only problem then was locating the ball."

Early in the second quarter, Pittsburgh added a 30-yard field goal by Gary Anderson to take a 10-7 lead. Aching ribs and all, Montana returned but his success was minimal. He completed two of his next four passes, but was sacked once and forced to scramble on another play. When the Chiefs gained possession with just less than 2:00 to play in the first half, Montana finally got hot, hitting three straight passes and moving the Chiefs to the Steelers' 42-yard line. But on a fourth-and-one play, Montana tripped over Allen's feet and fell to the turf. Ruled a sack, the play gave Pittsburgh possession near midfield with just 55 seconds to play.

O'Donnell only needed 37 seconds to add another Steelers score, as he found wide receiver Ernie Mills for a 26-yard touchdown. Mills broke a tackle by cornerback Jay Taylor and then spun away from a tackle attempt by safety Charles Mincy, sprinting into the end zone and stunning the Arrowhead crowd. Gary Anderson's PAT kick made the score 17-7.

"We spent most of the day doubling Eric Green, and that put our cornerbacks in some difficulty, because they did not have the inside help that is normally there," said Schottenheimer. "That caused us some early problems."

As the Chiefs left the field at half-time, there was a smattering of boos from the partisan crowd.

"We deserved the displeasure," said Hackett. "At times we looked brilliant, at other times we couldn't catch, we couldn't throw. Part of it was getting used to what Pittsburgh was doing. The Steelers are one of the best defensive teams in the NFL. There were a lot of things they were doing that we had to sort our way through.

"But there is no reason to miss those passes, whether it was the receiver, the quarterback or the protection."

The Chiefs defense was having its problems as well.

"We didn't play very well, we showed more heart than we did ability," said cornerback Albert Lewis. "We didn't tackle very well, we weren't very physical. We were trying to create some cohesiveness with some new people in the lineup. We had some holes to fill, but that's no excuse for poor tackling."

In the third quarter, the Chiefs closed the gap with a 23-yard field goal by Nick Lowery. They tied the score early in the fourth quarter on a 2-yard touchdown run by Marcus Allen. That made it 17-17 with just under 9 minutes left in the game.

The Steelers came right back and scored as O'Donnell threw his third touchdown pass of the day, this one for 22 yards to tight end Eric Green. The Chiefs went three plays and out on their next possession and with just three minutes to play, Pittsburgh had possession of the ball and a 7-point lead.

On first down, defensive end Darren Mickell stopped running back Leroy Thompson for a 4-yard loss. Thompson got those four yards back on the next play, but on third down, Jay Taylor knocked away a pass intended for wide receiver Jeff Graham, forcing the Steelers into a punting situation.

All season, the Chiefs tried to produce big plays on the special teams but were seldom successful. With time running out on the season, it was time to make something happen.

"We had gone after a punt earlier," said Marty Schottenheimer. "And Kurt (Schottenheimer) kept after me to try to block another one. As we got closer to the play, Kurt finally said, 'I have to know.' I told him to go for it."

The Steelers expected the rush and figured it would come from one of the best punt blockers in NFL history: Albert Lewis. As Lewis jockeyed along the line of scrimmage, he drew all the attention of the Pittsburgh blockers.

They barely noticed Keith Cash.

"Everybody was keying on Albert, because everybody knows how good a punt blocker he is," said Cash. "Everybody went to Albert. He went inside and everybody followed him. I only had one man to beat and I gave him a swim move and beat him."

Cash blocked the ball just milliseconds after it left the foot of Pittsburgh punter Mark Royals. The ball ricocheted backwards, where it was recovered by Fred Jones, who returned it to the Chiefs 9-yard line.

It was the turning point of the game, maybe the season, for both the Chiefs and Steelers.

"There's no question that was the big play," said Schottenheimer.

Added Cowher:

"You just cannot have that. It's a turnover. It's worse than a turnover. It's a killer."

In three offensive plays after the blocked punt, the Chiefs gained just two yards. Montana called time out and Arrowhead was silent. As Montana walked over to talk with his teammates and coaches, he ran through the different options available for the fateful play.

"At that point, I was just trying to think of things that Paul might want to be doing," said Montana. "And once you've got the play settled, you have to remember that if the play isn't there, it's fourth down and you have to throw the ball somewhere. Or, you have to buy some time. You have to give somebody the opportunity to make a play in the end zone."

In the Chiefs' playbook, the play that Hackett and Montana settled on is called "flanker trail." But it is not a bunch of X's and O's that never change. There are a host of different options available from the basic play. In fact, as Montana talked with Hackett, the Chiefs made a change; they added a "shake" route for Birden. A shake is a post-corner route, meaning Birden would leave the line of scrimmage, cut towards the inside, and then quickly cut back towards the outside.

The change in Birden's route was suggested by Krieg because of something he had seen in the Steelers defense.

"What David talked about in this three-way discussion, was that we had run a similar play just a few plays earlier and they had responded in a three-deep configuration," said Hackett. "David came up with the idea that because of the way they were playing the corner, running a shake route could break something open for J.J."

The words of Chiefs radio announcer Kevin Harlan tell the story from there:

"The Chiefs are down by seven . . . two receivers to the right, one to the left. Backfield is split. Montana surveys the defense. Montana's got a receiver in motion. Back to pass Montana, cocks his arm, looks right, no one there, looks left, throws in the end zone.

"Touchdown!!!!! He's done it. Joe Montana has done it again. The quarterback with the Hollywood name has just laced a line drive pass into the teeth of the Pittsburgh defense and Tim Barnett has come up with the biggest catch of his career as a Kansas City Chief. What a play! What a sensational play!"

"I thought if we got single coverage, it would open up J.J. on the route, because it was a pretty good route," said Montana. "But the corner jumped pretty hard to the inside of J.J. I figured, 'Man, I might have him.' I looked over there and looked at him long enough that it gave Timmy a chance to sneak down the middle. I actually started out thinking J.J., but came back to Tim."

Said Hackett:

"As it turned out, the time Joe spent looking at J.J. on the shake route ended up opening up Tim in the middle of the field."

Barnett did not even know it was fourth down. He did not realize it could be the Chiefs last chance in the 1993 season. His thoughts were only of finding an open spot in the Pittsburgh coverage.

"I saw zone, so what I wanted to do was find a spot in between the zones and just sit there and try to make eye contact with Joe," said Barnett. "We made eye contact. Then he looked off the safety, pulling him to the left and I was wide open."

The Chiefs had a chance to win the game in regulation, but Lowery missed a 43-yard field goal. Eventually, Lowery won the game with a 32-yard field goal in overtime.

Kansas City 27, Pittsburgh 24.

As the game ended, Schottenheimer raced across the field to find Cowher. Schottenheimer gave Cowher his first job in coaching and before moving to the Steelers, Cowher was the Chiefs' defensive coordinator. These two talked on the average of once a week during the season, sometimes more. When Schottenheimer found his protege, he enveloped him in a bear hug.

"Look at the statistics; there were very few penalties, no fumbles turned over, no interceptions," said Schottenheimer. "It was a gallant effort by both sides. Today, it was our day."

Next were the Houston Oilers. The 1993 season had been turbulent for the talented Oilers, but they had overcome a host of problems to finish the season with an 11-game winning streak. They were considered the AFC's best club and in the view of many league observers, Houston was the only team capable of knocking off the Buffalo Bills *and* Dallas Cowboys. All the talk was of an all-Texas Super Bowl between the Oilers and Cowboys.

In the second week of the season the Oilers handed the Montana-less Chiefs a 30-0 defeat at the Astrodome. The Chiefs had lost four straight to the Oilers and had not won in Houston since 1983. Kansas City had not won a postseason game on the road since the 1969 American Football League title game victory in Oakland. All that made it easy for the Las Vegas oddsmakers to post Houston as a 7 to 8-point favorite.

Very few people felt the Chiefs could pull off the upset. One national radio broadcaster said the only way Kansas City would win was if the NFL told the Oilers the game was on Monday, not

Sunday. That 11-game Houston winning streak convinced most people the Oilers were unbeatable, even if the Chiefs did have a healthy dose of Montana magic.

"I'm not sure we should even go play," Schottenheimer said in the days before the game, sarcasm dripping from his every word. "Apparently we have no chance to win. Maybe we shouldn't even bother.

"I think we'll show up."

Adding fuel to the fire were the Oilers players. The 11-game winning streak, combined with the cocky defensive attitude fostered by coordinator Buddy Ryan, had Houston players talking big. Ryan gave evidence of the aggressive demeanor he prized by throwing a punch at Oilers offensive coordinator Kevin Gilbride during the last game of the season. Ryan also called Gilbride a "wimp" and said "he's got no business coaching in the pros."

When talking about Joe Montana and the Chiefs, Ryan's players followed his example:

Linebacker Lamar Lathon: "What about the (Montana) magic? I've seen a lot of magicians at magic shows blow a magic trick. As far as the Comeback Kid? We'll just see what happens on Sunday."

Defensive end William Fuller: "I wouldn't put him at the top of the list of quarterbacks that I wouldn't want to face in the playoffs. I might have said different at the first of the season when he was hot. That would have worried me, but not at this point."

Defensive end Sean Jones: "I never knew there was a mystique surrounding him. I don't psyche myself up by saying: 'Oh, Joe Montana, the Super Bowls, the comebacks.' I'm not one of those people. I don't get into that. We're not worried about playing him. He's the one that should be worried about playing us."

Veteran linebacker Wilber Marshall was worried about his teammates' comments.

"Hopefully, they're not saying that," Marshall said. "Hopefully they're thinking about him still being the greatest quarterback around."

The talk turned to whether Montana could withstand the pressure applied by Ryan's blitzing 46 defense. Publicly, Montana answered questions about the Houston defense with words of admiration. Privately, all the talk and doubters were motivating him even more.

"The last thing you want to tell Joe Montana is that he can't do something," said tight end Jonathan Hayes. "When you have accomplished everything that he has, you live for those moments when people doubt you and your ability. It gives you another chance to achieve."

One day at practice, Schottenheimer got down on one knee directly in front of Montana as he was taking snaps.

"He asked me what I was doing," Schottenheimer said. "I told him I wanted to see if there was any fear in his eyes."

There was no fear in the Chiefs eyes, only anger. The talking by the Oilers got under their skin. Offensive players were upset that all the talk was about what the Houston defense would do to Montana. The defensive players were upset that all the attention was on the Oilers defense.

"It's like our defense won't even be on the field," snapped Neil Smith.

Added Kevin Ross: "Did Buddy Ryan invent defense? Is he the guy who created the game of football? I think some folks down there are doing a little too much talking."

Tim Grunhard was so irritated about the cacophony coming out of Houston, that during his weekly radio show three days before the game, he guaranteed a Chiefs victory. "The only question is by how much we will win the game," said Grunhard.

Schottenheimer and his coaching staff were not saying anything publicly. Privately, however, they were thrilled to be facing the Oilers. Despite the lopsided loss earlier in the season, the coaches felt they had a good plan of attack against the Oilers' run-and-shoot offensive scheme. Over the years, the Chiefs learned that stopping the run was the key to slowing down Houston. Make an offense one-dimensional and the defense's task becomes much easier.

The Chiefs offense was not always consistent, but they had the perfect attack to hurt the blitzing Ryan style. Offensive coordinator Paul Hackett also had something in this game he did not have in the first meeting between the teams: Joe Montana.

However, he was not a healthy Joe Montana. Those sore ribs caused him problems in the days before the Houston game. Eventually, he received an injection of painkiller in the ribs before stepping on the field. And by the time he left the Astrodome, Montana had a sore left hand, a bruised left knee and a sore right ankle.

Montana and the Chiefs also left Houston with a 28-20 victory. He shredded the vaunted Ryan defense in the second half for three touchdown passes. By the end of the game, Ryan was not throwing punches at his fellow coaches; he simply stood on the sidelines muttering to himself.

"They made a big mistake," Ross shouted in the bedlam of the Chiefs' locker room after the game. "They woke up No. 19. Don't ever do that. Don't ever wake him up. They talked too much and look what happened: they are walking home with their tail between their legs."

The Oilers made a lot of mistakes on the field and the Chiefs seemed to take advantage of all of them. Despite an Astrodome-record crowd of 64,011, the Chiefs outplayed and outcoached the favorites:

—Houston quarterback Warren Moon was sacked nine times, as the Chiefs defense never allowed him to develop the throwing rhythm so necessary in the run-and-shoot offense. So harried was Moon that he ended up fumbling five times, losing two.

—Oilers running back Gary Brown averaged over 100 yards per game in the last half of the 1993 season. For the season, he averaged 5 yards per carry. But the Chiefs held Brown to 17 yards on 11 carries, an average of 1.5 yards per carry. In the second half of the game, Brown carried just four times for zero yards; by then Houston simply gave up on the running game.

—The run-and-shoot offense has four wide receivers on every play. The Chiefs have always felt the key to stopping that attack was hitting the receivers after the catch, limiting their chance for big plays. Houston receivers caught 32 passes, and while they averaged 9.6 yards on each catch, they averaged only 3.8 yards after grabbing the ball.

—Ryan loves the blitz, but Chiefs defensive coordinator Dave Adolph decided to gamble a bit himself, and he put in a whole series of blitzes for the Houston offense. They were especially effective, producing four of the nine sacks. Kansas City blitzed on 23 of the 52 passing plays.

—Ryan's defense had all kinds of problems. The Oilers sacked Montana just twice in 40 passing plays. They touched him only seven times total in the game, although several of those hits were vicious, leaving Montana dazed and in pain.

But Ryan backed away from his blitzing 46 defense. In the first half, Houston sent extra rushers on 13 of the 20 passing plays. In the second half, Ryan called the blitz on only five of 20 passing plays.

Despite all those advantages, the Chiefs still trailed the Oilers by six points with 9 minutes, 34 seconds to play in the fourth quarter. Defensively, the Chiefs were pressuring Moon and stopping Brown. But the offense was inconsistent. The best example came in the second quarter, when Willie Davis dropped a Montana pass at the Oilers' 5-yard line that would have been a touchdown.

"It was all my fault," said Davis. "I really can't tell you what happened. It was a perfectly thrown ball . . . I thought it was shorter than what it was, and when I got down there, it just sailed on me. It was all my fault."

Davis was upset, but Montana tried to soothe his feelings.

"I told him, 'Hey, you dropped one, I missed you on two others, we'll get it done,'" said Montana.

Added Davis: "By the time he got done talking to me, I thought it was *his* fault I dropped the pass. I couldn't wait to get back on the field."

Davis' drop was one of several long passing plays that did not connect in the first half for the Chiefs. But they made an impression on Ryan; he realized his defensive backs could not cover Davis and J.J. Birden in one-on-one situations. The pass rush was having trouble getting to Montana and the Oilers were in danger of giving up some mighty big plays.

In the third quarter, Montana found Keith Cash open for a 7-yard touchdown pass. After he scored, Cash saw a banner hanging from the stands with Ryan's picture on it, and fired the football at the likeness of the defensive coordinator.

Houston added a field goal to push its lead back to six points, 13-7. But with the Oilers blitz called off, Montana went to work dissecting the defense. The Chiefs took the lead when Montana found Birden open for an 11-yard touchdown. Moon fumbled on the next offensive play and Montana needed just three more plays to throw another TD pass, this one for 18 yards to Willie Davis, who made a remarkable catch in the end zone around Houston cornerback Chris Dishman.

The Oilers came back with a touchdown, as Moon hit wide receiver Ernest Givens in the end zone, as the Chiefs blew another coverage. But that score hardly bothered Montana. Kansas City went 79 yards on six plays, as Marcus Allen scored on a nifty 21-yard run. Allen started left, came back to his right for the handoff and then cut back to his left once he was into the Houston defense. Blocks by Tim Barnett and fullback Ernie Thompson opened the running lane and he cruised untouched to the end zone.

Allen's touchdown left the Oilers dazed and the clock ran out on their comeback hopes. When the final gun sounded, the Chiefs celebrated like no Kansas City team had in 24 years. Neil Smith collapsed on the Astrodome field with exhaustion and joy. He eventually had to be helped into the dressing room.

"Nobody believed in us," yelled Derrick Thomas. "You've gotta believe."

Marty Schottenheimer was the first person into the Chiefs locker room after the game. He stormed in, grabbed a soda and then flung a towel against a wall. "*!&@#$% Buddy Ryan," Schottenheimer shouted.

Later, when he met with the media, Schottenheimer was much more composed as he talked about what Montana meant to the Chiefs.

"He is a tremendous source of confidence for whoever lines up with him," Schottenheimer said. "Guys who have been there before can make a difference. They can lift the others around them to another level."

Physically, Montana was not in good shape after the game. He needed help to get his equipment off, and there were bandages on his elbow, his knee and his hand. But as he met the media, it was hard to tell he was hurting.

"It feels as good as ever," said Montana. "You know a lot of people have counted you out, said you would never make it this far and it feels good to be at this point, still in one piece. It's as good as I've ever felt."

In the bowels of the Astrodome, Carl Peterson stood off to the side, watching Montana answer questions from the media. He was asked if the trade for Montana was worth the price and effort.

"He was definitely worth it," Peterson croaked, his voice hoarse from the combination of a cold and cheering. "This is why we brought him here. Not for the regular season. It was never for that. We knew how to win those games. But these games, the ones in January, the ones that can get you to the Super Bowl.

"That's why we got Joe."

CHAPTER TWENTY-ONE

EPILOGUE

It is one of the truths of football: A team either improves or deteriorates. A step is taken forward or backward. No team stays the same. Those who think they have held their position lose ground because other teams are advancing, pushing those that are stagnant farther down the National Football League ladder.

In 1992, the Chiefs did not improve. Although they won 10 games and made the playoffs, they took a step backwards.

In 1993 the Chiefs improved dramatically, with 11 victories, two more in the playoffs and a division title. To take yet another step forward in 1994, Carl Peterson and Marty Schottenheimer knew they could not sit back and attempt to recreate the '93 magic. Changes were necessary.

Some alterations were mandated with the institution of a salary cap throughout the NFL. In 1994, all 28 clubs will work with approximately $34.6 million for player costs. For teams like the San Francisco 49ers and Washington Redskins, that means major alterations in how they operate their payroll. In the past, they have been free spenders, willing to keep larger numbers of players around and paying large salaries when necessary. Those days are gone.

For every franchise, the new rules have forced some alteration in philosophy and planning. With costs capped and players able to become free agents after just four years in the league, the NFL had a very different player personnel landscape.

"It has become a situation where it is more like college football," said Peterson. "With free agency after four seasons, we have to get players on the field more quickly. We have to find out if they can play and then get the maximum we can from them in the first four years, because chances are they won't be around after that.

"Like college football, we've got to get the talented freshmen on the field and make sure that by the time they are sophomores, they are contributing to our program. And just like college coaches, we can't become too attached to players, because they are not going to be around for nine or 10 years the way they have been in the past. A lot of tough decisions are going to have to be made."

For the Chiefs, the $34.6 million salary cap was close enough to their 1993 payroll that a complete housecleaning of the roster was not required. Plus, the team spent all of the '93 season working as if the cap was already in place.

"We spent the year playing capnomics," said Tim Connolly. "We learned last year about some of the problems we were going to have this year. That allowed us to prepare ourselves."

But there were going to be changes, big changes in the Chiefs. Within 100 days of the AFC Championship Game loss to Buffalo, the team:

• Saw three defensive starters leave via free agency — cornerback Albert Lewis, safety Kevin Ross and linebacker Lonnie Marts. Backup quarterback David Krieg departed as well.

• Released tight end and co-captain Jonathan Hayes, punter Bryan Barker, running back Harvey Williams and offensive lineman Reggie McElroy. The release of Hayes was tied directly to the pressure of the salary cap.

• Announced it would not make contract offers to a trio of free agents — running back Todd McNair, defensive back and special teams captain Bennie Thompson and wide receiver Fred Jones.

• Signed unrestricted free agents in defensive tackle Tony Casillas and cornerback Mark Collins. Combined, Casillas and Collins have four Super Bowl rings from their time with the Dallas Cowboys and the New York Giants respectively.

• Made a trade with San Francisco for backup quarterback Steve Bono. Yes, that's the same Steve Bono the Chiefs chased during free agency in April of 1993, before deciding to concentrate on making the trade for Joe Montana.

Despite the addition of Bono, Schottenheimer planned on Matt Blundin being the team's No. 2 quarterback in 1994.

• Selected two running backs — Greg Hill and Donnell Bennett — and two wide receivers — Lake Dawson and Chris Penn — with their first four selections in the 1994 NFL draft. Seven of the 10 Chiefs' draft choices were offensive players.

As the Chiefs went through their annual spring mini-camp in late April, there were 81 players listed on the roster. Nearly half—38—were names that were not part of the Chiefs at the end of the 1993 regular season.

"We need a lot of those 'Hi, My Name is. . .' tags around here," said defensive tackle Joe Phillips, who as an unrestricted free agent decided to stay with the team, signing a four-year deal for $7 million.

Said linebacker Derrick Thomas:

"I looked around and realized that I was one of the grizzled veterans. And I'm only going into my sixth season."

There were changes for Thomas as well. After spending the 1993 season at the rush-backer/defensive end position, Thomas was moved back to outside linebacker, the position he played in his first four NFL seasons.

"I'm happy they made the switch back," said Thomas. "That's where I feel more comfortable playing."

Said Schottenheimer:

"We ended up moving people around last year because of the way we were using Derrick, and all it did was cause uncertainty. He will still line up at defensive end in obvious passing situations, just as he has since he was a rookie. And at linebacker, he's going to have fewer opportunities to rush the passer."

There were other changes for the Chiefs as well. In February, they announced that the playing surface at Arrowhead Stadium was going to be changed to grass. After 22 seasons on artificial turf, the Chiefs will play their home games in 1994 on the real thing.

Ticket manager Phil Youtsey was hired away by one of the NFL's two expansion franchises, the Carolina Panthers. Radio play-by-play voice Kevin Harlan was lured away by the FOX network to do NFC games on television.

But the biggest changes came on the roster, mirroring those going on around the league.

Lewis was the first to leave, signing a four-year contract with the Los Angeles Raiders for $7 million. The Chiefs wanted to keep Lewis, but not at that kind of money.

"Albert had a good season for us in 1993," said Peterson. "But we could not commit that kind of money to a player who would be 34 years old and has missed so much time because of injury."

Ross was the next to leave, signing a three-year deal with the Atlanta Falcons for $4 million. The Chiefs did not plan to make a contract offer to Ross, so his departure was not a surprise.

"It was time for Kevin to move on and for this team to go on about its business," said Schottenheimer.

Marts signing with the Tampa Bay Buccaneers was a shock, especially for the size of the three-year contract: $3.3 million.

"We would have liked to have kept Lonnie," said Peterson. "But not at that number."

Krieg's departure was not a surprise. Just a week before he signed with the Detroit Lions, Krieg met with Peterson and Schottenheimer. He was told by the head coach that the Chiefs wanted him back, but he would have to be the third quarterback, behind Montana and Blundin. Peterson told him that as the third quarterback and because of the salary cap, he would have to take a big paycut from the nearly $2 million he was paid in 1993.

The Lions offered Krieg the No. 2 job behind Scott Mitchell and $800,000. When Krieg signed the contract, the Chiefs were forced to find an experienced quarterback to fill their No. 3 position. Eventually, they made a deal with the 49ers for Bono, giving up a fourth-round draft choice in 1995. San Francisco had to get rid of Bono because of their own salary cap problems.

This new free agency process ruffled a few feathers along the way. Lewis and Ross did not leave Kansas City quietly, as both players took shots at the Chiefs organization for not re-signing them.

"I'm done with them," Ross said of the Chiefs in a story printed by the *Rocky Mountain News* newspaper in Denver. "If you play with a team for 10 years and you commit yourself to the organization the way I did, you expect to be treated fairly. I don't think I was. They didn't extend my contract. If I'm not a priority, I don't want to be around."

Peterson refrained from firing back publicly.

"Both Albert and Kevin sued the NFL for free agency and won their suits," said Peterson. "They got what they wanted, but then they apparently did not want what they got.

"They helped bring about this new system of free agency and it's something Albert, Kevin and all of us are going to have to get used too. The old way is out."

Lewis especially, seemed to be talking out of both sides of his mouth. Late in the 1993 season, the Chiefs and the other NFL teams faced a December 23 deadline for signing players to contract extensions. If signed before that date, money could be front-loaded to the 1993 season and would not count towards the salary cap in 1994. The Chiefs made a contract offer to Lewis before that date. Lewis decided he did not like the numbers and turned down the offer.

If Lewis really wanted to stay in Kansas City, he had his chance to re-sign with the team. But he wanted more money. Lewis found that money with the Raiders through free agency, which is something he felt so strongly about that he sued the NFL. In the end, Lewis wanted everything: big money and a chance to stay in Kansas City. He ended up with big money.

To help replace Lewis, the Chiefs signed Collins, a nine-year veteran of the New York Giants. Collins is four years younger than Lewis and missed only a handful of games over his career because of injury.

"Mark Collins brings great physical skills to our team," said Schottenheimer. "He also has some leadership abilities that we feel were an important element."

The signing of Casillas surprised many Chiefs fans. Phillips and Dan Saleaumua held down the interior of the defensive line for the last two seasons. As an unrestricted free agent, Saleaumua carried a transition player designation. That meant the Chiefs could match any offer made to him by another team. It also guarantees the player he'll receive a salary equivalent to the top 10 players at his position. For Saleaumua, that meant $1.9 million per season.

Some fans and media felt the signing of Casillas meant there was no room for Saleaumua under the salary cap. In fact, the Kansas City Star reported that the Chiefs could not re-sign Saleaumua and the team was considering changing its defense to better utilize Casillas' talents.

It was just another incorrect *Star* story that annoyed Peterson.

"First of all, we expect to sign Dan Saleaumua," Peterson said. "He's already accounted for under the salary cap. You have to do that. A mere phone call to the league would have provided that information.

"No. 2, we are not changing our defense. We've never even considered it. That was news to Marty, Dave Adolph and the whole coaching staff. Just about everything in that story was wrong."

Despite the mistakes in that one story, a bit of a truce had been declared between Peterson and the newspaper. After many phone calls from editor Art Brisbane, Peterson finally agreed to have lunch. They discussed the problems between the parties.

"He admitted that the paper may have been overzealous in their story about the players by including civil cases with criminal cases," said Peterson. "Of course that's easy to say after the fact. I listened to him. He listened to me. I'm not sure you could call it a dialogue, but we did listen to each other."

The decision to release Harvey Williams did not come as a great surprise, since the former No. 1 draft choice dressed for just one game over the second half of the 1993 season.

"I would have liked to have kept Harvey, but our coaching staff felt there was nothing he could contribute so we made the decision to release him," said Peterson. "I still think Harvey can make a contribution in this league."

Before the start of the 1993 season, Schottenheimer went out of his way to make sure Williams knew he was the starting halfback. Everything the head coach said publicly was designed to pump up Williams' sometimes shaky confidence. Christian Okoye was released and Barry Word was traded, moves that confirmed Schottenheimer's belief in Williams.

"I thought it would be important for Harvey to understand that he was the man we expected to run with the football," said Schottenheimer. "Our intention with Marcus was that he would play 50 percent of the time, and part of that would be played at fullback.

"What happened to Harvey? The performance wasn't there. He'll tell you it was because he did not get enough opportunities. I would tell you he got opportunities and it didn't happen."

Williams told the *Star*:

"I could see from day one at training camp that it was all a smokescreen. I could tell the first game of the season what was about to go down. Marty wanted his guy Marcus out there."

Williams suffered a concussion in the Miami game, which was the last time he carried the football from scrimmage in the 1993 season. Not long after the game, rumors started that Williams had faked the injury. On the play where he was hurt, Williams fumbled the ball away for the second time in the game. Some of his own teammates joked that he just did not want to get up and have to face Schottenheimer's wrath.

But the head coach discounts talk of Williams faking the concussion.

"Our doctors were quite concerned," said Schottenheimer. "They thought he really got his bell rung. I don't think you can do something like that and fool the doctors. I think he was hurt."

Williams ended up signing as a free agent with the Los Angeles Raiders.

One of the toughest decisions the Chiefs made was releasing Jonathan Hayes. A leader in the locker room and one of the team's most active players in the community, Hayes was liked by everyone in the organization. The Chiefs hoped to re-sign him after he talked with other teams and Hayes promised to bring his best offer back to the team, with hopes they would match the numbers. But there were no guarantees he would wear the red and gold in 1994.

"It's all part of the business and I understand that, but it still hurts," said Hayes. "It's the first time in my life I've ever been told that my services were no longer desired."

Almost from the moment the AFC Championship Game ended, the rumors about Montana began floating through Kansas City and the NFL. The Montanas had put their house on the market and were not planning to return to Kansas City was the first. Montana was going to retire because of the injuries he suffered in the 1993 season came next. Montana's (pick one) wife/father/mother/children/agent/friends wanted him to walk away before he suffered an injury that could cause permanent damage.

But at no time did he seriously consider retirement. And his house never went on the market.

"At this point in your career the future always crosses your mind," said Montana. "You have to face the fact that the seasons are running out. I know that. But I don't feel like what happened to me last year was a sign that my body is falling apart. I had a hamstring pull. Troy Aikman had a hamstring pull and he's a good bit younger than I am. I hurt my wrist. Steve Young broke his hand. I had bruised ribs. Every quarterback in the NFL had bruised ribs. I had a concussion. Troy Aikman had a concussion in the playoffs.

"It was very disappointing to lose to Buffalo," Montana continued. "When you get that far in the playoffs, you want to go all the way. But after looking at the season as a whole, we have to be happy with what happened. It was the first year for the new offense and we accomplished a lot. That gives us a lot to look forward to in 1994."

Paul Hackett heard the rumors about Montana's retirement. He did not believe them for a second.

"Do you think he's going to end his career on that game?" said Hackett, referring to the loss to Buffalo. "No way. All he thinks about is that game. He doesn't think about any of the good things that happened. All he thinks about is Buffalo and what could we have done to have things turn out differently.

"That's where we failed. We did a lot of good things, but that's what stares you in the face every morning, that loss. That's what gets you motivated to get ready for 1994.

"Joe Montana can't step away from that. You don't lose the AFC Championship Game and step away. Not Joe Montana."